The Pop Documentary Since 1980

The Pop Documentary Since 1980

Aesthetics, Performance, Creativity

Richard Wallace

BLOOMSBURY ACADEMIC
LONDON • NEW YORK • OXFORD • NEW DELHI • SYDNEY

BLOOMSBURY ACADEMIC

Bloomsbury Publishing Plc, 50 Bedford Square, London, WC1B 3DP, UK
Bloomsbury Publishing Inc, 1385 Broadway, New York, NY 10018, USA
Bloomsbury Publishing Ireland, 29 Earlsfort Terrace, Dublin 2, D02 AY28, Ireland

BLOOMSBURY, BLOOMSBURY ACADEMIC and the Diana logo are trademarks of Bloomsbury Publishing Plc

First published in Great Britain 2025

Copyright © Richard Wallace, 2025

Richard Wallace has asserted his right under the Copyright, Designs and Patents Act, 1988, to be identified as Author of this work.

For legal purposes the Acknowledgements on pp. xi–xii constitute an extension of this copyright page.

Cover design: Ben Anslow
Cover image © Beyonce Knowles outside the MTV TRL Studios in Times Square New York City, USA - 28.02.07
Contributor: WENN Rights Ltd / Alamy Stock Photo.

All rights reserved. No part of this publication may be: i) reproduced or transmitted in any form, electronic or mechanical, including photocopying, recording or by means of any information storage or retrieval system without prior permission in writing from the publishers; or ii) used or reproduced in any way for the training, development or operation of artificial intelligence (AI) technologies, including generative AI technologies. The rights holders expressly reserve this publication from the text and data mining exception as per Article 4(3) of the Digital Single Market Directive (EU) 2019/790.

Bloomsbury Publishing Plc does not have any control over, or responsibility for, any third-party websites referred to or in this book. All internet addresses given in this book were correct at the time of going to press. The author and publisher regret any inconvenience caused if addresses have changed or sites have ceased to exist, but can accept no responsibility for any such changes.

A catalogue record for this book is available from the British Library.

A catalog record for this book is available from the Library of Congress.

ISBN: HB: 978-1-3502-1424-8
PB: 978-1-3502-1423-1
ePDF: 978-1-3502-1426-2
eBook: 978-1-3502-1425-5

Typeset by Newgen KnowledgeWorks Pvt. Ltd., Chennai, India
Printed and bound in Great Britain

For product safety related questions contact productsafety@bloomsbury.com.

To find out more about our authors and books visit www.bloomsbury.com and sign up for our newsletters.

For Audrey, Murray and Jarvis

Contents

	List of Figures	ix
	Acknowledgements	xi
	Introduction	1
	Historical Contexts: Aesthetic Rejuvenation, the Documentary Boom and the Streaming Wars	4
	The State of the Field	9
	Hierarchies of Value	13
	The Pop Star as Discursive Tension	21
	Chapter Overview	23
1	The Concert Film	27
	The Purpose of Concert Films	28
	Eventfulness	30
	Fragmentation	36
	The Constructed Performance	47
	Competing Regimes of Knowledge	52
	Conclusion	59
2	The 'Documentary Backstage'	63
	The Backstage as Cinematic Space	64
	Archive	68
	Intimacy, Domesticity and Observation	79
	Journeys	87
	Self-reflexivity	103
3	Songwriting	109
	Showing Writing	113
	Production Stories: Making *Sgt. Pepper's Lonely Hearts Club Band*	125
	Ownership and Control	141
	Conclusion	149

4	Fans	151
	Fan Representation as Pathology and Pedagogy	153
	The Mob and the Individual	161
	A Life-course Approach to Fandom: *I Used to Be Normal*	171
	Collecting: *Sound It Out*	177
	Music and Meaning: *Our Hobby Is Depeche Mode*	183
	Conclusion	191
Conclusion		193
Notes		199
References		211
Filmography		231
Teleography		239
Index		241

Figures

1.1	The concert film is used by Taylor Swift to manage a transition between the stadium pop of *Taylor Swift: Reputation Stadium Tour* ...	29
1.2	... and the 'cottagecore' indie-folk of *Folklore: The Long Pond Studio Sessions*	29
1.3	An exhibitionistic gesture as Venzella Joy stares into the camera lens in *Homecoming: A Film by Beyoncé*	33
1.4	David Byrne offers the documentary audience the microphone in *Stop Making Sense*	35
1.5	Katy Perry is 'held captive' in the 'Who Am I Living For?' sequence of *Katy Perry: Part of Me*	42
1.6	The 'spatial montage' of the varied point of view of *Awesome; I Fuckin' Shot That!*	43
1.7	Four points of view from the 'Crazy in Love' sequence of *Homecoming*	46
1.8	A Busby Berkeley-esque aerial shot that reveals the stage marks during the 'Burning Down the House' sequence of *David Byrne's American Utopia*	60
2.1	A candid image of Billie Holiday and Louis McKay (left) framed as if viewed on a photographer's contact sheet	73
2.2	Lady Gaga cooks lunch in the opening scene of *Gaga: Five Foot Two*	81
2.3	Billie Eilish's parents, Patrick O'Connell (left) and Maggie Baird (right)	84
2.4	Camera-phone 'selfie' footage in *The World's a Little Blurry*	85
2.5	Baird's more composed footage in *The World's a Little Blurry*	86
2.6	Michael Lindsay-Hogg takes centre stage in *The Beatles: Get Back*	95
2.7	Tom Berninger hides the screen as he edits the film that we are currently watching in *Mistaken for Strangers*	101
2.8	Kylie Minogue appears in Nick Cave's car in *20,000 Days on Earth*	105
3.1	The tedium of songwriting: George Harrison yawns as Paul McCartney (foreground) begins composing 'Get Back' in *Get Back*	115

3.2	Andrew Combs writes a song based on Chusy's prompts in *It All Begins with a Song*	119
3.3	Forest Glen Whitehead explains his process to the film crew in *It All Begins with a Song*	122
3.4	George Martin (left) and Paul McCartney (right) interrogate the multitrack tapes in *The South Bank Show*: 'The Making of Sgt. Pepper'	127
3.5	Parodying the 'producer-at-the-mixing-desk' trope in *The Life of Rock with Brian Pern*	128
3.6	The 'producer-at-the-mixing-desk' trope is reformulated by McCartney (right) and Rick Rubin (left) in *McCartney 3,2,1*	128
3.7	Howard Goodall stands amidst the expressive mise en scène of the 'Strawberry Fields Forever' sequence of *Sgt. Pepper's Musical Revolution with Howard Goodall*	133
3.8	Inter-generational conflict and the 'kitchen sink' inspirations of 'She's Leaving Home' are combined in the mise en scène of *Sgt. Pepper's Musical Revolution*	134
3.9	The more literal mise en scène of the production-focused sequences of *Sgt. Pepper's Musical Revolution*	139
4.1	The intimacy of the handshake in *Tokyo Idols*	160
4.2	Part of the archival montage of screaming fans – complete with expressive subtitles – in *When Pop Ruled My Life: The Fan's Story*	162
4.3	Dara wanting 'to be' Gary Barlow is depicted in *I Used to Be Normal*	173
4.4	Shane listening to music in his semi-furnished home in *Sound It Out*	182
4.5	Depeche Mode fans (left) and Russian military supporters (right) take part in their respective 9 May celebrations in St. Petersburg	188

Table

1.1	A Comparison of the Numbers That Appear in the Performance Sequences of *Part of Me* Compared with Their Position in the Original Concert Setlist	41

Acknowledgements

There are numerous people who have played a part in the development, research, writing and publication of this book. First and foremost, I want to thank the commissioning and editorial team at Bloomsbury – and particularly Barbara Cohen Bastos, Camilla Erskine and Veidehi Hans – for steering the project through the various stages of development and commissioning it in the first place. Thanks also to the readers whose attentive comments have greatly improved the finished manuscript.

The book developed out of my earlier research on film and television mockumentary and so there are numerous people whose contributions to *that* project have shaped this one and who deserve residual thanks, especially Stella Bruzzi, Gregory Frame, Paul Long, Derek Paget and Martin Pumphrey.

Aspects of this project were developed in various teaching spaces at the University of Warwick and I am particularly indebted to my 'Issues in Documentary' classes between 2017 and 2019 for their insight and – at times – endurance, especially when working with the material on songwriting that has become Chapter 3. I am also grateful to current and former colleagues for taking an interest in the project and providing insights in one form or another that have shaped my thinking. In this respect, I particularly want to mention Hannah Andrews, Charlotte Brunsdon, Jake Edwards, Lance Hayward, Julie Lobalzo Wright, Tracey McVey, James MacDowell, Rachel Moseley, Alice Pember, Richard Perkins, Alastair Phillips, Nicolas Pillai, Jason Potel, Daisy Richards, Mike Riding, Karl Schoonover and Leanne Weston. I am also indebted to the University of Warwick for granting a period of research leave to allow me to finish the book (almost) on schedule.

The Covid-19 context in which this book was developed meant that opportunities to share early versions of this work were relatively limited; however, I am particularly indebted to the Warwick University Film Society for providing a receptive audience and helpful feedback on an early version of Chapter 1 (and Issy Smith and Harry Russell in particular for inviting me to speak in the first place). A number of films that I have been working on in this book were screened in venues during Coventry's year as UK City of Culture in 2021, either as part of CineCov's Rock'n'Docs strand or at events associated with the '2Tone: Lives &

Legacies' exhibition held at the Herbert Art Gallery & Museum. I am especially grateful to Helen Wheatley for developing these events and for collaborating in their delivery (as well as for other discussions about the project too numerous to name). Additional thanks also go to the CineCov team, and the staff at The Tin and Coventry Cathedral for hosting these events, to Jeanie Finlay for taking part in a post-screening Q&A for *Sound it Out*, and to the audiences at that and the *Our Hobby Is Depeche Mode* screening for their enthusiastic discussion and perceptive questions that have helped shape the work in Chapter 4. I would also like to thank the parent accompanying a prospective student to a university open day earlier this year who made a very useful observation about the work of Paul Dugdale.

Although I am not a dedicated cricket fan, I need to thank the England, Australia and *Test Match Special* teams for their work during the 2023 Ashes series. All three provided a much-needed accompaniment to – and at times means of escape from – wrestling with what has become Chapter 1 of this book.

Closer to home, I am always indebted to my parents for their love, support and interest – and for bringing me up in a very musical household. In reality, the seeds of this project date back to the early 1990s, and specifically to the *South Bank Show* episode on *Sgt. Pepper's Lonely Hearts Club Band* that my Dad recorded for me, which ignited an enthusiasm for The Beatles and for stories of music production more generally that persist to this day. This programme features heavily in Chapter 3, and the screenshot included there is taken from the original off-air video tape.

My three children, to whom this book is dedicated, ensure that my world is constantly filled with love and song (and noise). Finally, but most importantly, my eternal thanks must go to Lauren Wallace-Thompson. You are relentless in your support and have been a constant sounding board as this project has developed. Your influence is tangible and your instinct for structure (and what needed to be cut out!) has been invaluable to seeing the book through to completion. I couldn't have done it without you and the book is substantially better because of your input. Thank you.

Introduction

On 31 August 2023, Taylor Swift surprised the US film industry by announcing the release of a film version of her monumentally successful *Eras* concert tour (Swift 2023). Within hours of the announcement, the film had broken AMC Theatres' single-day ticket sales record and *Forbes* was reporting that the company's share prices had risen by 2.5 per cent (Roush 2023).[1] This made the film the tenth highest-grossing documentary of all time before a single screening had taken place; as of January 2025, it is the highest, with worldwide ticket sales in excess of $261 million.[2] Produced and financed by Silent House Productions and Swift's own production company – Taylor Swift Productions – and primarily distributed and exhibited through a deal with AMC, *Taylor Swift: The Eras Tour* (2023) has been a disruptive force within the film industry, almost entirely bypassing the major Hollywood studios (Belloni 2023).[3]

Production was undertaken in secret and, with an exhibition deal that guaranteed at least four screenings per day at every AMC location in the United States, the lack of cinematic real estate meant that a number of films already scheduled for release near to 13 October 2023, including *The Exorcist: Believer* (2023) and a limited run of Martin Scorsese's *Killers of the Flower Moon* (2023), had to be moved or cancelled (Brueggemann 2023; Chapman 2023). The bypassing of the film industry's production sector was also concerning for studios given the wider context of industrial action undertaken by the Writers Guild of America (WGA) and the Screen Actors Guild-American Federation of Television and Radio Artists (SAG-AFTRA). Swift's approach demonstrated that exhibitors could find other means of financial security that did not rely on the studios as a supplier of product.[4] This created an unprecedented situation in which the Hollywood production sector received no financial reward from one of the biggest cinema events of 2023 and has established a precedent that other major artists have begun to follow; *Renaissance: A Film by Beyoncé* followed the same distribution model when it was released in November 2023 (Donnelly 2023).

Although Swift's commercial power is unique, and the film's success is unlikely to be replicated to quite the same extent, the combination of financial success with industry-shaking production processes demonstrates the current significance of the music documentary. The film did not emerge from a wilderness, but is part of a trend that sees the music documentary as a key site of struggle across the broader media ecosystem. Although Sarah Whitten (writing for CNBC) raised the potential for the Swift film to '[reinvigorate] the concert genre, which blossomed in the 1960s and 1970s', interviews with exhibitors included in the article make it clear that this has been developing for some time (2023). Particularly notable is the prominence of concert films within premium-priced 'event cinema' packages, and the year 2023 alone saw cinema releases of over a dozen such 'events', including *Coldplay: Music of the Spheres – Live at River Plate* (2023), Metallica's two-night live event *M72 World Tour Live from Texas* (2023), André Rieu's *2023 Maastricht Concert: Love is All Around* (2023) and the BTS 'solo documentaries' *j-hope IN THE BOX* (2023) and *SUGA: Road to D-Day* (2023). These join over twenty high-profile documentary features and series released in UK cinemas and on streaming platforms.[5]

The music documentary is in the middle of a prolonged period of visibility, something Michael Brendan Baker has called a 'rockumentary renaissance' (2014), and this book explores the aesthetics, meanings and purpose of the music documentary from the vantage point of this particular moment of commercial and critical prominence. As I will demonstrate shortly, the increasingly evident commercial impetus of music documentaries made over the past thirty to forty years (particularly in the twenty-first century) has tended to be treated with scepticism and critical disdain, yet these documentaries represent an important way in which pop stardom is shaped, consumed and interpreted. Rather than shying away from this aspect, I place it at the forefront of this study, deploying techniques of close analysis central to film studies as a means of interrogating the forms and functions of the genre and exploring the multiplicity of ways in which the music documentary since the 1980s has become – to use Raymond Williams's (1977: 121–7) well-known formulation – a 'dominant' space for the enactment of musical stardom, identity and commercial and creative endeavour. Rather than viewing the tension between art and commerce that is frequently apparent in these documentaries as representing a weakness – even a crisis – for their claims of significance or seriousness, I argue that it is a key source of their vitality.

The book demonstrates the importance of the music documentary as a component of the mechanisms that underpin pop stardom and also as a means of accessing, projecting and making sense of those mechanisms for the wider world. I am not primarily interested in setting out a history of the music documentary, nor in developing categories based on aesthetic approaches to documentation such as is exemplified in the work of Bill Nichols (1991), and so the structure of this book is neither a chronology of the music documentary since 1980, nor does it attempt to taxonomize the form (though elements of this do emerge in Chapter 2).

Instead, *The Pop Documentary Since 1980* offers an investigation of the narratives and aesthetics of access as they are articulated in documentaries about pop stars. The centrality of discourses of access speaks to some of the overriding concerns of the pop music documentary and the tripartite relationship between the star, the audience and the documentary representation. I argue that the music documentary forwards an aesthetic of access in numerous ways, including the creation of a 'documentary backstage'. Here the question of whether the documentary is genuinely able to provide access to the star is less important than the identification of strategies deployed by documentary makers to *suggest* that this heightened level of personal engagement and access has been achieved. I suggest that this assertion of access is managed through documentary methods such as the use of domestic locations and self-shot footage, the suggestion of privileged access to rare archives, the structuring devices of narratives of discovery and modes of self-reflection. In addition, the 'unity of fragmentation' that I argue characterizes the concert film is the means by which the experiential capacity of live performance is accessed in a way that constructs a depiction of a live event that is both 'truthful' and 'transformative'.

Discourses of access are also present in the consideration of acts of creative production and reception. Given that significant aspects of the creative process are internalized and subjective, the question of how best to access and understand these processes – or negotiate their *inaccessibility* – becomes key for documentary makers concerned with creativity. The multifaceted relationship that fans have with their idols also revolves around questions of access that raises ethical issues around power dynamics, especially when documentaries use images of music fans in ways that exploit these hierarchies of access.

A central contribution of this book, then, is to consider the centrality of narratives, discourses and aesthetics of access within the pop music documentary, and to suggest that it plays a key role in shaping the public perception of pop stars. However, this also raises broader theoretical, practical and ethical questions about the place of the documentary within contemporary pop stardom and the methods through which such 'access' is achieved or disclaimed.

Historical Contexts: Aesthetic Rejuvenation, the Documentary Boom and the Streaming Wars

The focus of this book is on pop music documentaries made since 1980. There are reasons for this grounded in the existing critical literature that I will set out later in this introduction, but just as important are a set of historical contexts that have shaped more recent music documentaries. The 1980s is the starting point because a number of key transitions in the form can be traced back to that decade. Most pertinently, this period saw a shift away from the prioritization of objectivity as a key marker of documentary truth via a self-reflexive 'turn' evident since the late 1980s, and apparent in films like Errol Morris's *The Thin Blue Line* (1988). This placed the structures of documentary enquiry within the purview of the documentary film itself and is, perhaps, epitomized in the pop documentary by the sequence in Molly Dineen's *Geri* (1999) in which the film-maker and the former Spice Girl discuss the extent of Dineen's editorial control on camera.[6] Although I do not go so far as Daniel Marcus and Almin Kara in referring to the mid-1980s as part of a 'contemporary' moment (not least because almost ten years have passed since *they* themselves made this argument), I do agree with their position that taking a relatively long view allows connections to be made between the 'emerging forms and tendencies' of recent documentary productions and the 'precedents' of this earlier period (Marcus and Kara 2016: 2).

As with the emergence of the direct cinema documentaries of the 1960s (of which more later), formal and industrial transformations are intertwined with technological developments. The continued evolution of portable cameras marks a continuity with the earlier period of the music documentary, but has resulted in some quite distinct aesthetic qualities. For instance, the use of Steadicam to shoot *Dance Craze* (1981), a film about the British 2Tone scene, creates a sense of proximity to the live performance sequences that relies on a smoothness of movement that is quite different from the jerky and unstable 'shaky-cam' of direct cinema produced by the use of handheld Auricon and Éclair 16mm cameras in films like *Dont Look Back* (1967)[7] and *Gimme Shelter* (1970). Furthermore, the use of remotely controlled cameras, drones and GoPro devices (as seen in films like *Folklore: The Long Pond Sessions* (2020), *The Eras Tour* and *Billie Eilish: The World's a Little Blurry* (2021), respectively) enables novel points of view because of the physical separation from an operator that was largely impossible in earlier periods, but which have become standard aesthetic features of recent music documentaries.

MTV, of course, also provides an important influence.[8] The channel – itself a relatively early product of satellite and cable television technologies – not only acted as a space for the exhibition of music documentary content but also influenced and refreshed documentary production through the ubiquity of music video aesthetics, which frequently stressed artifice and manipulation (especially with digital tools) over authenticity.[9] MTV's subsequent fall in importance for the music industry ecosystem of the twenty-first century – in 2002, Simon Frith suggested that it was by then 'better understood as a youth service than a music channel' (2002: 278) – has in turn left a space for music content that has been filled by social media and tube sites, but has also resulted in documentary content relocating to other spaces in the audiovisual ecosystem (Klein 2021). This includes those emerging from digital infrastructures like streaming services (see below).

There are also particularly important textual interventions towards the start of this period that continue to shape the form and have helped to determine the periodization of this book. The first of these is the intervention of the parodic mockumentary film *This Is Spinal Tap* (1984). Iversen and MacKenzie have argued that the incisiveness of the parody demonstrates that by the early 1980s, the music documentary was capable of eliciting a 'combination of audience and industry recognition' (2021b: 11). Thomas Doherty's contemporaneous review presents the less favourable view that *Tap*'s 'note-for-note assaults on fatuous rock music ... are less ferocious than the trashing given the "rockumentary" form itself', suggesting that 'it's the genre that's tapped out' (1985: 13). I have argued elsewhere that the intervention of *Spinal Tap* creates a rupture in the documentary representation of popular music, with those following in its wake having to negotiate its presence in order to avoid being tainted by its malignant scent (Wallace 2019: 87–92). This can manifest as momentary textual gestures, such as *Spinal Tap* guitarist Nigel Tufnel (Christopher Guest) appearing on a poster in the opening moments of the Blur documentary *No Distance Left to Run* (2010). Or it can be more structural in nature, as is evident in *Anvil! The Story of Anvil* (2008), which makes direct textual references to *Spinal Tap* in its narrative structure, the use of Stonehenge as a location and the replication of elements of its mise en scène (Wallace 2019: 88–92). Likewise, the interview sequences of *U2: Rattle and Hum* (1988) suggest a recognition of the clichéd vocabulary of the rock film, with drummer Larry Mullen Jr. requiring multiple attempts to describe the film as 'a musical journey' because of his bandmates' inability to keep their faces straight; significantly, these out-takes are 'left in' to show that the band are aware of their own clichés. The continued potential for the post-1984 music documentary to be read through the lens of *Spinal Tap* has led Iversen and MacKenzie to suggest that it 'marks the beginning of another phase of the genre' (2021b: 11), and the period covered by this book is congruent with the more self-reflexive, intertextual music documentaries that have emerged in order to avoid its long shadow.

A second significant film is the near-simultaneous release of Jonathan Demme's 1984 Talking Heads concert film *Stop Making Sense*. In his review of the film, Doherty places it in a direct relationship with *Spinal Tap*, suggesting that it '[evades] rock-doc cliches and rock-vid encroachment with equal agility' (Doherty 1985: 14). Described by Pauline Kael as 'close to perfection' (2016), *Stop Making Sense* is significant because it offered a moment of reinvigoration for the genre during which its aesthetic possibilities were reconsidered. For both Doherty and Kael, the film proposed a way forward for the music documentary in a context in which the genre was being snagged on the dual horns of incisive parody and low critical worth. Taken together, then, *Spinal Tap*, *Stop Making Sense* and the 1980s in general stand as the start of a period of generic transformation, the former posing the question of how to be innovative and interesting when making films about music in a context in which all of the clichés have been laid bare, the latter providing a range of possible answers to that question.

The other key context that defines the periodization of this book and speaks to the current prominence of the music documentary is a set of larger developments related to the viability – and visibility – of documentary cinema as a mainstream commercial form. When writing the introduction to the first edition of *New Challenges for Documentary* in 1988, Alan Rosenthal and John Corner suggested that documentary was 'going through a period where there was a drop in innovative creative energy and funding opportunity, perhaps also in audience interest' (2005: 1). By the time of the second edition in 2005, the pair were able to identify some signs of work 'that [appeared] to buck this trend' (2005: 2). In particular, *Bowling for Columbine*'s (2002) critical and commercial success demonstrated that 'the ability for a documentary film to break into popular theatrical cinema is still there, given the right combination of storytelling, directing ability and the presentation of a theme already felt as important in the public imagination' (2005: 2).

The first decade of the twenty-first century saw the fortunes of big-screen documentaries continue to change, with a range of high-profile films capturing the public's imagination and showing that documentary cinema could find mainstream success (Saunders 2010: 1–2). These included *Fahrenheit 9/11* (2004), Michael Moore's follow-up to *Columbine* and at that point the most commercially successful documentary film ever made, as well as *Touching the Void* (2003), *Super Size Me* (2004), *March of the Penguins* (2005) and *An Inconvenient Truth* (2006). By 2013, Nick Fraser, editor of the BBC's *Storyville* (1997–) strand, was able to claim that 'nowadays it's common to hear documentary film described as the new rock'n'roll', with Hollywood directors and actors eager to have their names associated with documentary projects (2013: x).

Music documentaries have contributed to this renewed critical and commercial landscape, offering a variety of different approaches to the subject of music that includes observational portraits of living music stars and archival portraits of dead ones, documentaries about specific genres of music, music scenes, particular gigs and iconic locations. There are documentaries about instruments and artwork, record labels, producers and production processes, songwriting and fans. There are the ever-present concert films, and even documentaries *about* documentaries. The genre has also received substantial critical acclaim, winning the Academy Awards for Best Documentary at the 85th (*Searching for Sugar Man* (2012)), 86th (*20 Feet from Stardom* (2013)), 88th (*Amy* (2015))[10] and 94th (*Summer of Soul (...Or, When the Revolution Could Not Be Televised)* (2021)) ceremonies.

Television has also played a prominent role. Although Simon Frith suggested in 2002 that there was an uneasy relationship between music and television in that 'it is rare to watch a television programme without music, and just as rare to watch a programme that is really about music' (2002: 278), the same argument could not be so easily made in 2024. Although my work here – and Chapter 3 in particular – stresses that there continues to be relatively few programmes that focus on musicality itself or that 'have changed the way we hear or understand a composer or composition' (Frith 2002: 280), the picture is more hopeful. Over the past twenty years, music programming has formed a core element of the Sky Arts channel and the weekend scheduling of BBC Four, and the BBC's annual coverage of the Glastonbury festival has become suitably mammoth (Weston 2021a; Weston and Samuel 2022). Furthermore, the *Classic Albums* (1992–2021) series and the television documentaries of composer Howard Goodall *have* made attempts to draw attention to *how* the music that we are familiar with operates.

The period of expansion within cinema exhibition has been augmented (and perhaps even superseded) by digital streaming platforms where music documentaries have become an important weapon in the streamers' battle for dominance. Tatiana Siegel has characterized this as 'a land grab' (2019), with each streamer securing high-profile music content to ensure its position within the marketplace. For example, through acquisitions and original productions, Netflix has developed a broad range of music documentary series and features that are comfortably placed alongside the rest of their documentary and dramatic offerings. These include observational portrait films (*I'll Sleep When I'm Dead* (2016), *Gaga: Five Foot Two* (2017) and *Miss Americana* (2020)), concert films (*Ariana Grande: Excuse Me, I Love You* (2020)], *Barbra: The Music … The Mem'ries … The Magic!* (2017), *Homecoming: A Film By Beyoncé* (2019]) and *Taylor Swift: Reputation Stadium Tour* (2018)), archival and expository films (*What Happened, Miss Simone*; *Rolling Thunder Revue: A Bob Dylan Story by Martin Scorsese* (2019), *Wham!*) and original series (*Song Exploder* (2020), *ReMastered* (2018–19), *Robbie Williams* and the non-US distribution rights to *The Defiant Ones* (2017)).

Tom Hemingway has argued in regard to the placement of comedy on Netflix that the association of particular comedians with specific platforms – Jerry Seinfeld or Adam Sandler with Netflix, for instance – functions as an important method of cross-promotion that helps to define an identity for both the platform and the comedian (2021: 110, 114). The same is true for music stars, where their appearance on streaming services helps to position both the platform and the star within the broader digital media economy. Thus, Netflix's deals with artists like Taylor Swift, Lady Gaga and Beyoncé act as an enticement for fans of those artists to subscribe to the service, while simultaneously associating the stars with a dominant global media brand.

This sense of cross-promotion is not limited to Netflix, and the other major streaming services have developed similarly productive relationships with music stars and film-makers. Apple, for example, holds the world screening rights to the Ed Sheeran documentary *Songwriter* (Stutz 2018) and has used its ownership of Spike Jonze's *The Beastie Boys Story* (2020), Todd Haynes's *The Velvet Underground* (2021), *Billie Eilish: The World's a Little Blurry* and *Selena Gomez: My Mind and Me* (2022) as a subscription incentive for its Apple TV+ platform. Similarly, Disney+ has taken advantage of associations with musical stars, including poaching both Swift and Beyoncé from Netflix and becoming the home of The Beatles online output, acting as distributor for Peter Jackson's *The Beatles: Get Back* (2021) series, the accompanying reissue of the 1970 *Let It Be* documentary and as European distributor of the *McCartney 3,2,1* (2021) series (produced by the Disney-owned Hulu platform). We can even see individual streaming services commissioning their own version of the same kinds of programmes, such as the way Netflix, Disney+ and Apple TV+ each have their own 'behind the song' documentary strands (*Song Exploder* (2020), *McCartney 3,2,1* and *Watch the Sound with Mark Ronson* (2021), respectively). This digital placement also creates an association with the kinds of 'quality' output with which these subscription services aim to be aligned. As Sudeep Sharma suggests, '[Netflix] has made feature-length documentary a core pillar of its service, both as a way to highlight its connection to quality cinema and to distinguish its catalog from more mundane forms of television programming' (2016: 143; Jenner 2018: 139–60).

The placement of music documentaries within the catalogue of high-profile streaming services is not just a matter of mutual image curation. There is also a substantial 'halo effect' on music sales and streams. As Justin Lacob, head of development for documentary studio XTR, has suggested, 'you're getting people in to watch the doc … you're then increasing downloads or streaming revenue. [Artists and labels are] taking a cut, and [streaming companies] [are] keeping those viewers in the ecosystem for longer. It all sends back to driving downloads, driving streaming revenue' (Terry 2021). The current boom in music documentary production is part of a highly commercial, and mutually beneficial, strategy to maximize subscription revenues and music sales (and streams) and as such is the epitome of 'the synergistic relationship between filmmaker, artist, studio, and record company' that Michael Brendan Baker has argued has been important to music documentaries since the 1959 *Jazz on a Summer's Day* (2011: 102). Disney+'s $75 million deal to secure the global screening rights to *The Eras Tour* only confirms this (Spangler 2024b). These contexts position the music documentary as a significant cultural form that has gained critical and commercial success and plays an important role in the creation and dissemination of the public image of music stars; and this book offers a detailed analysis of how this works at a textual level.

The State of the Field

In 2013, Michael Chanan noted that 'films about music and musicians have been a major strand of documentary since the 1960s, but you wouldn't know it from the attention they've received in documentary studies' (2013: 337). In the subsequent decade, this picture has changed substantially. Keith Beattie's (2019) film-specific BFI Classic on *Dont Look Back* (1967) has been complemented by three substantial edited collections – *The Music Documentary: Acid Rock to Electropop* (Edgar, Fairclough-Isaacs and Halligan 2013a), *Mapping the Rockumentary: Images of Sound and Fury* (Iversen and MacKenzie 2021a) and Kirsty Fairclough's forthcoming *This Me: Interrogating the Female Pop Star Documentary* (expected 2025) – that offer broad coverage and a wide range of perspectives. Benjamin J. Harbert's *American Music Documentary* (2018) takes an ethnomusicological approach to the analysis of five significant music documentaries, and Laura Niebling's *Rockumentary: Theorie, Geschichte und Industrie / Rockumentary: Theory, Narrative and Industry* (2018) offers a more text-based approach, but is currently in print only in German.

The bibliography of this book demonstrates clearly that discussions of documentary texts that relate to music are numerous and dispersed across a wide range of fields beyond those anchored within the field of documentary studies, including the intersection of music and television (Frith 2002; Huber 2011; Long and Wall 2010, 2013), the relationship between music documentaries and biopics (Andrews 2021: 158–67; Bingham 2010: 223–37; Brown and Vidal 2014; Tibbetts 2005; Wall and Pillai 2018) and the consideration of the oeuvre of particular artists (Neaverson 1997; Reiter 2008) or musical genres (Gabbard 1996; Scott 2019; Wall and Long 2010). In fact, a key challenge when writing this book has been to navigate the mosaic of perspectives on the subject while also retaining a space for my own voice. This is especially true given that I am also interested in moving beyond scholarship that speaks directly of documentaries, but also literature that concerns aspects of music culture that overlap with documentary concerns while not being explicitly *about* music documentaries, such as the operations of the music industry, processes of creativity and the nature of fan engagement.

Much of this literature will be explored in more detail in the following chapters, but I want to identify some broad tendencies within the existing scholarship that emerge as points of departure for my work here. There are several reasons why the book takes its starting point as 1980, but the principal one is that the preponderance of scholarship on the music documentary remains focused on a handful of music documentaries (mostly films) that have received levels of attention equal to the most written-about non-music documentaries. These are the documentaries that emerged from the direct cinema documentary movement of the 1960s and include *What's Happening! The Beatles in the USA* (1964) (McElhaney 2009: 63–90; Saunders 2007; Wallace 2019: 39–63), *Dont Look Back* (Beattie 2005, 2008: 59–81, 2019; James 2016: 200–12; Romney 1995; Rothman 1997: 144–210; Saunders 2007: 57–83), *Monterey Pop* (1968) (James

2016: 212–23; Plasketes 1989; Saunders 2007; Westrup 2021; Wright 2013), *Woodstock* (1970) (James 2016: 228–45; Plasketes 1989; Wright 2013) and *Gimme Shelter* (1970) (Harbert 2018: 24–66; James 2016: 286–99; Kael 1970; Kolker 1971; McElhaney 2009: 76–90; Saunders 2007; Vogels 2005: 74–99; Wright 2013).[11]

Gunnar Iversen and Scott MacKenzie suggest that this particular group of films 'helped shape both documentary form and popular music performances' (2021b: 2), and Laurel Westrup argues that *Monterey Pop* became the blueprint for subsequent concert films (2021). The influence on documentary cinema more generally is also acknowledged by Chanan, who suggests that *Dont Look Back* in particular can be understood as 'paradigmatic for documentary' (2013: 337). Chanan argues that this moment of flourishing was enabled by the combination of the philosophical underpinnings of direct cinema – the appearance of objectivity and non-intervention – with the lightweight camera and sound equipment, which encouraged the depiction 'of live music-making in its rightful place and for its own sake' and in so doing had the potential to 'restore the musical object to the social reality of its practice' (2013: 338). This is most visible in the 'festival' films *Monterey Pop* and *Woodstock*; however, Chanan traces it back to *Momma Don't Allow* (1956), a short film shot in a London jazz club that was both an emblematic example of the British Free Cinema documentary movement and a 'candid portrayal of a contemporary sub-culture' (2013: 338), and *Jazz on a Summer's Day*, Bert Stern and Aram Avakian's record of the 1958 Newport Jazz Festival, which Chanan describes as 'an almost ethnographic portrait of the audience in its natural habitat' (2013: 339).

This focus on the relationship between music (particularly live music) and its audience has led to the five direct cinema documentaries mentioned above being discussed collectively within an overarching 'rise and fall' narrative that is paralleled with the (particularly United States) counterculture of the time. According to this narrative, The Beatles (*What's Happening!*) represent a light of hope following the Kennedy assassination and *Dont Look Back* exhibits the maturation of musical, documentary and sociocultural forms and forces. These are followed by the utopian highs of *Monterey Pop* and *Woodstock* and, ultimately, the nightmare come-down of Altamont (*Gimme Shelter*) which stands in for the death of the countercultural revolution. Such an arc can be found in works by Iversen and MacKenzie (2021b: 2), George M. Plaskates (1989), Dave Saunders (2007), Jonathan B. Vogels (2005) and Julie Lobalzo Wright (2013), among others.

This scholarship forms an important background to my analysis here, but it also poses something of a critical obstacle in that this 'rise and fall' narrative suggests a closure that requires later texts to be understood as standing *apart* from this group. This also has the effect of positioning later documentaries as less worthy, in part because the self-evident significance of the direct cinema films has been retrospectively tied to this narrative. Some limited attention has been paid to music documentaries that have followed this counterculture cycle, and it is possible to identify an embryonic canon of subsequent works that could include *The Last Waltz* (1978) (Beattie 2008: 72–4; Grochowski 2019; Plasketes 1989; Sarchett 1994), *Dig!* (2004) (Stahl 2013: 64–99; Strachan and Leonard 2009), *Metallica: Some Kind of Monster* (2004) (Beattie 2005: 34–6; Scott 2019), *Searching for Sugar Man* (Cole 2013; Gardner and Moorey 2016; Helgesson 2013; Hyslop 2013; Lewsen 2013; Rommen 2013; Watson 2013) and *Amy* (Andrews 2017; Polaschek 2018). One aim of this book, then, is to look beyond this identifiable canon of works and suggest some of the ways in which the music documentary has operated over the past forty or so years, apart from the influence of direct cinema. The films and programmes chosen here reflect a variety of approaches to the theme of music, though they do so within what could be understood as a 'mainstream' framework, given the centrality of industry and 'the popular' in my work. This still leaves room for variety and the corpus of texts includes films that focus on mainstream pop acts like Katy Perry (*Katy Perry: Part of Me* (2012)) and Ed Sheeran (*Songwriter*), jazz stars (*Billie* (2019)) and rock, indie and 'alternative' artists (*Mistaken for Strangers* (2013)) as well as taking in a range of styles, including those that take fairly traditional observational and expository approaches to documenting their subject (*Billie Eilish: The World's a Little Blurry*) to those that make complex archival connections or deploy self-reflective techniques (*20,000 Days on Earth* (2014)) to open up spaces through which the nature of documentary representation itself becomes part of the enquiry.

Nevertheless, I would not want to give the impression that the corpus selection has been particularly schematic or has been designed to be either exhaustive or representative. I *do* make attempts throughout this book to ensure that the coverage is broad and that the key case studies are supplemented by numerous smaller examples to demonstrate the wider applicability of the ideas being developed. However, it is impossible to cover all bases and so there is an element of having to follow paths that are of most interest to me and I make no apologies for this. Furthermore, my subject has proved to be even more of a moving target than I had initially anticipated when drafting the proposal in Spring 2020. Certain of the contextual features have accelerated over the last five years in unpredictable ways, and the Covid-19 period itself produced a range of interesting texts which were themselves shaped by being produced in lockdown conditions. There are, therefore, films considered in this book in various levels of detail that had not been announced when planning this book and other selections have been made for pragmatic reasons related to access, whether that be their availability on streaming services, or because they have been (re)issued in cinemas and on DVD and Blu-Ray.

This book's focus on pop means that there is a prioritization of material that has either received a mainstream release itself or *concerns* mainstream music acts. This does not, however, mean that everything mentioned here is, or has remained, easily accessible. Those films that are not explicitly associated with a particular music artist are generally less likely to receive widespread distribution in the first place (see, for instance, some of the films discussed in the chapters on songwriting and fans). Television historians are intimately familiar with the difficulties accessing historical television programmes and that is the case for some of the documentaries discussed in Chapters 3 and 4, where I have had to rely on my own off-air recordings for some programmes and digital repositories such as Box of Broadcasts for others. The ephemerality of television is also a condition of the wider streaming landscape and the proprietorial landscape of the streamers means that the texts addressed here are spread across a range of subscription services, with some – such as *Taylor Swift: Reputation Studium Tour* – now inaccessible. I have tried to convey the character of each of the texts that I discuss here, but would recommend that where possible the original documentary be sought out for the sake of completeness.

Hierarchies of Value

One starting point in this endeavour is to consider some of the reasons why music documentaries made since 1980 have received less sustained critical attention. In order to do so, the relative success of direct cinema can act as a counterexample, and I want to consider three interlinked reasons for this neglect:

1. **Observation:** In appearing to stress their authenticity, direct cinema documentaries had a natural affinity with the discourses surrounding the rock and folk music that they documented. Since the 1980s, this approach has been supplanted by a much broader range of methods of documentary production that stresses hybridity, performativity and self-referentiality which raise the spectre of manipulation (and thus inauthenticity) as a key signifying strategy.

2. **Commerciality:** The above transformation has taken place within industrial contexts (in music, film and television) that have been eager to exploit the commercial potential of documentaries as products in their own right *and* as key sites of brand construction and image management.
3. **Pop:** These shifts have occurred in tandem with a broadening of the generic scope of the music that is the focus of these documentaries, with pop becoming more prominent and bringing with it the various cultural (and often gendered) associations of such a change.

Observation

We do not need to look very far to find scholarship that places particular value upon observational approaches to musical subjects. Iversen and MacKenzie, for example, argue that the Paul Anka documentary *Lonely Boy* (1962) '[promised] the audience something new and more real than the older, more expository documentaries' (2021b: 6), and David E. James suggests that direct cinema's 'advance over previous expository forms allowed an unprecedented immediacy and fidelity' (2016: 187). This stance is most strikingly articulated by Robert Edgar, Kirsty Fairclough-Isaacs and Benjamin Halligan in their dismissal of numerous music documentaries made since the late 1990s. 'How can it be,' they ask, 'that documentary, operating in the field of popular music, has strayed so far from ideas of objectivity and reportage – ideas that represent the fundamentals of the documentary form – and has become pure promotion?' (2013b: xi). Direct cinema is, of course, the documentary mode that comes closest to being defined by priorities of 'objectivity and reportage'. Such a position makes an explicit link between commerciality and low cultural value that I wish to challenge throughout this book by suggesting that documentaries made in the service of promotion (which – as I will argue – is most music documentaries) can still be engaging, complex and aesthetically interesting.

Brian Winston suggests that the 'hand-held casual aesthetic of direct cinema meshed perfectly with the anarchic oppositional world of rock' (2000: 52). At an aesthetic level, the sense of seriousness and authenticity that characterize both observational documentary *and* rock and folk music was conveyed through this roughness of the image; everything feels spontaneous. For James, this contributed 'notions of existential presentness ... as well as to an overall sense of cultural urgency – the same skein of values that sustained folk music and would soon transform rock 'n' roll' (2016: 188). Although these developments may have been organic, they were also used in a tactical way, and Robert

Strachan and Marion Leonard talk of direct cinema's *'supposed* "transparency" of approach' (2009: 285 – my emphasis), which implies that the mode's sense of unofficiality does not accurately reflect the real production context; all of these documentaries were commissioned in some way, and Jonathan Romney points out that there is a 'fine distinction between a job from behind the lines and an inside job' (1995: 87).

The distinction between what direct cinema's aesthetic qualities promised and what it actually delivered is now a well-trodden furrow that has implications for our understanding of the 1960s direct cinema music documentaries.[12] William Rothman, for example, suggests that we should understand the relationship between Bob Dylan and D. A. Pennebaker during the production of *Dont Look Back* as that between 'co-conspirators' (1997: 147). Such a realization shatters observational documentary's illusion of authenticity, and with it any sense of sincerity associated with the subjects of those documentaries. In making visible the inauthenticity of observational documentary, the inauthenticity of rock and folk music is itself revealed. Dylan not looking at the camera in *Dont Look Back*, for instance, is transformed from a signifier of an unobtrusive camera to an indicator that a performance of 'ignoring the camera' is taking place.

Nevertheless, the association of direct cinema with authenticity, objectivity and immediacy remains a residual characteristic of documentary cinema more generally. This can be contrasted with a concurrent stylistic shift from this congruent form of documentation towards approaches that are more diverse, self-reflexive and hybrid in nature. These qualities are often signified by a concurrent move from 'rough' to 'slick' that suggests construction and a professionalization (and thus commercialization) that could appear suspect if looked at on a purely surface level. This is especially the case when viewed through an evaluative lens that prioritizes the aesthetics of authenticity, even when such a thing is a fallacy. Although I want to argue here that the handheld roughness of the image does not 'guarantee' authenticity and truthfulness any more than aesthetically stylized documentaries guarantee fabrication, such a position is not necessarily an uncontroversial one.

Commerciality

As well as gesturing towards a preference for the supposed intellectual agenda of direct cinema, Edgar et al. also demonstrate a particular concern about the 'institutionalization' of the music documentary, and the genre is argued to be 'in crisis' because it 'has become so fully given over to commercial concerns'

(2013b: xi). Similarly, Chanan suggests that this commercial element, and more precisely the knowledge that 'many music documentaries are made at the bidding of the musicians (or their managers)', might explain their critical neglect, though he also suggests that 'this should not become an excuse for ignoring [their] filmic qualities' (2013: 337).

However, to overlook the genre for these reasons is to accept the implied argument that the music documentary has only recently become commercialized. Rothman's, Romney's and my own work has proposed arguments about the links between documentary display in direct cinema films and the construction of a star image (Romney 1995: 88–9; Rothman 1997: 154–63; Wallace 2019: 78), and uniquely, James's commentary on the 1960s music documentaries does not end with *Gimme Shelter* but extends to 1974's *Ladies and Gentlemen: The Rolling Stones* and re-frames the 'rise-and-fall' narrative as a nuanced engagement with commercialization. *Ladies and Gentlemen* is not primarily concerned with situating the Rolling Stones within their social milieu, but 'honing their image for its afterlife as a sheerly commercial brand' (James 2016: 287). This continues a strand of commerciality in the cycle that includes the *Dont Look Back* sequence in which Albert Grossman and Tito Burns negotiate Dylan's television fee, which places Dylan 'in the commercial system that his earlier protest songs had indicted' (James 2016: 207), and the contrast that James makes between the egalitarian spirit of *Woodstock* with the festival's status as a commercial venture and the film's position as a Hollywood product thanks to Warner Bros.' $50 million return on a $1 million investment (2016: 244).

Commercial entities have always played a crucial role in the production of music documentaries. Iversen and MacKenzie suggest that Columbia Records were given significant editorial control in the artist and song selection for *Jazz on a Summer's Day* in exchange for the provision of sound recording equipment (2021b: 6). Niebling is even more radical, arguing that texts as varied as the early sound Vitaphone shorts made for Warner Bros. in the 1920s and post-war radio and television programmes such as *American Bandstand* (1952–2002) contributed 'to a fundamental understanding of music documentation as a promotional instrument' (2021: 32). In this context, Niebling positions the direct cinema directors as 'sympathetic [*merchants*] of music culture' (2021: 32).

Commercialization is not, therefore, a new phenomenon for music documentary, and discounting a film's worthiness on that basis would seem misguided. Nevertheless, it should be recognized that the commercial context has intensified significantly since the early 1970s. James's account of the direct cinema films is striking in its detail of how limited their initial circulation was.

D. A. Pennebaker struggled to secure distribution deals for *Dont Look Back* and *Monterey Pop*, with both being limited to screenings in small theatres more likely to be showing pornography, and the challenging subject matter of *Gimme Shelter* meant that its release required private funding (2016: 211, 243, 259). Although these films are now considered important documentaries and have been widely seen (*Dont Look Back*, *Monterey Pop* and *Gimme Shelter* have all been released by The Criterion Collection, for example, alongside other direct cinema films), there is a discrepancy between their initial invisibility and that of more recent music documentaries. K. J. Donnelly argued in 2016 that 'rock documentaries remain firmly minority interest films' (2015: 77), but it seems difficult to sustain such an argument in a global media context where documentary films and television programmes are widely visible and aggressively promoted. Indeed, it is worth noting that as of December 2023, of the four 'non-serious' pop documentaries that Edgar et al. give as examples of the poor state of the genre (2013c: 21 n.19), *Justin Bieber: Never Say Never* (2011), *Michael Jackson's This Is It* (2009) and *Katy Perry: Part of Me* currently occupy the positions of second, eighth, and twenty-fifth highest grossing feature-length documentaries of all time worldwide (*Demi Lovato: Stay Strong* (2012), the fourth title, did not have a cinema release).[13]

There is some correlation, therefore, between box office performance – or perhaps the commercial power of the stars featured in these films – and the negative critical perception of these texts. Although this has not been a strictly determining factor in the corpus selection of this book, I have made an attempt to address a number of texts which *do* fit into the criteria of being both commercially successful *and* critically maligned. This does not necessarily make them uninteresting, and I discuss the Katy Perry film in detail in Chapter 1, for example, to make arguments about how the complexity of the mainstream concert film might go unrecognized because of this prioritizing of their commercial impetus as an evaluative framework.

Pop

The music documentary's movement away from observation and from prioritizing rock music (and prior to that jazz and folk) has also been seen as representing a movement away from seriousness. Such a view reinforces cultural hierarchies that emerged in the late 1960s as a condition of the new rock culture epitomized by the output of *Rolling Stone* magazine, and that continues to shape public tastes. Diane Railton has compared the delineation of rock and pop to the materialization of the bourgeois public sphere of the eighteenth and nineteenth centuries theorized by Jürgen Habermas. As Railton notes, 'just as the bourgeois public sphere was a starting point that facilitated the hegemony of bourgeois ideals and political power, rock culture served as the starting point for the hegemony within popular music discourse of particular ways of understanding and appreciating music' (Railton 2001: 322). Most notably, these debates enacted a split between mainstream 'pop' and the more culturally valuable 'rock', often drawn out along gendered lines. Thus both the bourgeois public sphere and the new rock orthodoxy were 'based on what are traditionally considered masculine values (reason, objectivity, the mind), and eschewed the traditionally feminine (emotion, the home, the body)' (Railton 2001: 322). The status of rock (and other forms of music that coalesce around the figure of an 'artist') continues to be elevated by the systematic disparagement of pop, just as film is often held up as superior to television, or so-called 'quality' television as superior to 'trash TV'.

Such attitudes towards pop persist. David Hepworth suggests that in popular music discourse 'pop music is about pleasure' whereas 'rock music is about, or at least allegedly about, worth, substance and … gravitas' (2018: 76). From a similarly sympathetic vantage point, Mike Jones suggests that

> 'Pop' is the faint sound of a soap bubble bursting – and pop products are treated, colloquially as well as in academia, as enjoying the same (dubious) qualities as such bubbles – they are short-lived and have gaudy surfaces below which lie hollow centers filled with hot air. 'Pop' is now almost a term of abuse – and 'pop fans' can be treated with considerable disdain not just by critics of pop but from within the general fields of popular musical consumption and popular cultural studies. (2002: 147)

Furthermore, as Jones reminds us, 'popular music is what it says it is, music that has become popular, and to become popular music needs to be disseminated and consumed in a mass way' (2002: 149). The façade of aesthetic directness – often understood as a call to physicality and movement (i.e. dance), rather than thoughtful contemplation (i.e. connoisseurship) – is combined with the commercial infrastructures through which popularity is enacted to produce an object (a record, a pop star, a documentary) that is doubly maligned because of its embodiment of a sense of superficial commercialism. Pop music is thus often positioned as inauthentic, unworthy and feminine, and viewed suspiciously as a result.

Again, this attitude is most visible in Edgar et al.'s work, where the music documentary's links to reality television and celebrity culture in the 1990s and 2000s are explored in relation to *Madonna: Truth or Dare* (1991) (known as *In Bed with Madonna* in the UK), which is viewed disdainfully because of the film's suggestion 'that the key tenets of the music documentary could be both scandalous, wildly entertaining, and overwhelmingly trashy' (2013c: 17). Furthermore, the evaluative hierarchies that have tended to separate rock, folk and other singer-songwriting traditions from pop are fastidiously re-enforced in the suggestion that by the early 2010s 'the music documentary is no longer reserved for "serious" musicians, as evidenced by the popularity of pop documentaries, often afforded a full theatrical release' (2013b: 18–19). Apart from exhibiting the discursive tendency that Hepworth contests, whereby pop music is framed as 'something a serious musician could shrug off without thinking' (2018: 76), these 'pop' films are placed in direct contrast with 'the more respectable quarters of the music documentary' which the authors most directly associate with Martin Scorsese's work (Edgar, Fairclough-Isaacs and Halligan 2013c: 19). I want to suggest that contrary to this position, taking 'pop' forms seriously allows us to think in detail about the mechanics of mainstream cultural spaces and that music documentaries that focus on pop stars place these concerns at their centre.

Taking these three aspects together, it is possible to identify a range of value judgements acting against the music documentary in its recent contexts. It is now more commonly 'pop' than 'rock'. Its commercial function is more visible than ever in both its content (selling pop stars/music) *and* the media contexts in which the form operates (competition between media platforms). This context is itself more hybrid in nature, being as much aligned with the 'notoriously hybridized' (Turner 2015) medium of television and streaming as it is with cinema exhibition, and reflecting the genre's own unstable aesthetic profile which is frequently 'an amalgam of documentary styles that have accumulated during the last several decades' (Stahl 2013: 73). Each of these discursive contexts has played a part in the genre's critical neglect or the channelling of critical attention towards established, 'safe' cultural objects.

Drawing on Chanan's position, I want to argue that it is a mistake to assume that the music documentary is fundamentally uninteresting *because* of these aspects and instead argue that it is precisely these contexts that charge it with cultural power. The landscape of the music documentary over the last three to four decades shows that it is a vibrant and significant cultural form that has gained critical and commercial success and occupies an important place within the creation and dissemination of the public image of the music stars that are its subjects. Rather than view these recent trends as a corruption of the documentary project and of a failure to reach the potential of the 1960s direct cinema films, I explore the position that these texts occupy *within* the commercial infrastructures in which they are located. One aspect that lies at the heart of this book, then, is how music documentaries negotiate their dual status as commercial products and works of culture, and I argue that this tension frequently makes them fascinating objects of study because these negotiations become a central facet of the texts themselves. Furthermore, I suggest that the underlying commercial impetus does not preclude music documentaries from being visually and sonically interesting. The aesthetic strategies of these texts are a primary concern because it is here – in their construction of a star image and their function as artworks in tension with that commercial process – where they make their meaning.

I am also interested in taking 'pop' films seriously, and the selection of films and television programmes examined in this book is deliberately chosen to represent a range of musical genres that can be found within the mainstream music documentary form. This prioritizes films that address 'pop' music, but I am also drawn towards Motti Regev's argument that 'pop' and 'rock' 'are obviously linked together in their sonic textures and in their cultural histories' (Regev 2013: 1) and that rather than looking to delineate between the two it is often more useful to consider the wider musical ecosystem encompassed by their overlapping. I do not subscribe to the idea that there is *no* distinction to be made between 'pop' and 'rock'; regardless of the aesthetic and industrial qualities, which are not in themselves uncomplicated, a cultural distinction has frequently been evident within discourses of taste and value, as I have already noted and as I explore further in Chapter 4. Nevertheless, maintaining such distinctions is not particularly valuable when considering the formal and cultural place of documentaries that focus on music and musicians operating across the rock and pop spectrum, which often have a great deal in common. I, therefore, prefer to think about the artists being considered in this book in line with Regev's notion of 'pop-rock', a useful term that

> refers to music consciously created and produced by using amplification, electric and electronic instruments, sophisticated recording equipment (including samplers), by employing certain techniques of supposedly untrained vocal delivery, mostly those signifying immediacy of expression and spontaneity, and by filtering all these through sound editing, modification, and manipulation devices. (Regev 2013: 18)

This allows for the consideration of the more expansive music documentary field and a wider range of case studies than has been the case with earlier scholarship on the 'rockumentary' (and this is the only time that this term will be used by me in this book). Thus, the inclusion of documentary work that focuses on Billie Eilish, Katy Perry, Nick Cave, The Beatles, Take That, Depeche Mode, David Byrne and Beyoncé has a logic to it that would be less convincing in a book that aimed to focus solely on either 'pop' or 'rock'. There are moments in this book (such as in Chapter 4) where I am specifically concerned with the discursive relationship between pop and rock as it is articulated in the wider culture, but in general, when I refer to pop music or pop stars, I am referring to the wider pop-rock field that Regev identifies; thus Katy Perry, Billie Eilish and Nick Cave are all understood as 'pop stars' despite their generic variance.

Similarly, the pop-rock approach also explains some exclusions. Apart from the marginal discussions of the early jazz documentaries included in this chapter and a short analysis of the use of archive and colourization in *Billie*, this book largely excludes the discussion of jazz. This is not to suggest that the jazz documentary is uninteresting; indeed, an argument can be made that similar developments to those I identify here have taken place in the field of jazz and that it is worthy of its own study.[14] Rather jazz falls on the margins of the pop-rock oeuvre, which, as Regev suggests,

> allows us to include in it a diversity of styles and musicians that ranges from the most raucous works of bands such as the Velvet Underground or Nirvana, to the most formulaic work of the Archies or Avril Lavigne, from the most experimental work of Sonic Youth or Brian Eno, to the most pleasing work of Take That or Beyoncé – while excluding the likes of, say, Johnny Mathis, *The Sound of Music* soundtrack, or the works of Barbara [sic] Streisand. (Regev 2013: 21)

The Pop Star as Discursive Tension

I have already noted the ways in which we can consider music documentaries to be commercial productions, acting in support of the public image of the artists that are their subjects, and Strachan and Leonard remind us that 'rock documentaries cannot be separated from the industrial context in which they are produced' (2009: 284–85). I want to suggest that recognizing this does not invalidate the music documentary as a significant cultural form but allows some of the tensions that operate between the music industry and its audience to come into view. Pop stars are central to this tension and Matt Stahl characterizes the pop star (in typically gendered terms) as 'a double figure':

On the one hand, she is a symbolic figure offered for our consumption, contemplation, and identification; she enacts forms of expression, autonomy, and desirability, seeming to encapsulate some of our society's most cherished virtues and values. On the other hand, she is a political and economic actor, a working person whose contractually governed relationship to her company is sometimes one of real subordination. (2013: 2–3)

Part of the role of the star is to obscure the fact that the first 'figure' is a product of the second. Mike Jones makes the argument that 'pop is ... a workplace, and its work is to create pleasure or the conditions of pleasure' and that overall the music industry 'is work masquerading as leisure' (2002: 156).

There is a clear resonance here with the ways in which the Hollywood musical has been theorized. Jane Feuer argues that the genre deploys a 'myth of entertainment' which occludes the labour involved in the production of entertainment and that 'the most complex type of film produced in Hollywood, paradoxically has always been the genre which attempts to give the greatest illusion of spontaneity and effortlessness' (Feuer 1977: 318). Similarly, in the seminal essay 'Entertainment and Utopia', Richard Dyer argues that the musical 'offers the image of "something better" to escape into', a utopian sensibility which provides 'temporary answers to the inadequacies of the society which is being escaped from through entertainment' (2002: 20, 25). For Jones, music serves a similar purpose: 'we dream other selves through it, imagine other lives ... Wherever music takes us it is always away from here' (2005: 246). The pop star plays a key role in this mediation, and ' "ordinary" life is made bearable by associating oneself with an artist (and/or star or celebrity) who lives an "extraordinary" life that might be enjoyed vicariously' (Jones 2005: 225). Rather than being seen in opposition to one another, then, we can instead see the 'pop star as artist/myth' and 'music industry as workplace' positions as going hand in hand, the former being deployed in a conscious and concerted manner to obfuscate the realities of the latter. As Jones suggests, 'the gaze of the audience [of pop music] must be distracted while the trick is performed' (Jones 2002: 156).

However, by placing commerciality at its centre, the contemporary music documentary draws attention to the industrial processes that go into constructing and projecting a star image and presents a self-awareness about its own place within those structures. The star is thus positioned as a near-mythical figure who is worthy of public adoration and documentary attention, and also as a worker whose efforts are shown in the documentary as well as being implicitly necessary for the existence of the documentary in the first place (they are workers *on the film* as well as being its subject). If the contemporary music documentary prioritizes anything, then, it is the exploration of the *relationship* between these two positions. It is engaged in a perpetual negotiation between justifying the worthiness of the subject – and thus upholding the extraordinary star image – while also demonstrating its documentary credentials by subjecting the star to scrutiny and examining the mechanisms and effort through which this success has been achieved. The complex tension that exists within the music documentary between a promise to reveal (and thus fulfil a documentary impetus) and its industrial requirements to fit within the acceptable parameters of a star's image is a fundamental consideration for this book and is bound up in the oscillation between ordinary/extraordinary, accessible/inaccessible and work/effortlessness that characterizes the star phenomenon more broadly. These two positions are fundamentally incompatible, however, and so the most interesting moments of any music documentary are often those where one position competes with the other.

Chapter Overview

The chapters of this book focus on four key spaces – sometimes literal; always discursive – in which both pop stardom and music documentaries are constituted and circulated, each of which forwards a different schema of access. These are:

1. The live performance space, usually a concert stage
2. The backstage space, which is also a space where the documentary asserts its efficacy
3. The creative space of music creation and promotion
4. The reception space of music consumption and the fan

Each of these spaces (and their respective chapters) contributes to a holistic picture of the tripartite relationship between the music star, the public and the documentary process itself. But this structure also represents a progression in how a sense of access to the star is articulated by the documentary framework. This is not necessarily a matter of literal physical proximity, but one which articulates a sense of intimacy, connection and understanding. Thus, a camera in the professional space of the concert performance might be able to come closer to the star than would be comfortable in a more observational space (such as a bedroom or dressing room), but there is an inherent distance maintained between the cinema audience and the pop star's sense of self. The sense of access increases across the chapters.

Chapter 1 examines the pop star at a distance, with the focus being on the various ways in which live performances are transformed into audiovisual texts. I suggest here that such texts should be understood as distinct from the live original, rather than as trans-media 'copies', and that far from being positioned as subservient to the experience of a live show, concert films function as cultural artefacts in their own right, and are not necessarily diminished by having the sense of liveness removed. This chapter also places the discursive construction of star images at its centre, exploring the ways in which concert films operate through what I refer to as a unity of fragmentation. The combinatory nature of concert films – produced through a multiplicity of viewpoints, an amalgamation of separate performances, the combination of on-stage meaning with off-stage action – establishes a mechanism by which musical performers use the on-stage space to cultivate alternative modes of performativity to that expressed in their 'off-stage' lives, and with it a density of meaning. One ironic result of this process is that despite their evident theatricality, moments of on-stage performance can sometimes result in more honest and spontaneous manifestation of an artist's musical persona than the 'backstage' versions discussed in Chapter 2.

Within the typical world of the music documentary, 'on-stage' finds its opposite in the 'backstage'. Adopting and adapting Jonathan Romney's notion of 'the backstage', Chapter 2 increases the film audience's proximity with the documentary subject and provides analysis of several films which assert their ability to gain access to, and elicit meaning from, the pop star through fundamentally different methodological (and thus stylistic) approaches. *Billie Eilish: The World's a Little Blurry*, *Billie*, *Searching for Sugar Man*, *Mistaken for Strangers* and *20,000 Days on Earth* address the fundamental performativity of their subjects, and of the documentary approaches *to* those subjects, and the impact that this has on the way the audience is asked to engage with the 'reality' of the person inhabiting the role of pop/rock star.

A key concern here is how the textual assertion of being 'backstage' (both literally and in terms of being 'out of the public eye') is established by the film-makers to promote a sense of access and intimacy. This creates a space through which different conceptualizations of 'authenticity' can be performed and articulated. This has wider implications for our understanding of how documentary subjects – even non-celebrities – perform 'being themselves' for the camera. Such a notion has previously played an important role in the music documentary's critical deprecation, given that the documentary enquiry itself becomes a catalyst for a particular kind of promotional self-performance even as it purports to interrogate that very process. The analysis here, then, moves beyond considering the ways in which authenticity is performed and constructed, to think about the self-reflexive ways in which this process becomes a structuring textual strategy in itself: a 'documentary backstage'.

More than any other artefact, the song is the defining component of the pop artist, and songwriting plays a key role in the curation of a musician's public image. However, the depiction of the creative process poses a particularly difficult problem for the documentary film-maker, given that much of it occurs in the inaccessible space of the songwriter's mind. Chapter 3 explores the representation of songwriting in the music documentary by unpicking an apparent paradox that lies at the heart of the visual representation of creativity more generally. For the work of art (the song) to function as a totemic component of the artist's mystique, it must appear to be the product of genius and, therefore, inexplicable and inaccessible; for it to be visible on film and explored as a documentary subject, it must be observable (or describable), and therefore appear as the product of labour. These two positions appear irreconcilable and this chapter explores the various ways in which this contradiction is negotiated. First of all, I examine the use of controlled staging to engineer situations in which songwriting can be observed and filmed, though argue that the focus is almost always on the 'progress' that results from moments of creativity, rather than the 'process' itself. In the second section, I discuss the ways in which the innovative labour of production and recording often comes to stand in for the writing process, through detailed analysis of a number of documentaries that focus on the writing and recording of The Beatles' album *Sgt. Pepper's Lonely Hearts Club Band* (1967). The final section explores the political strategies around representing songwriting as labour through the notion of ownership and authorship as it is articulated in the Ed Sheeran documentary *Songwriter* (2018).

The final chapter addresses the role that fans play in the music documentary. Although the focus of this chapter is a handful of films that make music fans their subject – *Tokyo Idols* (2017), *I Used to Be Normal: A Boyband Fangirl Story* (2018), *Sound It Out* (2011) and *Our Hobby Is Depeche Mode* (2007) – the fan has a ubiquitous, if transitory, presence within music documentaries and so the interaction of fan and artist across the genre more generally is a key site of analysis. The central argument is that fans' appearances in music documentary films are carefully controlled, with certain fan behaviours emphasized and others denied to project a particular star identity through association. Chapter 4 ends with a discussion of the ethical considerations that such treatment of fan subjects raises, especially given the power imbalance between them, their idols and the documentary makers, and the second half of the chapter examines the possibilities that emerge once the focus shifts from fans as a pathologized 'mob' to a collection of individuals with their own lives, beliefs and methods of engagement. Ultimately, an argument is made that the meaning of the pop artist articulated in the previous three chapters comes to find its clearest focus at the point of reception.

Overall, then, this is a book that argues for the place of the music documentary at the centre of the popular music star-making mechanism. At the same time, they are spaces that interrogate the popular music industry and contemporary documentary-making itself in a range of interesting ways. By placing discourses of access at their centre, music documentaries navigate an intricate tension between artistic and commercial imperatives and the analysis that follows examines this rich and complex set of relationships.

1

The Concert Film

The concert stage is one of the key sites where pop stardom is enacted. It is unusual in that it is part of a spatial relationship between star and audience that is both close and distant: close, because the star and their audience occupy a broadly similar physical space, and distant, because that proximity is only relative; they might temporarily share a postal address, but the audience remains some way away from the star and there is a vast numerical disparity between the individual performer and the mass audience that prevents genuine intimacy. This book begins with a chapter on the concert film because the onstage 'version' of the pop star is the most distant of those discussed here, with each successive chapter bringing us into greater proximity with the documentary subject. However, this distance does not mean that the concert film is straightforward, and the tension between documentary enquiry and star construction that I outlined in the introduction are visible within the onstage space of the live concert and the cinematic space of the concert film.

I argue throughout this chapter that the concert film should be understood as being separate from the live concert of which it is a record, that it deploys a set of aesthetic conventions that aim to 'enhance the effects of the musical performance' (Burns and Watson 2013: 103) for the viewer at home and that this is achieved through a narrative and editing schema that deploys what I call 'a continuity of fragmentation'. This aesthetic strategy enables a single, coherent performance to be assembled from a range of perspectives that prioritize a holistic view of the event that is not available to any one participant *in* that event (audience, performer or crew member alike) and is often composed of sonic and visual material assembled from a range of different performances in order to produce the best possible version of the event as the public-facing star text.

The Purpose of Concert Films

A range of different agendas, purposes and functions are held in balance by the concert film's varied stylistic qualities. We can see this in the different purposes ascribed to the sub-genre by critics, film-makers and musicians. Somewhat over-simplistically, Adrian Wootton suggests that 'most viewers watch concert films for one of two reasons: either they were not present at the concert being filmed, and so want to experience it vicariously, or they were and want to relive their memories of the event' (1995: 98). More convincing is Wooton's broader argument that the primary purpose of the concert film 'is to convey the essence of performance and the sense of an event' (1995: 100). Similarly, Laurel Westrup argues that concert films aim to produce 'the feeling of "being there"', with D. A. Pennebaker's *Monterey Pop* (1968) shifting the documentary perspective from being '*about* an event,' to '[placing viewers] *inside* it' (2021: 39). The experiential qualities of the concert film have also been recognized by Keith Beattie, who argues that in contrast to the factual regimes of knowledge often prioritized by documentary, 'the form of knowledge produced within this mode is subjective, affective, visceral and sensuous' (2005: 23).

Concert films also serve a commercial function. Although Wootton has described music documentaries as 'an adjunct of the marketing of music products by a global industry' (1995: 103), in more recent times they have proved to be box office successes in their own right, with five titles earning over $50 million apiece worldwide.[1] Beyond box office receipts, 'labels and publishers may benefit from concert films on several levels, ranging from negotiated licenses upfront for use of the music, to reaching new potential fans, to residual catalogue sales', as well as revenue from any soundtrack album (Donahue 2008). Niche and legacy artists like Rodriguez and Anvil can also find their careers rehabilitated by being the subject of successful documentaries. The concert film also has the potential to act as an enticement for audiences to buy tickets for future tour dates, a not inconsiderable outcome given the increasing reliance on income from concert ticket sales to offset declining record sales and underwrite musical careers in the streaming era (Krueger 2005; Papies and van Heerde 2017; Wlömert and Papies 2016: 325).

Alongside the commercial impetus, the artist can exploit documentary's capacity as a form of record to capture a particular moment in their career. U2's bass player Adam Clayton makes such a claim in *U2: Rattle and Hum* (1988), remarking that 'when a band is developing it goes through certain stages. And for us, we're not the same band we were when we recorded the *War* album,

Figure 1.1 The concert film is used by Taylor Swift to manage a transition between the stadium pop of *Taylor Swift: Reputation Stadium Tour* …

Figure 1.2 …and the 'cottagecore' indie-folk of *Folklore: The Long Pond Studio Sessions*.

for instance. And we captured that on *Under a Blood Red Sky*. And we just wanted to capture *this* period of the band.' Showcasing an artist at a moment of transition can also be advantageous for their future career. Steven E. Severn (2002) and Michael Brendan Baker (2015: 249) argue that *The Last Waltz* (1978) can be understood as an attempt to set Robbie Robertson (The Band's nominal leader) apart from his group at the moment of their splitting. Taylor Swift's *Folklore: The Long Pond Studio Sessions* (2020) can also be understood in this way, taking advantage of mandated social distancing during the Covid-19 pandemic to create an intimate live recording of her *Folklore* album that is drastically different to the spectacular stadium concerts captured in *Reputation Stadium Tour* (2018) and *Taylor Swift: The Eras Tour* (2023). Alongside her

Folklore and *Evermore* albums, *Long Pond* contributes to Swift's repositioning within an indie folk mode, and the mise en scène of the film – collaborator Aaron Dessner's timber-framed, rural Long Pond Studio; Swift's unfussy, 'cottagecore' clothing and understated hair and makeup – connects the songs (and the songwriter) with a musical genealogy associated with the likes of Carole King and Joni Mitchell (Figures 1.1 and 1.2).[2]

The concert film, then, acts as a site upon which a range of functions and purposes interact, including selling commercial products (tickets, albums, platform subscriptions), preserving particular moments of an artist's career, (re)positioning an artist in relation to their public and engaging with the experiential and affective aspects of live performance. This chapter is an attempt to explore this complexity by considering how these often-contradictory agendas inter-operate and are managed within these texts. This is not always straightforward, but does frequently result in films that are more complex than they are generally given credit for.

Eventfulness

The starting point for understanding the mechanics of the concert film, however, is to consider the ways in which the cinema audience is positioned in relation to the live event differently to that of the live audience. I argue that this should not be understood as an inferior replication of a live concert experience, where, as Herbert Molderings argues 'whatever survives ... is no more than a fragmentary, petrified vestige of a lively process that took place at a different time in a different place' (Molderings 1984: 172–3 quoted in Auslander 1999: 41). Instead, we should understand the creation of concert films as a process of transformation, with audiovisual techniques used to construct a filmic space that is related to, but distinct from, the original event. Such an approach opens up the possibility of considering concert films as having the capacity to function in aesthetically interesting ways. Landon Palmer, for instance, recognizes Spike Lee's achievements on *David Byrne's American Utopia* (2020) as legitimizing the film as 'a work of cinema' (2023: 1158), and my analysis here aligns with Susan Fast's argument about *U2 3D* (2008) that 'the film follows cinematic conventions, not the conventions of live popular music performance' (2013: 21). Thus, the sense of 'being there' that Westrup proposes is embodied in the concert film is not that experienced by any individual participant. Rather, through a regime of varied points of view, concert films construct a holistic, filmic (or televisual) space that transforms the live, present-tense event into a recorded, edited, past-tense representational space that is visually and sonically separate from the original event; that expresses its own aesthetic and experiential qualities; and that prioritizes the screen audience.

The privileging of the film's audience is addressed directly in one of the behind-the-scenes segments that are intercut with the performance sequences in *Homecoming: A Film by Beyoncé* (2019), which documents the star's landmark headline performance at the 2018 Coachella festival. In it, Beyoncé watches back footage of the rehearsals and questions how to best convey the energy of live performance to the documentary audience. She expresses particular concerns about the sound, noting that 'not only does Derek [Dixie – musical director of the show and the film] have to record the choir, he has to record the rumble of the structure. The stomps. He has to record everybody's "Hey! Ah!", and that adds another element of the performance that feels so good on the stage. And it's not translating on film.' Beyoncé's concern is to provide the film's audience with an experience of the performance that is proximate to the performers', and her clearly stated aim is to make sure that 'everyone out there can feel what we feel', the 'we' being first and foremost the people on the stage and not (necessarily) those in the crowd. That this discussion is included in the film itself provides Beyoncé with an opportunity to demonstrate the multi-layered and multimedia artistry that she is conceptualizing during preparation, while also offering a sense of the mediation process that has produced the film that we are now watching; we are asked to understand the performance on the stage, its reception in the concert venue and its representation on film as each constituting different experiences.

A momentary diversion into television aesthetics is instructive here, because although my object of study in this chapter is not live performance viewed via live television broadcast, debates around live television are one of the places where the mediation of live performance on screen has been theorized. In particular, Paddy Scannell's groundbreaking work on television's live broadcasting of nationally significant events (his study focuses particularly on the BBC's coverage of The Coronation of Queen Elizabeth II) is useful, given that he argues that broadcasting's task 'is to re-present the event in such a way as to proximate its eventfulness for those who are not there' (1996: 80). Crucially, Scannell is not arguing that television *replicates* the event, but that it transforms it, and in so doing creates a 'double articulation' of said event. The event as it exists in the geographical and social space of the world he calls the 'event-in-situ', whereas the 'event-as-broadcast' comes into being at the moment of transmission, takes place on viewers' screens and in their homes, and is constructed by broadcasting techniques and technologies (1996: 83).

A similar transformation is described by Jason Jacobs in his work on early live television drama in Britain, and he argues that such dramas should be understood as aesthetically constructed entities in their own right and not just 'photographed stage plays' (2000: 5). In particular, Jacobs argues that television drama has always been characterized by a desire 'to "get in closer" to the dramatic action, to become intimate with it' (2000: 6), and that this impulse manifested itself through 'a close-up style of multi-camera studio production' (2000: 8). The notion of intimacy through proximity is apparent in Scannell's discussion of the Coronation because of concerns raised by the Royal Family and the government 'of the general public having a more privileged access to the event than the privileged few in the Abbey itself' (1996: 81). This sense that broadcasting creates 'a new event' (Scannell 1996: 80) in the event-as-broadcast that is different to, and separate from, the event-in-situ and which also offers an experience that is fundamentally different to that experienced by attendees provides a useful theoretical model for this discussion of the concert film.

By understanding the concert film as a transformation of the concert event rather than an attempt to replicate it, the concert film is freed from the spatial and temporal logic of the original performance. As Susan Sontag notes, 'theatre is confined to a logical or *continuous* use of space', whereas 'cinema (through editing ...) has access to an alogical or *discontinuous* use of space' (1966: 29). Even if the film is a documentary and the subject a formerly theatrical event which *was* so constrained, these texts are first and foremost audiovisual works, not live performance pieces, and should be understood as such. This is a distinction that is understood implicitly by film-makers and can be seen in Jonathan Demme's reflections on why the audience is mostly absent from *Stop Making Sense*: 'In the cutting room we quickly discovered that there was always something far more interesting going on on stage than in the "best" of our audience footage. This led to the realization that if we pulled back from showing the live audience, it made our film feel that much more specially created for our movie audience!' (Locker 2014).[3] This has been taken to the extreme with Billie Eilish's *Happier Than Ever: A Love Letter to Los Angeles* (2021), made at the Hollywood Bowl during Covid-19, which removes the live audience entirely but does not fundamentally reorganize concert film aesthetics.

In order to demonstrate these ideas in more detail, I want to return to *Homecoming*, and specifically it's opening sequence, to consider how the documentary camera functions as a focal point for the performance and how moments that privilege those not in attendance at the concert makes visible the separation of the cinema and the live audiences. The first shot after

Figure 1.3 An exhibitionistic gesture as Venzella Joy stares into the camera lens in *Homecoming: A Film by Beyoncé*.

the titles is a stylistically extravagant tracking shot lasting 45 seconds that takes place on the runway of the Coachella stage. It begins with a medium shot of a drummer (Venzella Joy) dressed in a marching band outfit, who stares directly into the camera's lens as it moves towards her (Figure 1.3). The camera continues moving along the runway, past Joy and out into the Coachella crowd, with other musicians, flag-bearers and dancers standing aside until it reaches the one person not already looking in its direction. This is Beyoncé herself, styled as Nefertiti in a spectacular black, silver and gold outfit, who turns and follows the camera which is now retreating back down the runway, leading the other performers in a procession back to the main area of the stage.

This is a moment of cinematic spectacle that announces the star's arrival through a combination of camera movement, spatial proximity and exhibitionist performance that is reminiscent of Tom Gunning's arguments about early cinema. Describing the sensibilities of what he has famously called the 'cinema of attractions', Gunning argues that this is a cinema 'of exhibitionist confrontation rather than diegetic absorption' (2006: 384) and that a central component is 'the recurring look at the camera by actors. This action, which is later perceived as spoiling the realistic illusion of the cinema, is here undertaken with brio, establishing contact with the audience' (2006: 382). Although documentary cinema is not concerned with maintaining the unity of a fictional world and deploys direct address as one of its fundamental characteristics, in the concert film, directing such attention at the camera prioritizes the film's audience over the audience at the event.

There is a complexity here, though. As Beyoncé turns to face the camera there is a loud cheer from the crowd, suggesting that the image that we are seeing is also appearing on the large screens positioned around the Coachella site. This is, then, a carefully staged 'arrival', performed directly to the camera, but which fulfils a double purpose: one, to make the details of the live performance visible to the festival audience, the majority of whom cannot see the performers with any great clarity;[4] and two, to provide a dramatic and intimate opening to the film, with the proximity of the film's audience to the screen – and to the performer – being far greater than that of the live audience to the large screens at the venue.[5] It is also important that we are shown the direct feed of the camera's eye-view, rather than seeing Beyoncé's arrival on a screen within a screen that would constitute a spectator's eye-view. A similar moment can be found in Ariana Grande's *Excuse Me, I Love You* (2020), where the song 'Be Alright' is preceded by a short extract from the movie *The First Wives Club* (1996) projected on a large screen above the stage. Although we see a few seconds of this projection in situ, the film cuts quickly to a direct insert of the sequence, thus providing us with direct access to the clip that the live audience only sees at a distance. Such moments, and *Homecoming*'s exhibitionistic opening in particular, confirm the direct relationship that the camera has with the performance.

Examples of direct address are abundant in the concert film more broadly and often occur early in a film to establish the camera's (and thus the film audience's) status as a key receptor of the performance. This is the case with *Homecoming*'s opening shot, but two other indicative examples bookend *Stop Making Sense*. The first occurs during the opening performance of 'Psycho Killer' when, mid-performance, singer David Byrne makes a startling turn away from the concert audience to face a camera located in the wings. The second is towards the end of the film, when Byrne holds the microphone out towards the camera during the climax of the song 'Girlfriend is Better', inviting the audience to sing along to the repeated refrain – perhaps not coincidentally also the title of the film – 'stop making sense / making sense' (Figure 1.4). This reworks the inciting gestures usually aimed at live audiences to sing or clap along and can be read as an invitation to the cinema viewer to see themselves as participants in the performance.

More recent concert films have combined exhibitionist moments with 3D technologies to emphasize both the spectacular nature of the performance and the sense of intimacy, access and participation through a display of technological

Figure 1.4 David Byrne offers the documentary audience the microphone in *Stop Making Sense*.

accomplishment not unlike early trick films (such as those made by George Méliès), which Gunning argues can be most fundamentally understood as 'a demonstration of the magical possibilities of the cinema' (2006: 383). *Hannah Montana and Miley Cyrus: Best of Both Worlds Concert* and Justin Bieber's *Never Say Never* contain numerous instances where forward-facing gestures activate the negative parallax of the 3D cameras (Weetch 2016: 2), stretching out beyond the screen towards the viewing audience. Such moments are spectacular and privilege the cinema spectator through their proximity, but also because in order to achieve this effect the camera has to be placed between the performer and the concert audience, providing a moment of dramatic exhibitionism for the film viewer that is largely obscured for those in attendance at the live event (except, perhaps, as a mediated image on a distant 2D screen).[6]

Each of these examples emphasizes how a performance produced for the screen results in a materially different experience for the cinema audience than for the live audience in the venue. Although the in situ performance underpins the filmic events, its transformation into a mediated version opens up representational possibilities that *do not* depend solely on replicating the experience of being there. In the rest of this chapter, I want to suggest that these transformative processes operate through a structural dependence upon what could be called a continuity of interruption and fragmentation. This is an aesthetic regime in which varied points of view are brought together to form a holistic sense of a performance that layers multiple situated experiences on top of one another. In doing so, it creates a new performance. The second aspect that I want to consider is how this fragmented point of view holds in tension a range of knowledge regimes that shift between prioritizing information and experiential epistemologies that work to inflect the pop star's public personae.

Fragmentation

One of the primary ways in which a filmic performance space is constructed in the concert film is through a structural balance between unity (or continuity) and fragmentation (or interruption). This operates at every level of the concert film, from the macro (the sequence of events covered by the film) to the micro (how individual numbers are shot and edited). This is antithetical to the concert experience, which is generally experienced (barring intervals) as one uninterrupted performance sequence. However, I want to argue that the fragmentation of the concert film does not jar because it is carefully intertwined with a sense of coherence and continuity that allows the competing purposes and points of view to be articulated in ways that appear congruent and straightforward, but are actually quite complex.[7] This is achieved through the construction of continuous performance sequences made up of interruptions and fragments that are not dissimilar to the ways in which broadcast television has been understood as being simultaneously a continuous 'flow' of programme content that sweeps the viewer along in its currents (Williams 1974: 77–120) and a medium defined by its segmentation (Ellis 1992: 16–23) and a tendency towards constant interruption (Jacobs 2011). In this section, I wish to set out some of the ways in which this sense of a coherent, continuous whole, constructed from fragments, operates.

Fragmentation: The Macro

The first way in which fragmentation and interruption operates is at the macro level of narrative structure. Although K. J. Donnelly has suggested that in their purest forms, concert films can be contrasted with rock documentary because the former include the 'concert only' and the latter includes 'much besides the on-stage performance' (2013: 173, 171), in fact, the uninterrupted recording of a concert is rarely found in the most high-profile examples of the concert film. Instead, this approach tends to be found at the fringes of the evaluative spectrum, either in direct-to-video productions that Donnelly attributes to 'technicians'

(2013: 173) or in 'authored' films made by well-known directors such as Jonathan Demme (*Stop Making Sense*, *Neil Young: Heart of Gold* 2006), Julian Schnabel (*Berlin*) or Spike Lee (*American Utopia*). More common are films that prioritize live performance in terms of their structure and the proportion of their content but do not make it their exclusive focus, usually including some non-performance elements, such as an exploration of the performer's life, scenes set in the backstage area of the concert venue or details of the practicalities of staging the concert itself. This is even the case for the films made during what Baker calls the form's 'golden age' (2015: 246), such as *Monterey Pop*, *Woodstock* (1970), *The Last Waltz*, *The Song Remains the Same* (1976) and *Ziggy Stardust and the Spiders From Mars* (1979), which all contain numerous non-performance sequences.[8]

Some films establish the primacy of live performance by opening directly with a live sequence. This is the case with U2's *Rattle and Hum*, which begins *in medias res* with a pre-credits performance of The Beatles song 'Helter Skelter', filmed at Denver's McNichols Sports Arena. After the credits, we are relocated to a rehearsal space in Dublin, where The Edge performs the song 'Van Diemen's Land', and the band are interviewed. Although *Homecoming* alternates between performance footage and material exploring the creation and development of the Coachella show, with the exception of a handful of pre-credits shots of the crowd gathering, the first sixteen minutes of the film comprises a run of five numbers ('Welcome', 'Crazy in Love', 'Freedom', 'Lift Ev'ry Voice and Sing' and 'Formation').

Even when concert films do not begin so directly, live performance is invariably established as a key concern from the outset. The first full performance in Madonna's *Truth of Dare* (1991) ('Express Yourself') doesn't occur until around six minutes into the film, but the scenes prior to that number are all focused on aspects of her 'Blond Ambition World Tour'. The film begins in a Nice hotel room in August 1990, with Madonna discussing the fatigue and strain she feels having completed the tour. This establishes the tour as the main subject, and we are then taken back to April 1990, where Madonna narrates an account of the technical difficulties and inclement weather that affected the first dates in Japan, proclaiming that 'the only thing that kept me from slashing my wrists was the thought of coming back to America and doing the show the way it was meant to be.' These preliminary sequences are presented in black and white, but the film bursts into colour as the behind-the-scenes sequences of preparation give way to the onstage spectacle of performance, which also coincides with her arrival in America.[9] Live performance is thus centralized in the film, even when concert footage itself is absent.

Katy Perry: Part of Me (2012) takes a slightly different approach. Here a montage of backstage images of concert preparation – which includes the archetypal time-lapse shot of a concert stage being constructed – is paired with a set of text captions that establish the impending drama associated with the tour: 'In 2011 Katy Perry embarked on the largest tour of her career. It was a year filled with tremendous success and personal heartbreak.'[10] Although this text intimates that a larger story will unfold, the priority remains with live performance, and the opening creates a sense of anticipation by moving through footage of Perry doing costume fittings, her tour manager describing the fairy-tale theming of the show and shots of dress rehearsals and of the performers engaging in pre-show backstage rituals, until it ends with Perry located beneath the stage in a striking candy-cane dress, clutching a diamond-encrusted microphone. These images are intercut with shots of the waiting audience as Perry's voice-over suggests that: 'Since I was nine, my dream has always been the same. To be onstage in a glittery costume and to hear thousands of people sing along with me. This moment is my childhood dream come true.' This preparatory montage gives way to the first sustained performance sequences, the point of view of the film transitioning from the backstage to the onstage through a sequence of shots of Perry travelling up on a lift from below the stage and emerging into view above the stage to begin her performance of the opening song 'Teenage Dream'.

Although the first live performances in *Truth or Dare* and *Part of Me* are delayed by six and eight minutes, respectively, the scenes that precede them emphasize the 'readying' of these performances and ensure that the spectacle of live performance structures the films' narratives and holds together texts which often have a much more varied focus. This fragmentary structure is a systemic component of the mainstream concert film, and *Part of Me* can be examined further as an emblematic example of how live performance is used as a structuring device to impose a sense of continuity onto a highly fragmented – and quite complicated – sequence of events.

Most obviously, the film alternates regularly between offstage sequences and the live performances of individual songs. This is a common organizing structure for music documentaries that prioritize live performance and can be found in (among numerous others) *Ziggy Stardust and the Spiders from Mars*, *The Last Waltz*, *Rattle and Hum*, *Depeche Mode: 101* (1989), *Truth or Dare*, *Shut up and Play the Hits* (2012), *Never Say Never*, *Homecoming* and *The Long Pond Sessions*. The live sequences form the skeleton of *Part of Me* and the progress of Perry's 'California Dreams Tour' structures the offstage sequences, with the film providing occasional updates on its progress via on-screen captions that state the number of days since the tour began (e.g. 'Day 1', 'Day 89', etc).

However, while *Part of Me* might appear to have a straightforward structure, the further intertwining of the concert tour with the unfolding personal drama of the breakdown of Perry's marriage to Russell Brand and the film's interest in her biography mean that there are actually four separate chronologies operating concurrently throughout the film, each with vastly different temporalities, and none of which are conveyed in chronological order (though it often appear as if they are):

1. The live concert.
2. The progression of the concert tour from opening night to final performance. This is the timeline that is most emphatically drawn attention to by the 'Day X' captions.
3. The broader scope of Perry's career from her Pentecostal upbringing through to the success of her *Teenage Dream* album, which we see being toured.
4. The development of Perry's relationship with Russell Brand, from first meeting to divorce.

There are thirteen live performance sequences in the film, eleven of which are drawn from Perry's performance at the Staples Centre in Los Angeles on 23 November 2011. Thus, there is an immediate juxtaposition between the live performance sequences, which cover a single evening's worth of entertainment and the temporal expanse of the offstage 'tour' sequences, which cover the period from 20 February 2011 to 22 January 2012. This is another convention of the concert film. Both *Truth or Dare* and *Rattle and Hum*, for instance, exhibit the forward momentum of the tour 'journey' but contain performance footage from a limited number of dates: the concert sequences in the former were shot over three nights in Paris (Manning 2016), and in *Rattle and Hum* four dates – two in Colorado and two in Arizona – represent U2's 110-date *Joshua Tree Tour* of 1987 (McGee 2011: 112, 115).[11] This gestures towards a generalized tension evident in these films. On the one hand, a sense of unity accrues across the live performances and we gain a clear sense of what a complete Katy Perry concert is like. At the same time, by locating the single concert within the temporality of the tour, the Los Angeles performance also comes to stand in for – and could even be mistaken to depict – other dates as well.

This alternation of on- and offstage sequences means that we are not asked to experience the concert as an uninterrupted live performance. This is further apparent if we compare the order of songs in the concert setlist with their place in their respective films. An opening number in a concert film might be selected for the affective, spectacular or thematic dimensions of the performance, for instance, rather than maintaining strict concert chronology. 'Helter Skelter', which opens *Rattle and Hum*, was not the opening song performed that (or any other) night of U2's tour, and *The Last Waltz* begins with The Band's cover of the Holland-Dozier-Holland song 'Baby Don't You Do It',[12] which was actually performed as the final song in the third encore of their final ever concert.[13] Although *Part of Me* conveys a sense of what a Katy Perry concert might look like, and what the Los Angeles show in particular *did* look like, the chronology of the real concert setlist is not maintained (see Table 1.1). Five songs are omitted entirely, and their exclusion can be at least partly understood as an attempt to address the fact that live concerts and cinema films have different requirements when it comes to duration. Similar omissions can be found in *The Last Waltz*, *Stop Making Sense, 101* and *Shut up and Play the Hits*, with Johnathan Demme removing three numbers and an intermission from Talking Heads' set to bring *Stop Making Sense* in at a tight 88 minutes, and Martin Scorsese trimming the mammoth four-hour 'last waltz' concert down to 116 minutes.

Certain key songs *do* retain their setlist position in the film; all shows on the 'California Dreams Tour' opened with 'Teenage Dream', closed with 'Firework' and were followed by an encore of 'California Gurls', and this structure is retained in *Part of Me*. These are the only numbers that are not interrupted with non-performance footage (though they *are* all abridged), and although the gap between the main set and the encore is gestured to by the inclusion of a final interview sequence, this lasts barely 20 seconds in what is otherwise an uninterrupted five-and-a-half minutes of performance footage at the end of the film. These are also three of Perry's most well-known hits and provide a suitably exciting beginning and end to both the live show and the documentary film.

However, the internal sequencing of the numbers is frequently determined by the thematic links that are drawn between the biographical chronology and the mise en scène of the performance, with the latter generally becoming subservient to the former in structural terms. The early stages of *Part of Me* are thematically focused on the practicalities of production and interviews with Perry's key creative collaborators on the tour, including her makeup artist and stylist, are intercut with footage of the up-tempo hit 'Hot n Cold' (placed fourteenth in the original setlist, but second in the film). A clear thematic link is created between backstage discussion of the creation of Perry's live wardrobe and the displaying *of* that wardrobe in a live performance which features a carefully choreographed

Table 1.1 A Comparison of the Numbers That Appear in the Performance Sequences of *Part of Me* Compared with Their Position in the Original Concert Setlist

Setlist from Katy Perry Concert, Staples Centre, 23 November 2011	Songs in the Order They Appear in *Part of Me* (And Position in Original Setlist)
1. 'Teenage Dream'	1. 'Teenage Dream' (1)
2. 'Hummingbird Heartbeat'	2. 'Hot n Cold' (14)
3. 'Waking Up in Vegas'	3. 'Hummingbird Heartbeat' (2)
4. 'Ur So Gay'	4. 'Who Am I Living For?' (9)
5. 'Peacock'	5. 'I Kissed A Girl' (6)
6. 'I Kissed A Girl'	6. 'E.T.' (8)
7. 'Circle the Drain'	7. 'I Wanna Dance With Somebody (Who Loves Me)' (16)
8. 'E.T.'	
9. 'Who Am I Living For?'	8. 'Last Friday Night (T.G.I.F.)' (15)
10. 'Pearl'	9. 'Peacock' (5)
11. 'Not Like the Movies'	10. 'Not Like the Movies' (11)
12. 'The One That Got Away'	11. 'The One That Got Away' (12)
13. 'Thinking of You'	12. 'Firework' (17)
14. 'Hot n Cold'	13. 'California Gurls' (18)
15. 'Last Friday Night (T.G.I.F.)'	
16. 'I Wanna Dance With Somebody (Who Loves Me)'	
17. 'Firework'	
18. 'California Gurls'	

quick-change routine, with the numerous outfits being used as a metaphor for the indecisiveness of the song's central subject.

The performance of Perry's breakout single 'I Kissed a Girl' is placed alongside the discussion of her successful move to Capitol Records, the biographical impetus dictating the logic of the sequencing and also initiating a shift away from the overall thematic focus on 'readying' that propels the earlier scenes. More dramatic and emotional offstage sequences are paired with minor-key ballads linked thematically through their lyrics ('The One that Got Away' as Perry's relationship with Brand breaks down, for example) or their staging and choreography, such as when Perry – filmed in slow-motion – is ensnared in a web of neon ribbons during the performance of 'Who Am I Living For?', an image that parallels her publicist's description of Perry 'being held hostage' by a reluctant record company (Figure 1.5). This linking of onstage performance

Figure 1.5 Katy Perry is 'held captive' in the 'Who Am I Living For?' sequence of *Katy Perry: Part of Me*.

with offstage meaning is not unique to this film, and Burns and Watson argue of *P!nk: Funhouse Tour – Live in Australia* (2009) that that film 'mobilises private themes within the setting of public spectacle and this collides and juxtaposes intimate subjectivity and sensational display' (2013: 137). The interweaving of thematic, biographical and emotional timelines in *Part of Me* is complex, but is always tied together by the macro structure of the live performance sequences, even if this also results in the constant disruption to the chronology of the concert itself.

Micro-fragmentation: The Point of View of the Concert Film

The concert film is often framed as positioning the audience within the 'best-seat-in the-house' (Doherty 1985: 14), or, to return to Westrup's formulation, 'the feeling of "being there"' (2021: 39). Such statements naturally raise the question of what we might understand to constitute 'the best seat' when it comes to concert attendance. Furthermore, just as it was felt that the remote television audience of Queen Elizabeth II's coronation may have been granted a more privileged point of view of the ceremony than the physical attendees, there is an insinuation that what is on offer in the concert film is actually *better* than the best seat and might – contrary to both of the phrases above, which anchor the judgement of the experience with the live audience – involve points of view located in areas inaccessible to the average concert attendee: the areas directly in front, above or at the side of the stage; the dressing rooms; the technical spaces; and the stage itself.

The 'best-seat-in-the-house' framing also suggests a static and singular point of view. This is patently not how the concert film works and is, perhaps ironically, most apparent in *Awesome; I Fuckin' Shot That!*, the Beastie Boys concert film that uses the situated nature of concert attendance as a key aesthetic strategy. *Awesome* is composed of camcorder footage of the band's 2004 Madison Square Garden concert, shot by fifty audience members and with each angle explicitly aligned with a particular position within the audience. Cutting between these points of view retains the multiplicity of views common to the concert film but creates a disjointed, disorienting and ultimately frustrating experience that emphasizes the restrictions placed upon each individual camera position and the corresponding audience member. This is most explicit when the image cuts to the viewpoint of cameras that have moved to spaces outside of the concert floor/seating areas, such as when one person goes to the toilet, another goes to buy beer and a third attempts to find their way backstage. At such points, the onstage performance disappears from view entirely. The situated nature of each camera position in *Awesome* is also regularly emphasized by the screen fragmenting into a grid formation (Figure 1.6), bringing dozens of different camera positions together in a 'spatial montage' (Manovich 2001: 322–6) that provides an overall view of the concert while emphasizing the fundamentally different experiences 'of being there' felt by each individual camera operator.

Figure 1.6 The 'spatial montage' of the varied point of view of *Awesome; I Fuckin' Shot That!*.

However, *Awesome* is an outlier in aesthetic terms, in that it emphasizes the fragmentation of viewpoints over a unity of experience. Instead, I wish to argue that the point of view that is constructed in the concert film, more generally, is a varied one that doesn't align in its totality with either the concert audience or the performer, but extends beyond these single experiential relationships. Instead, the film audience occupies a wide array of spaces within the event space – including within the audience, among the players on the stage, backstage and in various locations not practically habitable by the audience in the venue – but does so in a way that aims to unite these varied points of view into a logical whole, a sort of 'event's-eye-view' that allows us to see 'the full perspective of the concert arena' (Burns and Watson 2013: 116). If the macro-fragmentation combines different elements of a pop star's public persona and brings coherence to multiple, fragmented temporalities, I suggest here that the micro-fragmentation determines how individual numbers are experienced, through the articulation and unification of a multifaceted, and often quite complex, point of view.

Westrup has argued that long takes played a key role in the maturation of the concert film because they have the effect of reproducing the spectator's point of view. This is evidenced through an analysis of a justifiably famous shot from *Monterey Pop* in which the cinema audience's view of Janis Joplin is reframed by the combination of a zoom and pan that 'signals a kind of shift of attention' that 'mimics the shifting attention of the audience' (Westrup 2021: 44–5). A similar point is made by Auslander in relation to the live televising of plays, when he argues that a 'multi-camera set-up enables the television image to recreate the perceptual continuity of the theatre' and that 'switching from camera to camera allows the television director to replicate the effect of the theatre spectator's wandering eye' (1999: 19). However, one of the tendencies that we can see that distinguishes the music documentaries produced since the mid-1980s is a shift towards a dislocated point of view that is congruent with an increasingly fragmented visual style.

The long take, for instance, is no longer the aesthetic bedrock of the concert film, which is, instead, built around a strategy of intense cutting that reflects broader shifts in mainstream cinema aesthetics since the 1980s, most notably the energy of MTV, YouTube videos and the 'intensified continuity' that David Bordwell (2002) has argued is characteristic of contemporary Hollywood action cinema. Indeed, it could be argued that the most effective way in which the experience of 'presence' is communicated to cinema audiences is in the kinetic energy that is visible in the moving bodies of the performers (and the crowd), experienced through the movement of the camera and generated through editing by the rapid cutting between camera positions (and thus points of view). As Burns and Watson suggest of the P!nk film, a 'sense of motion is created not only by the busy choreography on stage, but also by the camera movement … and the fast rate of editing … creating a dizzying sense of activity' (2013: 116). In *Part of Me*, eventfulness is constructed, then, not through the careful and sober observation of unfolding events, but through the spatial manipulation of those events through a montage of varied camera positions that replicates the specific energy of the song being performed (slower songs having slower camera movements and less frequent cutting, for instance).

It would be disingenuous to argue that this is not also a feature of earlier concert films, and Westrup's schema of key shot types within *Monterey Pop* infers a multiplicity of viewpoints (2021: 47). However, the decrease in average shot lengths also equates to an increased variety of points of view. To give just one example, the 'Crazy in Love' performance near the start of *Homecoming* lasts for 172 seconds and is composed of 58 shots taken from around fifteen different camera positions. The preponderance of these (43 in total) are shots looking towards the performance from a range of cameras positioned either directly in front of the stage (Figure 1.7a) or mounted to a crane located at a distance. However, these are punctuated by three shots looking down towards the audience taken from the top of the large-tiered pyramid-shaped stage structure (Figure 1.7b), one shot from a camera positioned *within* the performers on the structure, one shot taken from a camera located within the wings, one aerial shot (Figure 1.7c), one shot of the crowd and seven shots which exhibit a point of view which is more connotative than denotative, in that they all contain visual markers – film grain, a 4:3 aspect ratio, the accoutrements of super-8 mm film – that ask them to be understood as 'archival' in nature (Figure 1.7d). The overall effect is to replicate the energy on the stage with a stylistic energy unleashed by the frequent cutting and the relocation of the audience's point of view to spaces not available to the live audience. The average shot length of this number is a little over three seconds, and it is not atypical for this or other recent concert films. We can, then, argue that one aesthetic of documentary meaning-making (the long take and the audience's supposedly objective reading of it) has been supplanted with another (fast cutting to produce a filmic approximation of the kind of physical and sonic energy that might have been part of the original concert experience). Nevertheless, if the experience of going to a concert is evoked at all in the concert film, it is done so through the energy generated through aesthetic construction, rather than by straightforwardly showing a performance.

Figure 1.7 Four points of view from the 'Crazy in Love' sequence of *Homecoming*: (a: top left), the view from the audience; (b: top right), the view from the top of the structure; (c: bottom left), an aerial view of the performance; and (d: bottom right), the 'archival' point of view.

Another aspect of Westrup's and Auslander's points that I wish to examine, here, is the extent to which the use of multiple cameras, or camera technology that allows for the manipulation of either the location of the camera (such as dollies or cranes) or the scale of the image (zoom lenses), can really be said to replicate the experience of an audience member watching the event. Westrup argues that 'when we watch a performance, we do not necessarily experience it in long shot. Rather, we attend closely to what the drummer's doing during a solo, and then maybe to the way a singer brushes the hair from her face. Sometimes, we try to take in the whole spectacle of the band's interaction with one another' (2021: 44–5). Certainly, our attention as concertgoers will shift frequently throughout a performance. However, unless we have front-row seats, it is rare that we have the opportunity of doing *anything other* than watching a performance 'in long shot'; we only have a limited capacity to move around the venue, and we certainly can't do so spontaneously. Although this can be mitigated (as per Auslander) through the use of in-venue screens, it is still recording and vision mixing equipment that allows for greater proximity, not the physical affordances of our eyes and bodies.

This distinction between the human eye and the camera eye can be extended to a final way in which cutting or zoom effects differs from the perceptual experience of the live event. As Auslander himself admits, 'whereas in the theatre spectators direct their own vision, the television camera does not permit them to choose their own perspectives' (1999: 19). Instead, our attention is directed for us. Thus, the notions of cinematic mise en scène, camera movement, and editing become key features of the mediated performance. As Bordwell, Thompson and Smith remind us, at the most basic level, in any film, 'the filmmaker has to guide the audience's attention to the important areas of the image' (2019: 141). Because we do not view a performance 'in long shot' in the concert film, but through a fragmented point of view, our eyes have relatively limited freedom to roam across the images that we are shown, especially if the cutting is frequent. However, we *are* given privileged access to spaces and viewpoints that are not uniformly aligned with either the audience or the performer. Rather than replicating a change in attention, then, D. A. Pennebaker's pan and zoom in *Monterey Pop* brings Joplin's face larger and closer to the cinema audience than it ever would have been for concertgoers, an effect further emphasized by the scale of the cinema screen itself, which John Ellis reminds us is usually substantially larger than both the spectator and the people whose images appear on it (1992: 127–8). This is a characteristic that Elizabeth Marquis argues has the potential to imbue any image that appears on it with 'a particular semiotic intensity' (2014: 49). While the camera movement might *represent* a shift in the audience's attention, it does not *replicate* it, and so it is fundamentally transformative, changing the audience's spatial relationship with the object of their attention. We can see the same things happening every time there is a cut between spatially distinct locations in the concert film, and especially so when these spaces would typically be occupied by different categories of people. A cut from an audience position to that occupied by a technician or musician, for example, represents for the cinema audience a naturalized rupturing of the separation of performer and audience that is generally reinforced in the concert setting.

The Constructed Performance

All of the aspects discussed in the previous sections, from the moments where the camera occupies a privileged position in relation to the performance to the fragmentary point of view, signal clearly that the performance within the concert film is constructed *by* the makers of the film. This is not too radical a proposition if we understand concert films (and documentaries more generally) to be the product of film-making techniques. Marquis makes a convincing argument that the performances embodied by documentary subjects 'are forced to coexist with additional cinematic signifiers' and so 'are stripped of some of their communicative primacy' (2014: 50). Documentary subjects do not have 'semiotic independence', and 'directors select the elements of any given performance that will be filmed and finally included in an edited text and further mediate the way in which the chosen performance cues are rendered via framing and other filmic choices' (Marquis 2014: 50). Even without extra levels of manipulation, a documentary performance is already a construction, but when the performance is shot from multiple points of view (both spatial and temporal), this is compounded further. I have been arguing against the proposition that these shifting camera positions and the reframing of the image represents first and foremost a reflection of the live spectator's roving attention. But this opposition might be most strongly articulated by the way in which this fragmentation of a performance acts to produce a *new* performance on our screens – not dissimilar to Scannell's 'event-as-broadcast' – that is predominantly constructed through shifting temporal and spatial regimes. To return to Sontag, the concert film deploys cinema's 'access to an alogical or *discontinuous* use of space' (1966: 29) (and to this we should also add 'and time') to create a coherent single performance that is, nevertheless, a mosaic, unbound by the need to rigorously replicate the spatial and temporal continuity that is an inherent part of the live concert experience.

Although numerous concert films focus on a specific, significant performance, there are also many which stitch together several different performances into one coherent, but ultimately non-existent, 'master' performance. *Stop Making Sense* provides the template for this. Shot over four nights at Los Angeles's Pantages Theatre, the filmic performance was then constructed from this material. Thomas Doherty suggests that 'staying with the one venue permitted the lighting design a greater precision, complexity, and artistry than would have been possible on the road' (1985: 15), and Byrne recalls that 'during the shoot every day was spent re-balancing the lights so that the show would look to the camera as it did to the eye, as well as blocking out camera moves' (Locker 2014). This also allows fragments of four separate performances to be combined into a coherent whole, without the need to negotiate discrepancies in venue style and stage size. In examples like this, *Truth or Dare* and *Taylor Swift: The Eras Tour*, which was filmed across three LA shows in August 2023 (Spangler 2024a), there is an attempt to create a seamless single performance which hides the mechanics of production. For instance, one evening of the *Stop Making Sense* shoot was dedicated to filming wide shots of the stage, a strategy that provided coverage and flexibility in the editing, but also allowed for footage to be captured which excluded the onstage cameras used on other nights to film close-up material. This is a common technique in concert films – especially the 3D films which necessitate obtrusive shooting – where the close-up is often followed by a wide shot that erases the camera responsible for capturing the preceding shot. Such attempts to remove the logics of production and create a 'neat' version of the show have more in common with the logics of fictional narrative cinema than they do with documentary production.

Some concert films take the unusual step of highlighting the mosaic nature of the film. R.E.M.'s *Roadmovie* (1996) does this, with cuts between the three filmed concerts marked by regular changes in the band's attire *within* individual song performances. More prominently, *Homecoming* combines both of Beyoncé's Coachella sets (from 14 and 21 April 2018) into a single performance, with no attempt to hide that this is a composite performance, though the continuity of the editing means that this isn't initially easy to spot. The first instance of a switch occurs as Beyoncé moves towards the end of the runway (continuing the opening sequence described earlier in this chapter), where the gold and black Nefertiti outfit is replaced by an all-silver version. This transition is not obvious, and the change in colour can be easily attributed to uneven light conditions. The procession down the runway is also constituted in two halves, with each half being drawn from separate performances, and so if the initial switch is missed, the viewer might not register that a change has taken place at all.

These transitions become harder to ignore, however, once this prologue to the performance concludes and the pyramid structure housing the band is revealed. Up to this point, we could glimpse the dozens-strong performers dressed in yellow, mirroring the attire of the drummer who opened the film. However, as the music resumes, the ensemble can now be seen wearing pink, and from this point onwards, the film liberally switches between shots drawn from the two separate performances, highlighting these transitions through sometimes dramatic changes in hue.[14] Moments of transition between yellow and pink (and vice-versa) – and thus from one performance to another – are not always jarring, sometimes being accomplished within what appears to be a single uninterrupted shot. Towards the start of the opening number ('Crazy in Love'), for example, the image cuts between two separate shots taken from the same crane-mounted camera position, as it tracks right to left above the crowd, with the costumes changing mid-shot. Such moments of cinematic spectacle and technical dexterity speak to the precise direction required in both the live performance choreography and the cinematography to synchronize the dancers and the camera so seamlessly across two performances a week apart.

More frequently, single dance moves are completed across two (or more) shots, and it is not uncommon for these to be drawn from different performances, such as when match-on-action editing combines two separate 'hair-flick' movements performed and recorded seven days apart into one coherent action. At both micro- and macro-levels, this provides an experience unique to the film's viewer. The live audience saw either a pink ensemble or a yellow one, depending on which performance they attended. What nobody could have seen in person was both performances occurring simultaneously, though this is precisely what the audience of *Homecoming* experiences. The film provides a particularly useful example, because the use of colour makes visible the kinds of stylistic mechanics that are a common feature of concert films, but which are usually hidden from sight; here the constructed nature of the performance is laid out for all to see and is done so in a highly deliberate way, given that the same costumes could easily have been worn for each performance.

In such examples, the soundtrack provides the primary element of continuity that unifies the performance fragments into a coherent whole. Unlike the images, the soundtrack for each number *is* usually drawn from a single performance, recorded in high quality by recording engineers or the film's sound crew.[15] Rather than having the sound cut with the image, then, there is sonic unity through which the visual disunity is contained. This adds further complexity to the aesthetic operations in place here, because as well as being able to see two separate performances intertwined as one, we shift between different regimes of audiovisual synchronicity, with some images being synchronized to their live sound and others being synchronized to the sound recorded at an entirely different performance.[16] In the spirit of maintaining a sense of fragmented continuity, we are rarely given any insight into which sonic performances we are hearing or with which images the sound 'belongs', and so another distinction between the live event and the mediated representation is opened up.[17]

There are multiple reasons why such an effect might be desirable. Most notably, the process of amalgamation allows the construction of a coherent whole performance that can cherry-pick the moments from each recorded performance (and from each camera position within each of those performances) that are most interesting, most spectacular or demonstrate the greatest musical or choreographic proficiency. This can, in turn, lead to the most favourable view of the performing artist being forwarded through these constructions. This is further emphasized by the ways in which optical and digital manipulation can create sensational moments of spectacle through the distortion of ordinary space and time, another example of the exhibitionist tendencies at work in the concert film. Justin Bieber's *Never Say Never* makes frequent use of speed ramping techniques to speed up and slow down the image, and slow motion is clearly visible in the 'Who Am I Living For' sequence in *Part of Me* described earlier. Indeed, slow motion is widespread in the contemporary concert film. The 'Shake it Off' number in Taylor Swift's *Reputation Stadium Tour* film ends with an elongated slow motion sequence in which Swift and guest singers Charli XCX and Camila Cabello wave to the audience as coloured tickertape showers the stage and crowd. It highlights the star power of the three performers – and the specialness of the moment – by lingering on the singers and the crowd, but the sound is out of synch with the actions. This sense of temporal manipulation being used to emphasize star power can also be seen in Ariane Grande's *Excuse Me, I Love You*, where the singer's trademark ponytail is emphasized repeatedly by slowing down moments in which she flicks it through the air. In all of these examples, the music continues at a regular speed, creating moments of spectacular unreality and emphasizing bodily display (and thus star power) through a dislocation of sound and image that is felt by the audience, but does not create a noticeable dissonance.

Such observations naturally return us to the first question posed in this chapter, of what purpose is served by these texts. Apart from providing an enjoyable experience for the viewer, the most obvious answer is that they play a crucial role in the perpetuation – and modification – of the star image of the performers who are the focus of the films. The combination of fantastical elements with the documentary framework positions these stars as being both real and unreal at the same time – a clear parallel with the stars of Hollywood cinema. In this respect, the concert film fulfils a similarly unifying role as John Ellis suggests is performed by the movie for Hollywood film stars. As he argues, 'through the presentation of the star in photos, writing and radio, the elements of the star's persona are offered to the public, but in discrete bits and without movement' (1982: 4). Like the movie, then, the concert film – which also places emphasis on the pop star's musical output – acts to 'present the completeness of the star' (1982: 4).

The combination of coherent fragmentation, image manipulation and sound/image disunity has a number of consequences for how the cinema spectator is positioned in relation to the material. The first is that, contrary to Auslander's claim, the concert film is a clear example of Sontag's discontinuous use of both space and time. Although each individual performance fragment might have an indexical link to a particular spatio-temporal moment, this is rarely true of the overall combination, where the complete performance exists in a space that is purely filmic. This has the effect of positioning the concert film within an operational mode that uses techniques borrowed from fiction film-making[18] and which mobilizes affective and experiential regimes of knowledge alongside the more informative and illustrative regimes found within the observational capacities and continuities central to much documentary film-making. I want to conclude this chapter by considering how these competing regimes of knowledge are balanced.

Competing Regimes of Knowledge

The previous sections of this chapter have argued that the concert film is a form that balances an overall sense of unity with a micro-regime of fragmentation and that this results in an experience – and the construction of a performance – that is unique to the film. This results in a tension between the kinds of knowledge produced and embodied by concert films. The documentary impulse pulls in one direction, towards a regime of knowledge grounded in the informative and the factual (most clearly, the 'what' and the 'how' of the concert). At the same time, the transformative capacities of cinema move the representation of the concert away from the purely factual (and even, potentially, the truthful). This, in turn, can be understood in two different ways: as a turn towards an affective or experiential regime of documentary knowledge, or as a transformation that turns the factual into something akin to the fantastical and spectacular approach of the Hollywood musical. This final section will explore each of these aspects in turn to suggest some of the ways in which meaning and knowledge are produced within the concert film.

The Factual Space

There are two broad tendencies within the factual space: a behind-the-scenes examination of how the concert we are seeing has been created and a more self-referential reflection on the place of the film-making process within this construction.

Staging the Concert

It is not unusual for music documentaries that focus on live performance to also examine how the concert that we are watching has been put together. Although explicitly informative, this also creates a link with the backstage musical, where the oscillation between offstage preparation and onstage performance '[gives] pleasure to the audience by revealing what goes on behind the scenes' (Feuer 1977: 315). However, as Jane Feuer notes, such musicals also 'remythisize ... that which they set out to expose' by shrouding the final performances with an 'illusion of spontaneity and effortlessness' (1977: 315, 318). In concert films, informative sequences tend to occur towards the start to establish underlying effort and creative energy, while also allowing the pleasures of live performance to unfold in an increasingly uninterrupted way as the films progress. The portions of *Part of Me* that deal with the logistics of staging a tour, for example, are concentrated in the first third, and the final 30 minutes of *Homecoming* is composed almost entirely of performance footage.

These informative sequences can be direct and explicit. This is the case with *Homecoming*, where offstage sequences focus on Beyoncé's overall conceptualization of the show, an overview of the choreographing and rehearsal process, Beyoncé's physical training post-pregnancy, details of her diet, reflections on balancing work and motherhood, designing costumes and the overall process of how to direct a headline show and a documentary film simultaneously. This is a common approach taken in such films that I have gestured to already in this chapter and that I have discussed in detail elsewhere (Wallace 2021a), and so I will not repeat it here. However, some other brief examples include a sequence in *Never Say Never* in which Justin Bieber practises an acrobatic jump from a spring-loaded platform through a trapdoor onto the stage, a demonstration by the lighting designer in *101* and nearly all of *Jennifer Lopez: Halftime* (2022) and *This Is It*, the latter of which is composed solely of rehearsal footage due to Jackson's unexpected death preventing the concerts themselves taking place.

Stop Making Sense takes an even more extreme approach by incorporating these backstage practical elements into the spectacle of the performance itself. The first half of the film is structured around a narrative, of sorts, in which Talking Heads's stage is constructed as the concert progresses. As David Byrne notes on the DVD commentary,

> the whole staging of the show seemed to me to be the most obvious idea in the world. To construct a show where you saw what it took to construct a show *in* the show. And you start with an empty stage with absolutely nothing on it, and you put the stuff on the stage during the show that it takes to make a show – the lights, the amps, the instruments, the players, everything – and then you proceed to use that stuff. So everybody sees what it takes to make a show, and then they see that stuff put into action (Byrne et al. 2009).

The film begins with Byrne performing 'Psycho Killer' alone on an empty stage, the bare brickwork, lighting rigs and ladders visible around him, with band members and their accompanying instruments emerging one at a time for subsequent numbers, assisted by stagehands wearing black in the tradition of Kabuki theatre (Byrne 2013: 62–3). By the start of the sixth number, all of the band members are present on stage, and by the end of the interval (which is edited out of the film), screens have been erected onto which decorative images are projected that reflect the character of the songs being performed. As Byrne acknowledges, 'there are two conversations going on at the same time' in the film, 'the story and a conversation about how the story is being told' (2013: 64). The concert, and thus the film, place the staging of the show at their centre, and the shift between performance and information is most apparent when the documentary camera focuses on the work of the stage crew wheeling the instruments about the stage and doing the work that normally happens before the performance starts.

This direct approach is complemented by subtler insights present within the performance itself. One such example occurs towards the start of *Homecoming*. After Beyoncé has completed the flamboyant catwalk procession that opens the performance, a camera positioned in the wings catches a glimpse of her being ushered offstage, replacing the poised onstage personae with a different kind of physicality necessary to undertake a costume change and relocate herself from the side of the stage to the top of the large performance structures in under two minutes. Although we do not see the rest of this backstage manoeuvre, this brief shot hints at the kind of labour that is occurring out of sight to sustain the performance. This focus on labour is also teased out in shots of the performance that are styled to look like super-8 mm film recordings (discussed earlier – see Figure 1.7d). The shift to a narrower aspect ratio (4:3 instead of 16:9), a shallowed depth of field, a lingering shot duration and possibly also elements of slow motion act to focus the attention on the physical effort and concentration exhibited by the performers; Beyoncé's breath control is particularly visible, for instance. This reflexive and affective focus on labour provides a glimpse of the physicality that goes into making Beyoncé's gruelling performance so spectacular, but the brevity of the shots ensures that they don't overwhelm the illusion of effortlessness.

Mounting the Film

The concert film is also somewhat interested in signalling its own processes of construction. The most obvious way in which this occurs is through the visibility of cameras – usually on the periphery of the frame – whose presence has become a naturalized element of the concert film's mise en scène. These cameras are not usually intrusive, though the performer *might* draw attention to them, such as when Beyoncé waves into the lens, when Dave Gahan of Depeche Mode ushers D. A. Pennebaker onto the runway alongside him towards the end of *101* or during the exhibitionist moments described earlier in this chapter.[19]

Some concert films include sequences in which the technicalities of production are directly addressed *within* the film itself. The opening 10 minutes of Martin Scorsese's Rolling Stones concert film *Shine a Light* (2008) provides a particularly interesting example of this. Scorsese plays a prominent role in the sequence, as he and Mick Jagger negotiate logistics related to stage design and camera placement within the venue. Cross-cutting between New York (where Scorsese is located) and London (where the Stones are), the film opens with Jagger looking at a model of the stage, which he describes as being 'like a doll's house', before we cut to Scorsese standing on the stage itself, framing potential shots and considering where to place the cameras. Jagger is concerned that, 'they whiz around all the time, and it's very annoying to the audience and to everyone on the stage, and it's dangerous.'[20] Conversely, Scorsese counters that 'it would be good to have a camera that moves, that swoops down and in and out, and tracks along the side, somehow.' We then see the band in New York familiarizing themselves with the stage, while Scorsese rehearses the camera movements and tests the lights, which, because they are designed with the film cameras in mind, offer a different experience for the band than normal stage lighting would do. The lighting designer warns Scorsese that 'if Mick stands in front of the light for more than 18 seconds he's gonna burn', and drummer Charlie Watts questions the necessity of the intense lighting rig. 'That's normal movie stuff, is it?' he asks. Thus, the tension between the different needs of the live and the film audiences, and the band members as live performers and film stars, is articulated directly as are the questions of how the performer presents themself to those different audiences and how the presence of the film cameras might, in fact, *alter* the performance.

A moment of drama is also created during this opening because of Scorsese's anxieties about the unavailability of the intended setlist, and he is seen in the gallery fretting about the resultant inability to plan camera positions:

> I really would like to know what the first song's gonna be, because if the first song opens on a guitar riff, a guitar intro, we have to make sure we're covering… Which guitar? Usually, it's Keith. We have to know that! But if the keyboard begins and then Mick starts signing, then we need two of three cameras to be on Mick.

Scorsese's frustration is intercut with shots of Jagger going through piles of paper trying to determine the ideal running order, demonstrating that this is a task that requires careful consideration. Since the Beacon Theatre concerts that Scorsese is recording take place during a larger world tour, Jagger can be seen compiling the setlists for other dates at the same time, giving a sense of his overall process. The collaborative nature of this concert – as being staged by both the band and the film-makers – is again reinforced by Jagger's paperwork including one list of songs under the heading 'include songs given to Marty' and another labelled 'Martin Scorsese Suggestions', the inference being that this is a concert that in design and execution has been staged to be filmed.

Instead of receiving the setlist a week ahead of schedule, as agreed, Jagger addresses one of the cameras in his hotel room directly, humorously recognizing the last-minute nature of the task: 'All done, Marty. On the night. An hour before the show.' This uncertain arrival of the setlist means that Scorsese's visible anxiety adds a level of tension to the film's opening that stands in for both the audience's and the band's pre-show anticipation. Although the setlist was surely delivered to Scorsese with some time to spare, it's eventual arrival is edited into a quick-cut montage that combines a shot of the venue's lights going down, Scorsese telling his crew to 'get ready to go', the MC welcoming the Rolling Stones to the stage and a CGI crane shot of the theatre's marquee, at which point the paper is delivered into Scorsese's hands, and as the opening riff of 'Jumpin' Jack Flash' rings out, Scorsese's tension is released as he announces: 'Set list! Ok! First song!', and the image cuts to a medium close-up of Keith Richards playing guitar. At this point, the focus on the interrelationship between Scorsese's and the band's preparations gives way to a more concentrated (though not entirely uninterrupted) view of the performance. However, this opening reveals the practical and technological aspects of the film-making process and asks the viewer to understand what follows as a product of (authored) film-making, as much as it is a simple record of a live performance. It also gives a clear sense of the negotiations that have to take place between musician and film-maker for the documentary to make it to the screen in the way that it does.

The Affective Space

When translated to film, the manipulation of speed, the dislocation of sound and image, and the forwarding of a spectacular star personae, positioned within the exuberant mise en scène of a stage production creates a sense of an event that is fantastical. The spectacular slowing down (or speeding up) of the performer's actions (Grande's hair flicks, for instance) positions them as operating in a space that is not always governed by the laws of physics, and the spectacular changes of colour in *Homecoming* have an otherworldly quality because the performance space that is constructed is not a real space, but one only made possible through cinematic trickery. This is also true of the switch between the verité-aligned black-and-white aesthetics of the backstage and the vibrant colours of the onstage sequences in *Truth or Dare*, *Rattle and Hum*, *Shine a Light* and *Homecoming*, which create moments of fantastical spectacle not dissimilar to Dorothy's (Judy Garland) emergence from the monochrome domesticity of the Kansas ranch house into the vibrant Technicolor fantasy of Oz in *The Wizard of Oz* (1939). Even when such stylistic flourishes are less visible, such as the decoupling of the soundtrack from the image, concert films are replete with moments where there is an aesthetic – and thus perceptual – movement from 'real' to 'fantastical' performance spaces.

The move from offstage to onstage (both in terms of literal location and the documentary approach to its subject) is frequently concordant with a reorientation of the documentary material from one anchored in the real world to one open to the fantastical possibilities of cinematic manipulation. This shift also tends to correspond to a broader transition from a mode of documentary engagement which prioritizes the factual and where the documentary image is 'rich in [factual] visual information' (Plantinga 2013: 41) as to how a concert is staged and which cultivates knowledge of that process, to the experiential, where the provision of factual information is displaced by a focus on knowledge that is – to repeat Beattie's phrase – 'subjective, affective, visceral and sensuous' (2005: 23).

Elsewhere, I have suggested that throughout the documentary film *101*, D. A. Pennebaker uses a documentary-based iteration of what Rick Altman has called the musical's 'audio dissolve' (1987: 77) to marshal the transition between these two empirical spaces, as the focus shifts from the practical to the experiential (Wallace 2021a). This is particularly apparent in a sequence in which Depeche Mode's soundcheck of the song 'The Things You Said' gives way to the full concert performance, the sound of the live show bleeding across before the image itself follows. However, the stylistic transformations that I have already discussed in detail provide the fundamental ways in which this shift occurs, creating an audiovisual space which encourages an affective and embodied engagement with the live performance.[21] This shift from a focus on the processes of a performance to an attempt to convey its experiential qualities is congruent with Richard Dyer's influential notion that the musical offers audiences a view of 'what utopia would feel like rather than how it would be organised' (2002: 20) (though I have suggested that in the factual sequences, concert films often attempt to do both). It is this shift from organization to feeling that is captured in these moments and that activate the possibility of an affective response to the film that might approximate, in a reformulated way, the experience of the live concertgoer. This is then combined with the stylistic aspects of the shooting, camera movement and editing to create a filmically constructed space in which the energy of any particular performance is conveyed through style as much as it is through the performance, that is, in any case, already constructed *by* these filmic processes.

This is, then, one way in which the 'truth' embodied in the music documentary is articulated through a tension between competing aesthetic and hermeneutic regimes. On the surface – and within the offstage/onstage dichotomy – the concert stage would appear to provide a highly performative vantage point from which to observe the documentary subject; it is the one space in the public world of the pop star where we can be certain that a performance is occurring. Auslander, for example, argues that during live performance, 'what musicians perform first and foremost is not music, but their own identities as musicians', something he describes as their 'musical personae' (2006: 102). A live pop concert is, then, a space of multi-layered performance, in which the artist can be understood to be playing a role that is, in turn, responsible for the onstage actions of playing and performing music. This is something identified by Nick Cave in one of the interview sequences in *20,000 Days on Earth* (2014), where he suggests that a transformation takes place at the moment of arriving on stage where the performer moves from a state in which 'you can't really understand how you can do the show' to a situation in which 'you get taken away' and 'forget who [you] are'.

This view is also articulated by Selena Gomez in *My Mind and Me*, when she describes falling in love with the 'escape' of performance. Implicit here is a suggestion that the onstage version of Cave and Gomez represents a substantially different performance of the individual to the offstage version. Although Cave's suggestion that he becomes 'somebody else' could be understood as indicating inauthenticity, Gomez's sense of 'escape' indicates a freedom for self-expression. It is, then, possible to understand onstage performance as being a more honest articulation of a star's persona, in part because it foregrounds and centres its performativity, but also because it is a space free from the constraints of social self-performance. Just as David Byrne has recognized the fundamentally 'artificial' (2013: 46) nature of being on stage, he also recognizes that the carefully structured space of the well-rehearsed and finely choreographed performance does not close off opportunities for authenticity (2013: 59), arguing that:

> In musical performances one can sense that the person onstage is having a good time even if they're singing a song about breaking up or being in a bad way. For an actor this would be anathema, it would destroy the illusion, but with singing one can have it both ways. As a singer, you can be transparent and reveal yourself onstage, in that moment, and at the same time be the person whose story is being told in the song. (2013: 79)

In fashioning an entirely new performance out of the fragments of multiple previous performances and a range of different points of view, the concert film has the capacity to place the honesty and truthfulness of live performance under the microscope and may, ironically, offer a more truthful experience of the pop performer because the layers of artifice are made visible, are explored and are drawn attention to, while also offering the space for moments of authenticity to break through.

Conclusion

I want to end this chapter with one final example to show how many of the aspects that I have identified up to this point inter-operate and how the complexity of the concert film in general – and the comparative sophistication of individual examples – lies in how well these aspects are balanced in order to achieve their desired effects (and affects). The interrelationship of viewpoints and how they contribute to produce both an affective experience and a documentary investigation is apparent throughout Spike Lee's film of David Byrne's *American Utopia* Broadway residency, but perhaps most strikingly towards the end of the performance of 'This Must Be the Place (Naïve Melody)', where the choreography creates a particularly startling effect. The band is set up with portable and wirelessly amplified instruments, so that they can move fluidly around the stage and combine their playing with complex choreography. They are dressed in uniform grey suits, with bare feet, and as the song reaches its instrumental coda, the personnel form themselves into three lines on the stage, with Byrne, Bobby Wooten III (bass) and Angie Swan (guitar) in the front line. On cue, the three lines begin to move, always facing the front but alternating between upstage and downstage directions. This creates a disorienting effect, especially as Byrne does not remain within his initial row grouping, advancing both further forwards and backwards than his compatriots and thus creating a spatial disparity as he moves in and out of synch with the three lines throughout the routine. The spectacular choreography is enhanced by the chiaroscuro lighting, and we observe it from a range of spaces that varies the proximity we have to the performers from a wide view that approximates that of a spectator in the front seat of the circle to a worms-eye view inches from Byrne's feet.[22] The energy and artistry of the choreography is captured by emphasizing the 'out-of-step' nature of Byrne's movements within the performance of a song which is known for the way its homely, almost sentimental, central groove repeats across its duration.

However, the crucial moment occurs midway through this coda where a single shot is included from a camera rigged directly above the stage and we are treated to a bird's eye view of the choreography, which offers a similar vantage point to that found in *Homecoming* (Figure 7.1c). This shot changes the nature of the performance that is constructed for us. On the one hand, it tames the disorienting choreography by clarifying exactly where everyone is in relation to one another on the stage. In so doing, it provides clear insight into the mechanics of the performance, as we can clearly see the white lines drawn on the otherwise empty stage, indicating the marks that the performers have to hit to achieve the desired effect. This enables us to understand how the complex movements are realized as well as making visible their hyper-rehearsed nature and the labour that has gone into getting it right. It is emblematic of the concert film's complexity, however, that this shot is not limited to providing a moment of documentary

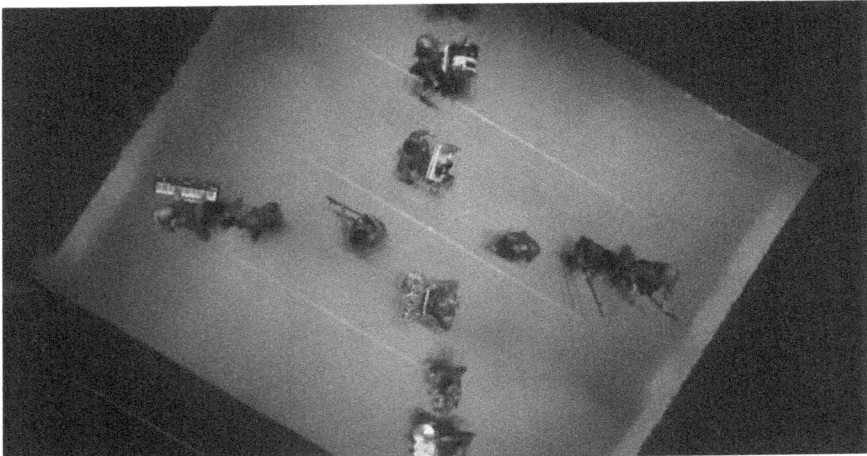

Figure 1.8 A Busby Berkeley-esque aerial shot that reveals the stage marks during the 'Burning Down the House' sequence of *David Byrne's American Utopia*.

insight, but contributes further affective elements to the performance. The 'impossible' viewpoint (except, perhaps, for a technician situated in the lighting gantry) emphasizes the informative capacity of the documentary aspects of the film, yet it also unlocks its cinematic potential, and the combination of the bird's eye view with rhythmic and regimented movements that are almost hypnotic in their regularity is Busby Berkeley-esque (another shot from this angle later in the film is even more overt in this respect, see Figure 1.8). Crucially, these oppositional ways of reading the image (as informative documentary *and* as fantastical spectacle) are mobilized simultaneously through the careful unity of the image fragments. They are beautiful images placed in a combination that is only possible as a product of cinema, and they engender an experience that is informative, exciting, moving – and available only to the film's audience.

2

The 'Documentary Backstage'

Perhaps *the* fundamental relationship explored by music documentaries is the one that exists between the performer and the performance. This is often understood as being an oscillation between reality and artifice; that the star – when in public – is wearing a metaphorical mask that the documentary-maker attempts to strip away to offer what Keith Beattie calls 'unmediated glimpses of the "real" person behind the performance' (2005: 25). This has been described as both a 'master trope of the rockumentary' (Beattie 2005: 25), and an 'enduring [motif]' (Strachan and Leonard 2009: 289) that can also act as an evaluative framework through which the relative success of any particular music documentary can be judged.

This tension between the 'real' and 'artificial' has often been formulated in terms of a juxtaposition of two opposing spaces that are inhabited by pop stars in their daily lives and in the documentary representations *of* those lives: the stage and the backstage. The concept of 'the backstage' has usually been explored in music documentary scholarship in terms of what its separation from the onstage space suggests about the different registers of performance that might be observed or the different kinds of information that we might expect to be revealed in each respective location. More fundamentally, these spaces are understood to exist as real-world spaces – the concert stage versus the dressing room, for instance, or the press conference versus the hotel room – in which access to the 'truth' of a documentary subject is contingent on how performance-based that space is in the world outside of its documentary representation.

In this chapter, I wish to develop arguments made by Jonathan Romney and Keith Beattie about the performative nature of *all* spaces in the music documentary and the nuanced modes of performance found there. However, taking cues from the work of Dean MacCannell and Carl Plantinga, I argue that rather than understanding the backstage as a space that is constituted outside of documentary mechanisms, and then accessed *by* those mechanism, we should instead understand there to exist a multiplicity of backstages, some spatial, some rhetorical, and some textual (the sense of backstage access could be constituted in the edit, for instance). These overlap but find their focus in a documentary articulation of backstage access that is first and foremost a structuring *audiovisual* device enacted *by* the documentary rather than *for* it. What emerges through this device – we might even call it a documentary method – is not necessarily the stripping away of layers of performance but rather a means of engaging *with* the performance itself. The chapter begins with an introduction which sets out the conceptual terrain of this chapter, and my reformulated understanding of how the backstage functions in recent music documentaries. The rest of the chapter demonstrates how this notion of a 'documentary backstage' works through the analysis of a range of recent music documentaries that constitute this through different aesthetic and narrative means. This chapter, then, increases the proximity to the documentary subject from that seen in the previous chapter; from the public space of the stage, to the – implied – private space of 'the backstage'.

The Backstage as Cinematic Space

In the second part of the television documentary series *Journey to Fearless* (2010), Taylor Swift's mother Andrea leads a group of fans into an area of a concert venue that is clearly beyond the means of access of most concertgoers; we see the edge of the stage along with the support rigs and scaffolding that are usually kept beyond the audience's view. The space is introduced to the tourgoers – and to the viewer of the documentary – by Andrea in the following fashion: 'alright, well, you were promised a backstage tour and this is about as backstage as it gets. Because this,' she says as she taps the raised platform behind her, 'is Taylor's stage, and you're in back of it'. This moment speaks to the potency of the backstage as a conceptual space within the star image of the performer through an inversion of expectations. The tourgoers *are* backstage in the literal sense that they are *behind the stage*, but a comic undertone punctuates Andrea's description and highlights the difference between being literally backstage at a Taylor Swift concert (seeing the scaffolding; meeting the technicians; getting a glimpse of how the stage show is put together), and being symbolically backstage at a Taylor Swift concert (being invited to meet the star and experience for oneself their mythical status).

It is the latter version of backstage that Romney suggests holds particular power within the myth-making process when he describes it as 'a sacred space' that 'underpins the institution of stardom' by upholding a separation between performer and fan (1995: 83). As he suggests, 'the audience is not normally permitted behind the sacred veil' (1995: 83), and as we see in *Journey to Fearless* this can even be true for those given privileged access to the literal backstage spaces of a concert venue. Romney suggests that the backstage 'may be literally the space behind the stage, or it may generally be the "off-screen" of in-concert fantasy – the tour coach, the hotel room, the interview situation in which stars "play" themselves off duty' (1995: 83). In other words, everywhere where the star is but the public are not. Although Romney hints at the impure nature of such a separation between onstage performance and backstage authenticity, he argues that this *is* often upheld in the backstage sequences within music documentaries that suggest 'an element of demystification' by demonstrating 'how the illusion of onstage spontaneity is the result of careful planning and struggle against seemingly insuperable odds' (1995: 83). This demystification positions the onstage as a space of falsification, and by implication the backstage as a space of reality. Such moments, then, 'promise … to reveal the star as he or she really "is"' and that 'backstage is imagined as a far more "real" space than the stage on which the artists do their work' (1995: 86).

I have already destabilized the notion that the onstage space is inherently less truthful than offstage in Chapter 1, but Romney makes it clear that 'backstage, particularly when cameras are present, is no less a space of display than the stage itself' (1995: 86). In some respects, it can even be understood to be *more* performance-driven, given that it isn't subject to the same rituals and expectations as the concert stage where 'the rules of behaviour … [are] always determined simply by the presence of a watching audience' (1995: 87). As Philip Auslander asserts, concerts are 'highly ritualized and convention-bound events' in which the interaction between audience and performer is carefully regulated by social cues dictated by the specificities of the venue, the musical genre and the performance itself 'letting the audience know what to expect from the interaction, what not to expect, and how to respond' (2006: 107). Such a perspective erodes the separation of onstage and backstage along lines determined by the presence/ absence of performance, by acknowledging that self-performance is ever-present, even if its extent is not always clearly delineated.[1] As David Hepworth argues, 'the theatrics in pop don't begin when the lights go down. Keith Richard is Keith Richards twenty-four hours a day. That's why he's endured' (2018: 72).

Beattie builds upon this recognition to make arguments about the nature of performative display evident within music documentary, drawing parallels with reality television and the audience's search for an authentic self that emerges through performance (2005: 24–7). This, Strachan and Leonard remind us, is all part of the image-making process and that 'the rockumentary deals with stars who are part of an industry where the control of image and persona is of paramount value', and that 'rock documentaries are clearly part of the marketing of popular music acts' (2009: 291). Romney suggests that by the early 1990s the idea of the 'real' backstage had been exposed as a fallacy in increasingly visible ways by self-reflexive documentaries such as Madonna's *Truth or Dare* (1991), which is explicit about backstage being yet another space of and for performance (1995: 90). Thus, it is important to view the material recorded in these 'sacred spaces' not as intimate footage that captures the star 'as they really are', but instead as a fundamental part of the star-making machinery.

In each of these cases, however, backstage is still understood as a space that exists prior to the filmmaker's arrival, and what we find in the documentary is a version of a pre-existing reality that may be modified by the camera's presence. What I want to argue here is that music documentaries are instead composed of several different 'backstages' that are all operating at once. The physical backstage spaces over which the performing artist has control are conveyed to the documentary audience through a second backstage – a documentary backstage – which is under the control of the documentary maker, and which is constituted *by* the documentary itself, during pre-production, shooting and editing. This idea of the documentary backstage brings together several theoretical approaches to documentary that relate to the most fundamental questions of what documentaries are and how they function.

In 1987, Carl Plantinga conceptualized the documentary form through observations 'about the way *we think* about documentaries' (1987: 44) and how this differs from fiction films, by developing philosopher Nicholas Wolterstorff's theorizations of 'projected worlds' in art and literature. Wolterstorff suggests that in fictional works the diegesis is 'projected' through utterances (or prose descriptions, brush-strokes, spoken dialogue, mise-en-scène, etc.) in order to communicate its status to its audience. Plantinga argues that documentaries project worlds in much the same way, and that particular projections might be common within specific sub-generic forms and have become naturalized by audiences. For example, in nature documentaries 'it is commonplace ... that filmmakers eliminate any trace of human existence in films about wildlife and wild areas', such as by framing shots 'to leave the telephone pole out', or by using audio takes 'without the sound of an airplane flying overhead' (2005: 113). Such choices are not enough to constitute deceptive or fictionalizing practices, but they 'may lead to a romantic and inaccurate conception of nature as something that is wholly free from human influence' (2005: 113). I wish to contend here that 'the backstage' is one such world that is projected across the music documentary, and that its basis is grounded in fact – these are real people in real spaces – but is also a representation that functions to instil the music documentary with an experience of access, proximity and intimacy that is *projected* by the documentary text as much as it is a genuine component of the pro-filmic events themselves.

This sense of intimacy operates in a number of ways, the most obvious being the dual sense of closeness that it implies: a physical proximity granted to the filmmaker that allows them (and us) to approach the subject directly, and a sense of access to their private spaces and interiorities, both physical and psychological. As Lauren Berlant suggests, intimacy involves a sense of 'something shared … within zones of familiarity and comfort: friendship, the couple, and the family form' (1998: 281). Berlant also suggests that, like documentaries, 'intimacy builds worlds' (1998: 282) and the projection of a documentary world that suggests such personal closeness has the effect of generating 'an aesthetic of attachment' (1998: 285). On the one hand, then, intimacy is conveyed through the suggestion that the documentary maker has been accepted into the star's private spaces (their personal 'backstage'). But intimacy is also formed around the potential for risk in the personal/private being made public via the documentary, and so is also intertwined with a sense of trust; as Ian Goode suggests, 'the revelatory possibilities of … access depends on the trust of the stars concerned' (2015: 70). Richard Dyer has argued that a key signifier of authenticity within the star image is 'the use of markers that indicate lack of control, lack of premeditation and privacy' (1991: 137) and part of the purpose of these intimate documentary encounters is to convey precisely this. Intimacy suggests risk, risk suggests a lessening of control, this in turn suggests a trust in the documentary maker not to misrepresent, and trust suggests intimacy.

This function is activated by Plantinga's other key observation, which is that documentaries project worlds through an 'assertive' stance (1987: 49), and that 'what the filmmaker asserts, in the first instance, is that the images, sounds, and other materials presented are … *veridical representations* of whatever the documentary takes as its subject' (2005: 111). This can be usefully combined with Dean MacCannell's work on back 'regions' of tourist settings, but in a way that breaks down the on/off binary. MacCannell's recognition of the 'tourist's desire to share in the real life of the places visited, or at least to see that life as it is really lived' (1973: 594) mirrors that of the documentary project, but like documentaries, back 'regions' are demarcated to arrange particular – and differentiated – touristic experiences of authenticity. These range from the explicitly touristic at one end to the entirely private at the other, with a range of fluid categories in between, including, for example, 'a front region that is totally organized to look like a back region' and 'a back region that may be cleaned up or altered a bit because tourists are permitted an occasional glimpse' (1973: 598).

My argument here is that the music documentary operates in a similar fashion, in that it presents to its audience a framework of access that *seems* to function along the lines of an onstage/backstage binary, and that it asserts that this is how we are to understand its projected world. In fact, it operates more closely to MacCannell's continuum of access. As Beattie suggests of *Dont Look Back* (1967), 'we are permitted backstage, but not granted access to the "real being"' (2005: 29). Such an understanding resolves the tensions that exist between the documentary inquiry and the need to preserve the artist's control over their image. As MacCannell argues, 'just having a back region generates the belief that there is something more than meets the eye; even where no secrets are actually kept, back regions are still the places where it is popularly believed the secrets are' (1973: 591).

Music documentaries generate the belief that the backstage is a space that is worthy of exploration, and project a documentary backstage that asserts access to this space, and provides an experience of 'transparency' (1973: 596), by upholding an onstage/offstage binary that masks the 'tidied' nature of what we are seeing. The validity of this projected backstage is upheld by the assertive stance taken towards it, and enacted through the documentary exploration of this space. Rather than understanding the documentary maker as a pioneer on an expedition to access and interpret untrodden ground, then, we can instead see them as a tour guide, taking us into tightly controlled territory.

It is, therefore, less interesting to me to be able to determine the extent to which the device of the documentary backstage is capable of 'getting behind the mask' – something that we can never know for sure – than it is to examine the methods through which documentary makers attempt to convince the audience that this has been achieved. The rest of this chapter examines a range of music documentaries that each take different narrative, aesthetic and self-reflexive approaches to the projection of the backstage world and I examine how the documentary backstage is constructed and asserted as a 'veridical representation' through four key approaches: the archive, observation, the journey, and self-reflexivity.

Archive

Except for sequences used to contextualize the pasts (and more specifically the childhoods) of contemporary music stars (see the next section of this chapter), the archival mode is overwhelmingly found in documentaries about subjects who are dead, whose careers are largely in the past, or whose activities cannot be accessed anew in a direct way. *The Kids Are Alright*, the 1979 documentary about The Who, set a template for this kind of documentary, compiling archival interviews and performance footage to tell the story of a band amid a period of uncertainty following the death of Keith Moon. Although rarely adhering to the archival aesthetic so purely, more recent examples that place significant weight on archival materials to tell their subject's stories include (and this is a very partial list): *The Devil and Daniel Johnston* (2005), *Amy* (2015), *Cobain: Montage of Heck* (2015), *What Happened, Miss Simone?* (2015), *Janis: Little Girl Blue* (2015), *The Velvet Underground* (2021), *Moonage Daydream* (2022) and (in a somewhat unusual way) Peter Jackson's *The Beatles: Get Back* (2021).

In this section, I want to consider how archival materials in music documentaries convey a sense of access (or a 'backstaginess') to star performers who are no longer alive through a dual process of textual 'resurrection' – bringing the artist and their historical context back to life – and by emphasizing the 'hidden' truths that can be found within the archival material. These texts assert that documentary mechanisms can achieve backstage access to the dead through the (re-)configuration of the archive, and in so doing find new ways of understanding the lives (and, often, the deaths) of their subjects. My key case study is the 2019 documentary *Billie* which concerns the jazz and blues singer Billie Holiday. The film uses and combines archival materials in a multitude of interesting ways, but I want to focus on two in particular: how a specific archive of 'found' audio material is used to suggest a sense of unique insight when combined with other audiovisual materials; and how colourized images reorientate and complicate the sense of 'pastness' encoded in the archival sources. Together, these two strategies construct a textual space – another documentary backstage – which asserts a sense of privileged access to the past.[2]

Although there are ontological and epistemological difference between footage located in official archives and that 'found' elsewhere, a delineation emphasized by Michael Zryd (2003), Jaimie Baron has argued that it is helpful to consider '"foundness" as a constituent element of all archival documents, whether they were "found" in an archive or "found" on the street' (2012: 103). Baron argues that within documentary texts, 'this "foundness" ... exists in contradistinction to documents that we perceive as produced by the filmmaker specifically for a given film' and that it is this sense of coming from a different place that imbues the archival document with 'its aura of "authenticity" and enhances its seeming evidentiary value' (2012: 103). This 'foundness' is often communicated explicitly through textual – and textural – features, as Beattie suggests: 'damaged, scratched or water-marked film evokes a degree of historical authenticity in the suggestion that the film survived the vicissitudes of the era it represents' (2004: 128), and, indeed, the subsequent years.³ This creates what Baron calls a 'temporal disparity' that characterizes our experience of archival documents incorporated into appropriation films (2012: 105).

This can be illustrated by returning to the shots from *Homecoming: A Film by Beyoncé* (2019) that I described in Chapter 1 as expressing an 'archival point-of-view' (Figure 1.7d). These shots eschew the 16:9 HD look of most of the film and instead emulate Super-8mm and 16mm film footage (complete with visible sprocket holes, a 4:3 ratio and filmic texture) to create a link with the heritage of direct cinema music documentaries, especially the colour 16-mm film stock used in the filming of *Monterey Pop* (1968) and *Gimme Shelter* (1970).⁴ This emphasizes the film's function as an act of record, but also expresses the significance of that specific concert event. Beyoncé was the first Black woman to headline Coachella, and the faux-8mm material renders it as aesthetically 'historical' at the same time as the surrounding HD video demonstrates its contemporary significance. In moving between two contrasting aesthetic styles, each of which contain different connotative associations, Beyoncé is both figuratively and literally 'making history' in that the act of staging and filming the concert is historically significant, and its representation has the aesthetic qualities of a historical artefact. By using the aesthetics of the concert film and of observational documentary more generally, she cements her position as a leading artist in a range of fields (music, live performance, videography, documentary filmmaking) that have tended to exclude Black women, and she pre-emptively memorializes these achievements by making them look archival. In this case, the *fabrication* of archival signifiers demonstrates the potency of the 'archival effect' as a marker of cultural significance and historical veracity.

More generally, temporal disparity allows the filmmaker to take advantage of the evidentiary quality of the archive by framing it as an 'outside object', free of their interference. This is the case with Nick Broomfield and Rudi Dolezal's *Whitney: Can I Be Me* (2017), where contemporary interviews are combined with a cache of previously unseen footage recorded during Whitney Houston's troubled 'My Love is Your Love World Tour' in 1999. Captions emphasize the external nature of the footage ('A documentary crew was given unprecedented backstage access') and its unique qualities ('This footage has never been shown') in order to emphasize the temporal disparity between the archive and its reuse, stress its evidentiary qualities and support the film's central thesis that the unsettled backstage events of the 1999 tour had a direct influence on Houston's untimely death thirteen years later (and her daughter's three years after that). Through the process of being recontextualized from present-tense observational footage into past-tense historical evidence, this archive functions as a key pillar in the 'documentary backstage' that Broomfield and Dolezal construct, as if they are detectives for whom the footage acts as a substantial trace from which they (and we) can gain 'unprecedented' insight into Houston's life and death.

In *Billie* we can see a similar deployment of an archival 'find': a collection of audio interviews recorded throughout the late 1960s and 1970s by journalist Linda Lipnack Kuehl. Captions tell us that Kuehl was compiling material for a biography of Billie Holiday by recording 'hundreds of hours of interviews with those who knew her best'. However, the book remained unfinished due to Kuehl's death in mysterious circumstances in 1978. As with the Houston footage, the Holiday interviews are framed as found artefacts which convey a sense of deep and unique access to their subject's personal and professional life. In part this is due to their 'never before heard' status, which is emphasized by the aforementioned captions.[5] Also significant are the multiple levels of temporal dislocation, the two primary relationships being between the duration of Holiday's life (1915–59) and the creation of Kuehl's interviews (from the late 1960s to 1978), and that between Kuehl's death (1978) and the interviews being included in the documentary (2019). This has several complex (and sometimes potentially contradictory) effects. On the one hand, the primary subject of the documentary is doubly distant, as Holiday's life is accessed through oral history accounts that have themselves become historical artefacts. At the same time, this double-distancing offers a way of bringing Holiday into greater proximity with the viewer of the film because the tapes metaphorically resurrect those who knew Holiday, and they in turn resurrect her. Many of those interviewed are famous jazz performers who are themselves now dead, and so the interviews provide a greater variety of accounts of Holiday's life than could be attained in the present day.

These temporal disparities, therefore, have practical affordances for how the interview material is used. Although generally heard asking questions, there are occasions where Kuehl's voice adopts a more editorial tone, negotiating a path between the testimony that she is recording and her ability to publish the material legally. During an interview with Earle Zaidins, Holiday's lawyer, Kuehl attempts to clarify certain facts relating to alleged acts of domestic violence committed by Holiday's third husband Louis McKay. Zaidins calls McKay a 'pathological liar' and suggests that on one occasion he hit Holiday over the head with a telephone and threatened her with a gun, but states that 'I don't want to put this on tape.' Kuehl makes it clear that without his testimony 'I can't say it, write it because I'm liable and [McKay's] alive and he's tough. I'm in trouble, not you.' At a purely practical level, the temporal disparity allows the claims to be made public in James Erskine's film because everyone involved is now dead, including the journalist who made the recordings. The film has greater access to the testimony because there is no risk of a defamation lawsuit.

This speaks to the second major disparity that Baron argues constitutes the 'archive effect'. This is the 'intentional disparity' that occurs when an archival document in a compilation film 'generates the dominant sense of coming … from a different intent' to that of its recontextualization (2012: 110). For the most part, Erskine combines the audio recordings with archival photographic material in an illustrative way that maintains the 'denotative function' of the archive to 'reinforce the exposition established in a voice-over or to complement comments made by witnesses or experts' (Beattie 2004: 128). This has the effect of playing down any intentional disparity between the original context of the interviews and that of their reuse in the documentary. However, there are moments where this relatively stable schema is disrupted, creating instances where the intentional disparity is foregrounded and the original intended use for the audio interviews as part of the research process for a book comes into collision with their reuse in a documentary film.

The Zaidins/Kuehl conversation is one example, because as well as now being among the dead, Kuehl is also absolved of any legal responsibility because her editorial negotiations around the interview are included in the documentary in a way that would not have been possible in the book. Erskine is thus able to flag the contentious nature of the material through a demonstration of Kuehl's own careful consideration of the legal ramifications of making the claims public. This also has the effect of marking the testimony as opinion, rather than a presentation of fact. Thus, temporal and intentional disparity are signalled simultaneously by the inclusion of the 'backstage' discussions around the interview material; we hear the process by which the evidence used by the documentary to make its case was procured and the 'off the record' nature of the discussion adds emphasis to the claims being made about McKay's violent temperament.

McKay's abusive nature is also signalled visually in one sequence through the atypical inclusion of stylized elements of the film apparatus. Instead of the photographic images being cropped to fit the frame as they are in the rest of the film, candid shots of Holiday and McKay are framed within the context of a photographer's contact sheet, which conveys the sense that the photographs

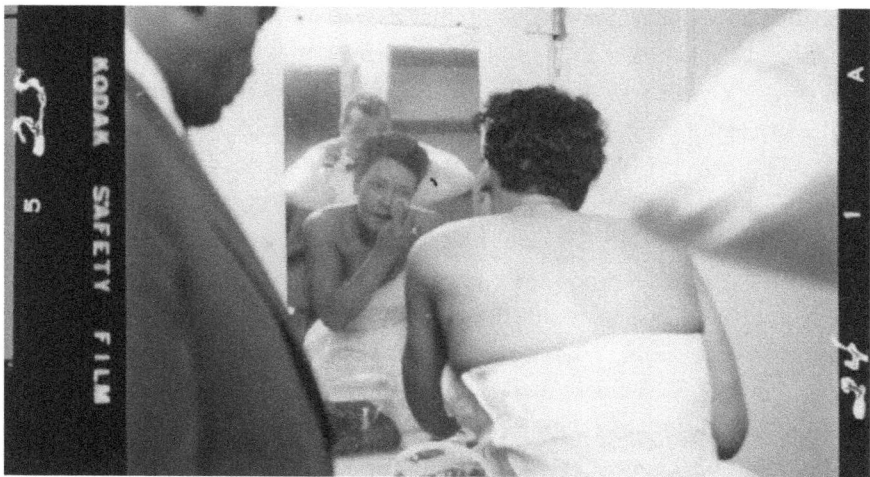

Figure 2.1 A candid image of Billie Holiday and Louis McKay (left) framed as if viewed on a photographer's contact sheet.

having been discovered unprocessed (Figure 2.1). The screen flashes sharply as the images progress from one to the next in a manner suggestive of being caught in a camera flash, but which is also implicitly violent. The self-referentiality of the apparatus also indicates a more general shift from a denotative to a connotative function, and the rupturing of the straightforward presentation asks for the images to be read in a non-literal way, as if indicating a revelation of violence through these stylistic touches. At such moments, backstaginess is signalled through Erskine's editing, the archive being reshaped and recontextualized to forward an argument about Holiday and McKay's relationship which is not contained in the images themselves, but which becomes part of their meaning through the visibility of the cinematic and photographic infrastructure, something that also emphasizes the intentional disparity by which these photographs can come to function as evidence of actions that they do not actually show.

This kind of intentional disparity also plays a significant role in Erskine's ability to connect the fates of Holiday and Kuehl. Using Kuehl's recordings, Erskine constructs a story about Holiday's life that lays significant blame for her fate at McKay's door. But this isn't just achieved through the testimony that Kuehl gathers *about* McKay, but from the inclusion of her own sense of unease about McKay's character, as expressed in her conversation with Zaidins. Kuehl's reluctance to accuse McKay because 'he's alive and he's tough [and] I'm in trouble, not you' is immediately followed by Kuehl's sister Myra Luftman noting – in a present-day interview – that 'in the process of interviewing for the book Linda had been threatened by people within the world that she was travelling'. Thus, the fates of Holiday and Kuehl reflect upon one another through the evidentiary use to which the archive is put. By including the contextual circumstances surrounding Kuehl's archive in the film, Erskine asks us to reassess what the archival material can tell us about its subject (Holiday) through the retrospective lens of future knowledge about the fate of the person who created the archive (Kuehl). This connects discussions of violence within Holiday's life with Kuehl's own death, and reminds us that the same people who were present in the late 1950s were also involved in Kuehl's interviews, and intimates that her death might have been related to her attempts to chronicle the earlier violence against Holiday. It is central to the success of the documentary backstage that is constructed for the film that an assertion can be made that it is uniquely within the film's gift to put forward such a hypothesis about these event, because it alone can link them in thematic and stylistic ways.

Before moving on to the next section, I want to give the film's inclusion of colourization techniques some consideration as another device which conveys a sense of intimacy and access. On the face of it, the use of colourized footage to connote a greater access to truth seems counter-intuitive. As Leanne Weston suggests, black and white's '[evocation] of pastness' situates the artefact within a particular historical context, and brings with it an 'association with authenticity, value, and seriousness' (2021: 225). This echoes Paul Grainge's assertions that monochrome footage has the capacity to produce both 'the *aura of the archive*' (2002: 3) and 'the aura of recorded history' (2002: 129). There is an implicit paradox here, as the monochrome image's potent claim to authenticity is upheld through an in-built sense of temporal distance and a representational strategy that stresses an aesthetic *dislocation* from the real world. Maxim Gorky's remarks upon viewing the Lumiere brothers' films in 1896 remind us of the fundamental strangeness of black-and-white cinema: 'Last night I was in the Kingdom of Shadows. ... Everything there – the earth, the trees, the people, the water and the air – is dipped in monotonous grey. Grey rays of the sun across the grey sky, grey eyes in grey faces, and the leaves of the trees are ashen grey. It is not life but its shadow' (2005: 6). The monochrome image epitomizes cinema's abstraction from everyday life, of the transposition of a noisy and colourful world into a 'soundless spectre' (Gorky 2005: 6). Although observational forms have reenforced the link between black and white images and documentary truth, such images can be understood as inherently strange and distant when compared to their pro-filmic original.

Colourizing such footage, then, is a complex undertaking. On the one hand, it would seem to remove many of the signifying traces that are contained in the original monochrome footage, removing it from its historical context, disrupting the 'authentic' status that is derived – at least in part – from a pastness signified by a separation from the colourful 'now', and thus undermining its evidentiary qualities. At the same time, colourizing the footage reduces the temporal disparity in the image, and in undermining the 'archive effect' has the potential to produce what we might call an 'immediacy effect' instead. By converting the black and white to colour, the connotations of 'pastness' are replaced by their opposite; a sense of 'nowness'. Colourization, then, has the potential effect of making the image less strange, and bringing it into closer proximity with the world as it is/was, rather than how it has previously been represented.[6] This reorganizes the sense of proximity embedded in the image from one in which there is a strong relationship between the image and its historical context but a weak one between the image and its contemporary moment, to one in which the relationship between the image and its historical context is weakened in order to strengthen the proximity between the image and its experience in the present day. This has the potential to foster a greater sense of access and immediacy between the archive and its audience.

Grainge notes the propensity for magazine editors in the late 1980s to advertise their newly full-colour publications as being 'more "exciting" and "livelier"', than their monochrome precursors (2002: 2), and Weston talks about colourization having the potential to '[bring the past] "to life"' (2021a: 222). This is a view embraced by Marina Amaral, the photographic colourist responsible for the colourizations in *Billie*. She argues that her intention 'is to build a bridge between the present and the past', arguing that although 'when we look at a black-and-white photo [we understand] that the past was as colourful and vivid as our present', in general '[we] can't feel the "essence" of this' (Freeman 2018). Colourization processes are controversial, particularly when it comes to the upholding of historical veracity; a monochrome image is not an accurate reflection of how the world really was, but it does not contain false colour information that might misrepresent the past. Amaral's process involves a painstaking amount of research:

> It's not as simple as picking up a big bunch of crayons and applying random colours over an image. Before I even start to colourise, I do an in-depth investigation of all the elements of a photo, because I want, I need to identify as many of the original colours as I can. ... What separates the good colourist from the bad one ... is not technique but their respect for history. (Freeman 2018)

Amaral asserts that because of this lengthy research process, 'the craft of adding colour is similar to the work of a historian, and becomes almost an archaeological process' (Sanderson 2018). Rather than playing up the 'archive effect' through the aura attached to the monochrome image, in *Billie* the filmmakers have instead opted to collapse the distance between the pro-filmic event and its reception, and thus also between the viewer and the archival documentary subject. Colour connotes privileged access to Holiday, not otherwise available, and especially not to viewers of the original monochrome images.

Not every sequence/image of Holiday in *Billie* is colourized, and the film is able to have its cake and eat it too, by using monochrome images to uphold the historical veracity of the film's account and imbue it with an archival aura, while creating a sense of proximity, intimacy and access at crucial moments through the newly coloured footage. This also has the effect of making the colourized photographs appear as if they are presented in their native colour, rather than *as* colourizations, as might be the case if the film was uniformly colourful.

The effects of this intertwining of a monochrome pastness and a colourful immediacy can also be detected *within* the colourized footage itself. Throughout this discussion I have used the word 'potential' to discuss the possible affordances of colourization – the *potential* to bring the past to life; the *potential* to override 'the archive effect'; the *potential* to make the image less strange – because the results (whether by accident or design) are rarely so straightforward. In *Billie* it is not the case that the colourized version straightforwardly replaces the monochrome original, but instead both versions exist alongside one another, creating a textual dissonance that pulls our attention in competing directions; towards the veracity of the monochrome past and the immediacy of the colourful present.

Perhaps the most notable examples of colourization in *Billie* are the live performances of 'Strange Fruit' and 'I Loves You, Porgy' taken from the 18 March 1959 edition of Granada Television's *Chelsea at Nine* variety programme. This was Holiday's final television appearance, and one originally broadcast in black and white, as all officially scheduled British television programmes were until 1967.[7] These images display this technological and textural dissonance in abundance. The footage itself was shot on videotape, and is unusual for surviving television of this period in that it exists *on* videotape.[8] The image density and its attendant textural qualities are technologically contingent, and are characteristic of television broadcast in Britain between 1936 and 1964, Hong Kong between 1957 and 1973, and almost nowhere else in the world. Unlike the colourized photographs, which have an image density defined by the high definition of 35mm film, the 405-line television image has significantly less visual information than both contemporaneous moving image material shot on film, or more modern images shot on high-definition video. It lacks sharpness, there is a fluidity to the image that is characteristic of field-based video, and the low definition causes a strobing effect across Holiday's jumper whenever she or the camera moves. In contrast to the still images in *Billie* that are colourized in a vibrant and detailed way, Amaral's colourizations of the Granada footage are broadly sympathetic to both the technological characteristics of the image *and* the period in which they were produced.[9] However, there are some subtle elements of technological and textural dissonance, as we see an image coloured in sympathy with 1950s US television technology (colour television was introduced in the United States in 1954), but applied to a British system which would never have carried colour information of this type (US colour broadcasting used the more highly defined 525-line NTSC system as opposed to the 405-line British system). However, this combination functions in a way that generally accords with a popular sense of what 1950s colour television might look like.

These moments, then, fulfil two purposes at once. They speak to the historically situated nature of the original footage, expressed through their technological specificity and through the visual characteristics or their aesthetic limitations, and the colourized footage appears to be *of* 1959 and not 60 years later. Nevertheless, these moments also fulfil the potential of bringing the past to life. Amaral makes the following argument about the relationship between colour and history: 'I think human beings respond very powerfully to very simple stimuli. And one of them is colour. The whole thing about history, whatever medium or discipline you're working in, is that it's always about trying to create a connection to a world that's gone. And I personally haven't come across any more immediate way of doing this' (Sanderson 2018). Both the immediacy of the connection *and* the 'gone-ness' are equally important, working in dialogue. The addition of colour to these sequences helps to create and maintain this connection, by making the images less 'strange'.

This is a particularly appropriate incongruity in the specific context of its use as the driving component in a sequence concerned with Holiday's controversial recording of the song 'Strange Fruit' (which takes as its subject matter the lynching of Black Americans in the Southern United States), the song's position within Holiday's life story, and its (and Holiday's) relationship with the broader political struggle around racial equality. Grainge has argued that colour and black and white have fundamentally different tonal and mood qualities and that 'a monochrome movie is not simply a film without colour but has a tonal quality that is often used quite deliberately in genres like film noir' (1999: 626). The sense of access to the documentary subject engendered by colourization can be understood as connoting a change in tone and mood, an intentional disparity that has a fundamental effect on how we are asked to engage with the footage. Both performances are imbued with added power because the distancing effect of the monochrome is eradicated. Such moments reflect a common understanding of (especially digitally) colourized footage as 'being simultaneously of the past *and* the present' (Grainge 1999: 632) and in this sense watching the colourized Holiday singing 'Strange Fruit' and 'I Loves You, Porgy' engenders a contradictory sensation of having 'immediate access to 1959'.

This does not necessarily mean that our relationship with the footage is a smooth one. My analysis here suggests that colourization removes the boundaries between the modern viewer and the historical past, and creates a smoother passage between the two through the removal of strangeness. However, this sense of access might instead manifest as a moment of jarring disconnection, a moment of what John Corner refers to as the documentary tendency of ' "making strange" that which may have come to be familiar' (2003: 96–7) (see Chapter 3 for more on this). Just as Ben Highmore reiterates John Ellis's argument that old television discourages a nostalgic engagement because the reality of old television jars with our 'sentimental desire' (2013: 49), seeing Billie Holiday in colour creates another kind of dissonance. As the promotional material for Billie emphasizes, 'while most of the filmed and still images that exist of Billie are in black and white, the world that she lived in was as bright and colourful as the 21st century' (Concord n.d.). The colourized images are jarring, because we *expect* to see Holiday in black and white and our reassessment of Holiday is partly created through a jolt of dissonance, rather than a smoothness of connection. At the same time, the self-reflexive nature of this sympathetic colourization, with its complex set of temporal relationships, subtly draws attention to itself *as* a colourization – as a new colourization dressed up to look like old colour – and in so doing, forms a key part of the film's documentary backstage address, by gesturing towards the uniqueness of this particular representation as distinct from the colourless original.

The use of the archive in *Billie* and *Whitney* demonstrates the wider strategies by which the archive can be used to project a documentary backstage that asserts the documentary's privileged ability to assess and convey truth. Both films use the independence and the 'foundness' of their archives to formulate arguments about the lives (and deaths) of their central subjects and do so by asserting the evidentiary characteristics of their visual sources, but also how the documentary form is uniquely placed to present such arguments through the combination and recontextualizing of this visual evidence. This closes the gap between the audience and the historical figure and asserts a sense of 'backstage' access to their lives that is otherwise unobtainable.

Intimacy, Domesticity and Observation

As noted in the introduction, it is rare for modern music documentaries to exhibit a single unified aesthetic mode. More usually, a range of elements work in combination to examine different aspects of a star's public and private persona. Archival home movie footage might be used to explore a person's childhood, for instance, and carefully staged interviews might allow the star to reflect on a particular aspect of their career. Nevertheless, for documentaries made about pop artists who are still in the public eye – and thus exist in the cultural 'present' – observational techniques remain the most likely aesthetic framework upon which these other elements are hung. At its most fundamental, this involves a camera crew following a star as they go about their daily life.

Despite being more than sixty years distant, perceptions of observational documentary engagement carry the residual rhetoric of the American direct cinema filmmakers of the 1960s, who used lightweight cameras and portable sound equipment to produce documentaries that redefined the aesthetic possibilities of the documentary form, including in key music documentaries such as *Dont Look Back* and *Gimme Shelter* (see the introduction). Observational documentary is the mode that is most directly shaped to give the appearance of an indexical relationship between the film and the pro-filmic events. Robert Drew, the pioneer of the movement, 'believed that his film crews were so unobtrusive and mobile that they could record "reality" without influencing it' (Cousins and Macdonald 2005: 250) and this particular approach offered the appearance of 'discreetly obtained footage' (Saunders 2007: 9), stressed 'the nonintervention of the filmmaker' (Nichols 1991: 38), and thus conveyed the suggestion that it offered 'the observing, recording, and presenting of reality without controlling, staging and reorganizing it' (Issari and Paul 1979: 13).

As I noted in the Introduction, such claims were naïve at best and duplicitous at worst, especially the claims about non-interference. As Stella Bruzzi argues, 'the core of direct cinema is the encounter before the camera, the moment when the filmmaking process disrupts and intrudes upon the reality of the world it is documenting' (2006: 78). This realization has led to a reorganization of observational principles in which the crew observes the subject, but does not attempt to uphold the pretence that they are invisible or that their actions are having no effect on the world around them. There is, therefore, an interactive element readily apparent in the observational sequences of recent music documentaries, where the star and the crew engage in a process of mutual recognition, and thus shift regularly between what Thomas Waugh has called presentational and representational modes of documentary performance (Waugh 2011: 72–92). There are moments where the star 'presents' themselves to the camera in an explicit way, and other moments where the priorities of their personal or professional life lead to something akin to a 'representation' of what their life would be like were the cameras not around.

If the level of interaction is different to the direct cinema documentaries, one of the aspects of continuity between the two periods is the emphasis on observation offering a particularly intimate form of documentary practice, in which the filmmaker and the subject are brought into physical and temporal proximity in order to convey – as direct cinema filmmaker Richard Leacock once put it – 'the feeling of being there' (Winston 1993: 43). This dual sense of proximity carries with it connotations of privileged access and intimacy that is both central to the construction of a 'documentary backstage', but is also a key aspect of the marketing of music documentaries as being 'deeply intimate' (Apple TV+ Press 2020) 'unfiltered' (Netflix Media Center 2017), and 'raw and emotionally revealing' (Netflix Media Center 2020).

The emphasis on proximity and access grounded in techniques of observation is central to the framework through which the illusion of genuine intimacy is maintained, and this constitutes the documentary backstage in the observational form. There are numerous aspects of these films that could be the focus of such a discussion. For example, a common trend in recent music documentaries (particularly about women) is a focus on aspects of physical and/or emotional vulnerability that might previously have been hidden from the public's view, and which embody a 'confessional' mode which combines 'reflexivity about the business of being a celebrity, emotional interiority and self-criticism' (Redmond 2015: 2). Mental health is central to *Miss Americana* (2020), *Selena Gomez: My Mind and Me* (2022), *Geri* (1999) *Framing Britney Spears* (2021), *Lewis Capaldi: How I'm Feeling Now* (2023), and *The Devil and Daniel Johnston*, and the pressures of fame overshadow *Gaga: Five Foot Two* (2017), *Katy Perry: Part of Me* (2012) and *Billie Eilish: The World's a Little Blurry* (2021), the latter containing a sequence in which Eilish shows her diaries to the production team, including details of her mental health struggles and history of self-harm.[10] *Five Foot Two* and *The World's a Little Blurry* focus on their stars' struggles with physical injuries, and each contains sequences where performers undergo painful physiotherapy

(Lombardo 2017). These documentaries place themes of vulnerability, resilience and emotional openness as key sites of meaning, and through these displays of emotion indicate privileged access not otherwise provided within official imaging related to the star (though, of course, by becoming the subject of the documentary they *become* part of the image-making process).

In the rest of this section I want to focus in particular on the way in which observational proximity combines with themes of domesticity, family and 'home' – the 'zones of familiarity and comfort' that Berlant (1998: 281) argues are key setting for intimate engagement – as a structuring framework through which the projected world of the documentary backstage is enacted. In recent years, 'the home' has replaced 'the road' as a key setting for music documentaries, taking the place of the tour bus or the changing room as the key space of backstage display. As such it reflects the wider domestic concerns of reality television series such as *The Osbournes* (2002–5) and *Keeping Up With the Kardashians* (2007–21). We can see this in the way that documentaries like *Five Foot Two* and *Miss Americana* establish the relationship between star and camera through a domestic context that sees them performing ordinary tasks in the company of other family members. *Five Foot Two* opens with Gaga at home, dressed in tracksuit bottoms and grey leotard as she cooks lunch with her mother (Figure 2.2) and feeds her dogs. The sense of being 'in private' is emphasized by her casual outfit and by the prominence of ordinary domestic labour; it is significant that Gaga is the one doing the cooking/feeding, rather than this being done *for* her. Although *Miss*

Figure 2.2 Lady Gaga cooks lunch in the opening scene of *Gaga: Five Foot Two*.

Americana begins with a scene of music-making, this similarly takes place in the home, is relaxed practice rather than energetic public performance, and Swift shares the piano keyboard with her pet kitten.¹¹

The familial context is vividly laid out in *The World's a Little Blurry*, which will be the focus of the following analysis and presents an aesthetics of intimacy through the thematic focus on family. This is somewhat unsurprising; Eilish was 16 years old and living with her parents when production began. Furthermore, the majority of Eilish's music has been co-written and produced with her brother Finneas, and so hers is a professional life that is inseparable from family infrastructures.¹² In various interviews, both director R. J. Cutler and cinematographer Jenna Rosher have spoken about their desire to adhere to the observational principles of verité shooting (Douglas 2021; ShotDeck 2022; Vincent 2021). To achieve this and minimise disruption within the 'very cozy' space of the family home (Vincent 2021), the on-site crew was restricted to three people: Cutler as direct, Rosher as cameraperson, and Jae Kim as sound recordist. Rosher also notes the camera – a Canon EOS C300 MarkII with a monopod rig – being partly chosen because 'it's got a low profile and it's lightweight' (Pennington 2021), the discretionary capabilities replicating the discourse around the technologies of direct cinema.

Nevertheless, the film embodies and acknowledges the implicit interactivity involved in making documentaries, and Rosher upholds the revelatory potential of observation, without making claims towards invisibility, objectivity or non-interference. Discussing the documentarist's presence in the filming space – and referring to the commonly deployed designation of the fly-on-the-wall – Rosher makes it clear that 'we're not flies. We're human beings, with bodies. We have a presence and we're there. It's not about "pretend we're not here". No, we're here, but with respect and compassion and curiosity' (ShotDeck 2022). In this she mirrors a statement made in 1964 by Albert Maysles – one of the key direct cinema filmmakers – who suggested that it was an advantage for the filmmaker and their technology to be openly visible because it encouraged a relationship 'like a non-directive therapist' because 'the relationship is one of a real person listening' (Haleff 1964: 23). This exhibitionistic aspect of the filmmaker-subject relationship was also shaped by Eilish's well-documented enthusiasm for the mockumentary sitcom *The Office: An American Workplace* (2005–13), the fake documentary informing real documentary production practices, with Eilish requesting that Rosher's camera be brought closer 'so that she could make contact with it' (Vincent 2021) in a way that reflects the fourth-wall-breaking gestures of the sitcom characters.¹³

Crucially, the intimacy of the documentary backstage that is projected by Cutler requires the viewer to feel like the camera is positioned *within* the family unit, rather than on the outside looking in, as is often the case with classic observational documentary. This is achieved through the on-screen depiction of a comfortable and trusting relationship between subject and filmmaker, and the careful integration of audiovisual material shot by family members. For Rosher and Cutler, familiarity and trust are determining factors in the success of the film. The pair spent hours sitting in with Eilish as she learned to drive (ShotDeck 2022) so that she became comfortable with their presence, and Rosher suggests that the long shoot meant that mutual trust between filmmaker and subject developed in tandem with a sense of familiarity and comfort (Vincent 2021). Rather than becoming 'invisible', the cameraperson instead becomes something much more prominent: 'You're just part of their world all of a sudden, and you're just on this ride with them' (Vincent 2021).[14] The crew, therefore, become *part* of the events being documented, rather than outsiders peering in.

To give just one example of the film's 'baseline' style, the sequence in which Eilish dives away from home alone for the first time after passing her driving test sees a shift from an observational style as Patrick O'Connell (Eilish's father) gives advice on how to be safe, to a more interactive mode once his daughter has driven away as he reflects to the camera about being a parent to grown-up children. This is a touching moment that O'Connell shares with Rosher, but this emotion is compounded when Eilish's mother – actress Maggie Baird – enters the discussion, upset that she has missed this important moment because she was on the phone. At this point the camera takes a step back and the shooting returns to a more observational mode, capturing a moment of transitional negotiation between two parents that is both tender and familial (Figure 2.3).

This general sense of familiarity is augmented by other stylistic features that act on the observational footage shot by Cutler and Rosher to make assertions about the film's intimacy. The most important of these is the incorporation of footage not shot by the documentary team. This occurs several times in the film but is most prominent in the early sequences that cover the period prior to Rocher and Cutler's arrival in February 2019. This includes home movie clips of Eilish and Finneas as children, adopting what has become a familiar method of representing the early years of a generation of pop artists who grew up in an era of affordable home movie and camera phone technology.[15] This footage is supplemented by sequences recorded by another documentary crew during 2018 – including a live performance in Salt Lake City and a single talking-heads-style interview (ShotDeck 2022). Most significantly, coverage of the recent

Figure 2.3 Billie Eilish's parents, Patrick O'Connell (left) and Maggie Baird (right), observed talking in *Billie Eilish: The World's a Little Blurry*.

past comes from Eilish's mother, who's 'premonition' that 'this was going to be something big' is manifested in a cache of iPhone and GoPro footage of Eilish and her brother writing songs and discussing their development around the family home (Douglas 2021).

There is an important distinction to be drawn between the home movie footage and the iPhone material shot by Baird. On the surface, all of this material should contain the 'foundness' of the archive, that I discussed in the previous section of this chapter. However, the sense of temporal disparity conveyed by each is different. The historicity of the home movies is clearly apparent. Billie and Finneas are much younger, the footage exhibits the textual, and textural, characteristics of SD home movie technologies, and we are not asked to view these moments as indicating temporal proximity between audience and subject. Baird's iPhone footage is different. In the first place, the 'present tense' that it depicts is broadly contemporaneous with Rosher and Cutler's footage and is edited into their material in a way that maintains the 'vivid form of "present-tense" representation' that Bill Nichols (1991: 40) argues is characteristic of the observational form. Movements between Baird's and Cutler's images are rarely signalled and do not create the same sense of temporal and intentional disparity as is found between Cutler's material and the home movie footage. Instead, Baird's material is incorporated in *The World's a Little Blurry* in a strategic way to assert a 'documentary backstage' grounded in familial intimacy that creates a halo effect that carries over in Cutler's footage.

The opening moments of the film emphasize this. The beginning of Eilish's song 'Ocean Eyes' – her first released song, and her big break – is heard over the Apple Original Films logo. This is quickly revealed to be not the finished song, but a pre-recorded backing track, as a snapshot of iPhone footage locates us in a garage or workshop space as Eilish sings the verse into a microphone. This is the first of several 'song production' sequences in the film, and through it Cutler addresses Eilish's rapid rise to fame with economy, while also establishing the domestic framework in a stark and direct way. The scene – a single shot of Eilish recording vocal takes in the family's garage – last a brief ten seconds before it is placed in its historical position by an ocean blue caption that states: 'When she was 13, Billie Eilish posted a song called *Ocean Eyes* online.' The vocal-free backing track continues to play under the caption until a leap forward in time is signalled by camera phone footage of Eilish and Finneas elsewhere in the house reacting with understandable excitement to the first radio play of the song on the Los Angeles-based KCRW radio station.

This sequence – which ends with another caption: 'Three years later …' – lasts 55 seconds, but sets up the thematic and aesthetic framework in a very deliberate way. The footage of the family listening to the radio comes from two separate sources. The first of these is Eilish's own camera phone, recording her reactions in portrait 'selfie' mode (Figure 2.4). As such, it is signalled as being amateur footage aligned with the unconventional aspect ratios of social media sites like Instagram, Snapchat and TikTok. However, the second source for this sequence, Baird's iPhone, has a less amateurish quality (Figure 2.5). It has a landscape

Figure 2.4 Camera-phone 'selfie' footage in *The World's a Little Blurry*.

Figure 2.5 Baird's more composed footage in *The World's a Little Blurry*.

framing that is in sympathy with film and television standards, and Baird is more disciplined in her framing. She appears keen to catch clear views of her children's reactions and the quiet pride of their father, who observes the scene while folding the washing (the most domestic of tasks). Although Baird can be heard exclaiming that KCRW is 'the coolest radio ever' and briefly appears in her own frame, there is an inherent stability to the image that is sympathetic with the professional observational material shot by an actual documentary crew that is introduced after the 'Three years later…' caption, where a hand-held camera records footage of Eilish greeting her fans in Salt Lake City. Where the temporal and intentional disparity of Eilish's camera phone footage is played up, that of Baird's is played down.

This opening minute, then, functions as more than a simple record of the 'time before the start of the film'. It also creates a framework for the documentary backstage through the present-tense immediacy and observational quality of Baird's composed images, which locate the documentary point of view *within* the family itself. Although the KCRW playback is significant because of its fundamentally public nature ('Ocean Eyes' being broadcast widely for the first time and the implications that this will have for Eilish's career), it is also a deeply private moment for the family who celebrate with ecstasy, joy and pride together and alone. However, by including the footage in *The World's a Little Blurry*, we are also invited into the household, and the same inference is transferred onto Cutler's material through the sustained assertions of closeness, intimacy and access to both the star and her family. The sympathetic technical quality of Baird's footage allows Cutler to include it alongside his own crew's material in a way that frequently makes it difficult to distinguish between the two, and there are sequences later in the film where Baird's footage fits seamlessly alongside Cutler and Rosher's coverage. Their footage is inflected by the aura of intimacy that is genuinely contained in the shots filmed by Baird from within the family and Cutler uses this to enhance the sense of proximity evident in his own footage. In doing so, he projects a documentary backstage on the back of genuinely intimate access drawn from elsewhere.

This does not mean that Cutler and Rosher are not able to capture important and intimate moments for themselves. The sequence of Patrick meditating on Eilish's independence is testament to the crew's position as a confidante to the family, and the moment when Rosher accompanies Baird into Eilish's bedroom to wake her with the news that she and Finneas have received six Grammy nominations also speaks to the sense of trust that is pervasive in the film. But the sense of being 'backstage' in the family is a construction that is skilfully established through the deployment of Baird's observational footage of her own family and the halo effect that it projects over Culter and Rosher's material.

Journeys

In the two previous section I have considered ways in which particular aesthetic approaches – observation and archive – assert their film's close relationship with their subject matter. In this section I want to consider how a documentary backstage can be constructed through narrative strategies, and particularly how the framework of a journey can be used to emphasize proximity and intimacy. The journey is a narrative mode common within documentary film and television, providing a clear sense of forward momentum in texts as varied as *Salesman* (1969), *Burden of Dreams* (1982), *Around the World in 80 Days with Michael Palin* (1989) and *Tracking Down Maggie* (1994) where the filmmaker or their subject (pursued by filmmaker) undertake a literal journey from one location to another. Stella Bruzzi has argued that the focus of journey films is the 'encounters and meetings that are often accidental and unplanned' and that therefore 'a preoccupation with an end point rarely predominates' (2006: 81). This is partly a condition of production, where material is gathered in an unplanned way, and as Dai Vaughan and John Ellis variously suggest, the shape of a documentary is often 'discovered in the course of refining the material' (Vaughan 1999: 134). Ellis suggests that the editing process is 'inevitably one of attributing meaning to events in hindsight' and that 'the construction of narrative is the construction of a chain of consequences, which by definition can be done only with hindsight, in the knowledge of the end to the story' (2012: 69). This allows the material to be given a sense of structure – which may be narrative or thematic in nature – that may not have been understood at the point of shooting. As Ellis argues, this ending 'need be neither boringly predictable nor entirely satisfactory in tying up all the loose ends', and indeed an eschewing of the latter temptation can function as 'the guarantee or sign that the film has been manufactured from material that was gathered from reality' (2012: 69–70). Music documentaries that employ a journey structure often have titles that are emphatic about the tension that exists between the journey and the destination. *Finding Fela* (2014), *Searching for Sugar Man* (2012), *What Happened, Miss Simone?* and Netflix's *ReMastered* (2018–19) series, which focuses on musical controversies, and includes episodes called 'Who Killed Jam Master Jay?' and 'Who Shot the Sherrif? A Bob Marley Story', all suggest that the substance of the film will involve a quest, either for answers to the titular questions or a search for insight into their subject's lives. In all cases there is some indication that the main focus will be the process through which these 'searches' are enacted, but also of something having been 'found' by their conclusion.

In documentary production, there are (at least) two journeys taking place concurrently: that taken by the documentary subject (who might also be the filmmaker) which is congruent with the shooting phase of the documentary (or may precede it); and that of the construction of the film itself, which extends beyond the shooting into the editing, distribution and promotion phases of a film's production. Both journeys are contained within the final documentary text, but the filmmaker can prioritise one journey over the other. Within music documentary, the 'tourfilm' narrative most clearly prioritizes the documentary subject's journey, with the structural trajectory and limited timeframe imposed by the duration of a concert tour fitting neatly with the 'crisis structure' (Mamber 1972b) device emblematic of 1960s direct cinema (see the discussion of *Part of Me* in Chapter 1 for more on this). Within the tourfilm structure, certain narrative devices recur, such as the preparation for a significant concert performance, as in *Gimme Shelter* and *Depeche Mode: 101* (1989) (Wallace 2021a), and concluding moments of vehicular departure that provide a sense of closure to proceedings, such as when Bob Dylan – describing himself as 'the vanishing American' – leaves his triumphant Royal Albert Hall gig in the back of a taxi in *Dont Look Back*, The Rolling Stones depart Altamont in a helicopter in *Gimme Shelter*, or The Beatles return from America at the end of *What's Happening! The Beatles in the USA* (1964). Such moments act to impose what Bruzzi calls 'a clear ending' that '[gives] coherence and logic to the potentially incoherent and illogical material observational films could easily unearth' (2006: 82). Each of these texts combines two endings into one: the end of the tour is also the end of the film (even if this is not a chronologically accurate reflection of events).[16]

However, in this section of the chapter, I want to focus on a number of music documentaries that construct a documentary backstage by shifting the focus towards the filmmaker's own journey of production. Bruzzi suggests that what the journey documentaries that she examines all have in common is a sense of reflexivity, in that the journey narrative functions 'as a means of probing the nature of documentary, the documentary subject and nonfictional representation' (2006: 81). In these journey films the documentary backstage is signalled by this self-reflexivity, and that by showing the ways in which documentary makers position themselves as part of the events that they document there is an implied openness to the representation that we see. Although the primary focus will be on two texts (*Get Back* and *Mistaken for Strangers* (2013)) that in taking a 'making of' approach place the production context of music documentary under the microscope, I want to begin by offering some brief views of how a sense of intimacy and proximity is conveyed in two more straightforward journey films, Wim Wenders's *Buena Vista Social Club* (1999) and Malik Bendjelloul's *Searching for Sugar Man*.

Searching for and Rehabilitating the 'Forgotten' Star

In *Buena Vista Social Club* and *Searching for Sugar Man*, the narrative device of the search is mobilized in quite different ways. Wenders's film focuses on Nick Gold, Ry Cooder and Juan de Marcon González's project to locate and record with a group of ageing Cuban musicians and singers who had been active in pre-revolution Havana, and who – at the time of the film's production – were in their 70s and 80s. The documentary is composed of concert and rehearsal footage and a series of interviews with the veterans, and although the *Buena Vista Social Club* album was recorded prior to Wenders's involvement, the film is formed around a number of journeys: Cooder and company's story of searching for the musicians; the individual biographies of the performers, who each recount how they came to be musicians as well as the details of their lives in pre- and post-revolution Cuba; the ensemble's literal journeys to Amsterdam and New York to perform; and, finally, the journey of global (re)discovery engendered by the album and the documentary. *Searching for Sugar Man* makes a different journey, as it follows two South African music fans as they search for an answer to the question of what happened to Sixto Rodriguez, a Detroit-based musician who released two albums in the early 1970s and was hugely successful in South Africa, but who disappeared from view and is said to have committed suicide onstage during a particularly bad performance.

The journey motif is established in the opening moments of both films with images of their respective subjects in transit. In *BVSC* we see Ry Cooder and his son Joachim travelling the streets of Havana in a motorcycle and side-car, while *Sugar Man* begins with shots of a car containing Stephen Segerman, a record shop owner and one of the aforementioned fans, travelling along a coastal highway near Cape Town. Both Wenders and Bendjelloul open up a space for intimacy and access by taking the viewer on a journey that begins from a position of relative ignorance – the musicians who are the subjects are not well-known stars and/or there is some kind of mystery to be solved – to one of proximity, as the artist is 'discovered' by the documentary and brought into a proximate relationship with the filmmaker and the audience through an on-camera interview.

In *Sugar Man* this occurs in quite a complicated way because the fundamental narrative trajectory is largely determined by the path already trodden in South Africa in the 1990s by Segerman and music journalist Craig Bartholomew-Strydom. The questions that the film poses at the outset – who was Rodriguez and how did he die? – are the same as those investigated by the pair twenty years earlier. Although Abigail Gardner and Gerard Moorey have suggested that the film 'uses a combination of interviews, archive footage, and animation to reconstruct a search for Rodriguez already undertaken' (2016: 174), the film is not a straightforward account of two men's search told fifteen years after the fact. Instead, Benjelloul uses a range of devices to place himself – and thus, the film – *within* that search, and thus allows the documentary to claim some responsibility for (re)discovering Rodriguez and providing intimate 'backstage' access to him in a way that moves beyond that provided by the South African fans in the 1990s.

The film adheres tightly to a narrative structure that has been variously called a 'fairytale' (Hyslop 2013: 490), a 'narrative of rebirth' (Rommen 2013: 471), and 'a story about the second coming of the great rock 'n' roll messiah' (Lewsen 2013: 455). It has also been criticized for its oversimplification of the social, racial and political contexts of both 1960s Detroit (Cole 2013; Davies 2012; Rommen 2013) and Apartheid-era South Africa (Helgesson 2013: 483; Lewsen 2013: 456; Titlestad 2013: 469; Watson 2013: 487), as well as for its smoothing over of any 'rough edges' of Rodriguez's story, such as the omission of Rodriguez's musical activities after the mid-1970s, which included a number of international tours (Lewsen 2013: 456 fn.2; Rommen 2013: 471; Titlestad 2013: 467). Timothy Rommen argues that these omissions are necessary to maintain the purity of the quest narrative (2013: 471), and Hugh Spearing, a marketing executive for StudioCanal, explains how the marketing campaign around the film recognized that Rodriguez was not a well-known figure in the UK, and attempted 'to preserve the mystery as much as possible' by 'presenting the film as a detective story in which clues are pieced together' (Grant 2012).

The first half of the film focuses on the South African fans' historical search for clues in the mid-1990s, something that Simon Lewsen says consists 'of dead ends and idle speculation', that acts to shroud its musical subject in mystery (2013: 455). Rodriguez's mythical status is emphasized, here, through the absence of direct and verifiable information, and the emphasis on hearsay and anecdote places the audience at a considerable distance from the musical subject, not least because in replicating the South Africans' journey the documentary does not initially challenge the duel misconceptions that drive the film's narrative: that Rodriguez is dead and that he is well known outside of South Africa. As such, the documentary begins with a perspective that emphasizes the distance between Bendjelloul and his subjects that is temporal (from Rodriguez's life in the 1960s and 1970s; from the South Africans' search in the 1990s), spatial (South Africa instead of Detroit) and epistemic (there are no 'cold facts'). This sketchiness is emphasized by a handful of CGI sequences which imagine a stylized version of Rodriguez within the milieux of Detroit in the late 1960s, but does so in a way that emphasizes the imagined nature of the images and the mutable history that arrives from the second-hand sources. This history is contingent and malleable, being worked over and rewritten, and Rodriguez's life story becomes a sort of palimpsest that is erased and rewritten as new information is gathered. The most obvious example of this is when the contested stories about his death are overwritten entirely at the halfway mark by the revelation that he is still alive and has been living out of the limelight as a manual labourer in Detroit since the commercial failure of his albums *Cold Fact* and *Coming From Reality*.

Up to the middle of the film there are two separate principal journeys, that of Segerman and Bartholomew-Strydon's search in the 1990s and that of Bendjelloul exploring the pair's earlier detective work from the vantage point of the 2010s, with the film prioritizing the first of these. However, the balance shifts as the film approaches its central revelation and Bendjelloul's own investigation takes precedence through the assertion that it is the documentary journey that is able to gather the 'proof of life' that Segerman and Bartholomew-Strydon struggled to secure in the 1990s. For example, while Bartholomew-Strydon is only able to give brief oral testimony of his failed attempts to 'follow the money' noting that he 'just got to a lot of closed doors', Bendjelloul gains on-camera access to key record company figures, including Robbie Mann of RPM Records, Rodriguez's first South African label, who suggests that 'if you can find out whoever the person was who owned Sussex Records, then you will find out what happened to the money.' Bendjelloul's intervention shifts the focus of the search from the 1990s into the present day, decreasing the separation between audience and subject by relocating the search from South Africa to Detroit, and adds tangibility to the investigation by replacing second-hand hearsay with first-hand testimony.

The notions of access and intimacy have implicitly structured the film up to this point. An investigation is always a quest for answers and information that will bring the searcher closer to something; the truth, perhaps, or into proximity with an individual. As such, Segerman and Bartholomew-Strydon can be understood as stepping stones in Bendjelloul's own journey towards an intimate on-film encounter with Rodriguez. The proximity between filmmaker and subject shifts at a rapid rate once it is revealed that Rodriguez is still alive, and the documentary pivots to provide a much more concrete approach to the singer that is grounded in conventional documentary methods; an interview with the subject himself, and a chronological overview of Rodriguez's musical career and his subsequent work as a labourer using interviews with colleagues, family members and a collection of old photographs. The answer to the question of who Rodriguez is, is delivered by the documentary film's investigation and not by the South African fans who first posed the question, and their earlier discovery is displaced by Banjelloul's investigation at this point. It is Bendjelloul's documentary camera that is able to make the trip to Detoit and present Rogriguez on screen as a tangible, concrete human being, and the interview plays up the intimacy of the encounter by appearing to take place within Rodriguez's home. The transformation from distance to intimacy is complete aesthetically when the CGI tracking shots of Rodriguez in Detroit are reconfigured in the present day as live action, with the real Rodriguez and the real Detroit overwriting their animated, intangible counterparts.

Both *Searching for Sugar Man* and *Buena Vista Social Club* end with their subjects making international journeys from spaces of obscurity into spaces of visibility. These are both literal journeys and figurative ones. Rodriguez literally travels from the obscurity of Detroit to the popularity of South Africa, though in another temporal slight of hand, he does this in archival footage of the concerts that took place in 1998 after Segerman and Bartholomew-Strydon had located him for the first time. The Cuban musicians in *BVSC* are shown wandering the streets of New York City in amazement, many making that journey for the first time. In these moments both films highlight the 'cosmopolitan privilege' (Helgesson 2013: 483) of free movement that is available to the filmmakers (and to Ry Cooder) but that has been denied to the documentary subjects up to this point: the wider political contexts meant that the South Africans felt 'cut off' from the rest of the world and from Rodriguez (Gardner and Moorey 2016: 175), and the same is true of the Cuban musicians and the United States.

Wenders's 'identification with travel and the road as metaphors for life' is abundantly apparent within *BVSC*, not least in the argument forwarded by Inge Fossen that 'the poignant point of the film is that Castro's revolution obscured the musicians and their music' and that 'the dramatic curve of the picture is thus one of triumphant vindication, of an almost heroic kind' (Fossen 2014). However, Tanya Hernandez raises the less comfortable argument that '*Buena Vista Social Club* idealizes the past and reinvents it to support the notion that socialist Cuba does not appreciate the talent of its populace in the way a White North American like Ry Cooder can' (2002: 67). We can also add Wim Wenders and Malik Bendjelloul to this category, as in both cases their films contribute to this narrative of (re)discovery and resurrection, especially in a commercial sense. Both films assert spaces of backstage access through narratives of discovery in which they play a key part, and the journey of BVSC and Rodriguez from obscurity into international stars is the fundamental endpoint of each film, both in narrative terms and in their legacies. Both films were critically acclaimed (*BVFC* was nominated for an Academy Award for Best Documentary in 2000, and *Sugar Man* won said award in 2013) and commercially successful (Grant 2012), and were central to the commercial resurrection of their respective artists musical output. However, in visualizing their own processes of discovery through the framework of the journey, they also act to construct a documentary backstage by demonstrating their own self-reflexive role in the popular rehabilitation of these two artists.

Making the Documentary

While the documentaries examined so far prioritise the journey undertaken by the documentary subject, this concluding section examines two documentary texts where the balance shifts towards the journey undertaken by the filmmaker in their own attempts to complete the documentary that we are currently watching. In these documentaries the relationship between filmmaker and subject is made available, and the documentary backstage is formed around the unveiling of the mechanics of how a person is transformed from an individual into a documentary subject. In other words, the place of the filmmaker within the film we are watching is not occluded as part of an attempt to preserve a sense of 'who the artist really is when the cameras aren't there'. Instead, the artist is revealed through their on-screen discussions with the documentary maker(s) about how the film that is being made about them will function.

Although the focus of this section will be Tom Berninger's documentary *Mistaken for Strangers*, which is ostensibly about Ohio-based indie rock band The National's 2010 European Tour, I want to first turn to the footage of The Beatles shot by Michael Lindsay-Hogg and his team in January 1969 as the band made what became the *Let it Be* album and documentary film (1970). This footage has since been re-edited by Peter Jackson into the three-part Disney+ documentary series *Get Back*, and significant extracts have also appeared in *The Beatles Anthology* (1995) television series and Ron Howard's *The Beatles: Eight Days a Week – The Touring Years* (2016) documentary. The availability of different version of this footage offers an interesting example of how the prioritization of the journey narrative can be reoriented from a focus on the subject to that undertaken by the documentary maker.

The original *Let it Be* film condenses dozens of hours of footage into a tight 80 minutes, which focuses on the tensions between the band members as they rehearse material in the sterile space of Twickenham film studios and later the Apple Studios in Savile Row in preparation for a live performance that is also to be filmed and included as the conclusion to the documentary.[17] The film is, therefore, fundamentally about The Beatles' creative process. Glyn Johns, the original musical producer on the sessions, recalls a key editing decision imposed upon Lindsay-Hogg by the Beatles' manager Allen Klein:

> Klein decided that there was too much footage involving other people and it should concentrate more on the four members of the band. So this meant that there was no interaction between The Beatles and anyone else, which, in my opinion, ruined what had been a much more interesting film. (Womack 2019: 189)

Much of this material is reinstated in *Get Back*, where Lindsay-Hogg becomes a key participant in the series (he is entirely absent from *Let it Be*) (Figure 2.6). Indeed, much of the intra-band tension that is documented seems to be a direct

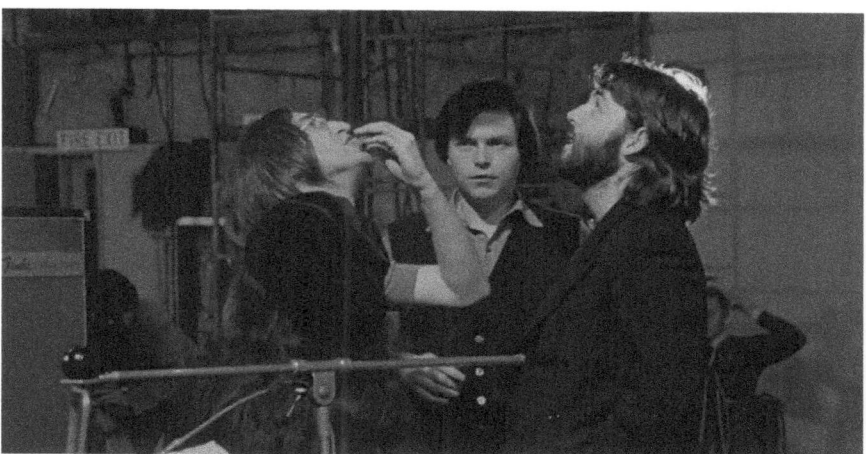

Figure 2.6 Michael Lindsay-Hogg takes centre-stage in *The Beatles: Get Back*.

result of the strain placed upon them by the production of the television special, and thus the presence of the documentary crew itself. There is a repeated sense of distaste for any of Lindsay-Hogg's proposals for a suitably epic location for the final concert – staging the concert in an amphitheatre in Libya, for example – and the filmmaker seems largely oblivious to his part in exacerbating the tensions that are leading to a reciprocal ill-will towards his ideas. The production of the television special, and the presence of Lindsay-Hogg in particular, then, are central to the story that is being told in *Get Back* – indeed, they define the 'crisis' being faced by the band – and in the hands of Jackson, this becomes a documentary about the making of the *Let it Be* film (and ultimately the *Get Back* series itself), something that is sidelined in Lindsay-Hogg and Klein's version of events as shown in the original documentary.

Lindsay-Hogg's absence from *Let It Be* and his omnipresence in *Get Back* demonstrate the kind of slight of hand required by observational documentary makers to convey the impression that their presence had little impact on proceedings. In *Get Back* we are asked to understand the events we see as being largely constructed and shaped by the interventions of the documentary-maker, even though Lindsay-Hogg frequently restates that he is attempting to capture footage without his subjects knowing. By reframing the material as a 'making of the *Let It Be* documentary' we are shown how laborious the endeavour was for the band, given that all of the work being done here – writing songs, arranging them, rehearsing them, recoding them, making decisions about the television special, discussing the staging and the location – is entirely in the service of the two documentary productions that emerged from the footage. We are constantly reminded of the position of the musicians as labourers within a commercial system. The *Get Back* series stresses 'backstage access' through the strategic and lengthy (the series is nearly eight hours long) deployment of an archive that explores both the act of music making but also the act of making a documentary, including the decisions being made about approach, structure and purpose, the key relationship between the musical personnel (the band and their management, engineers and producers) and the documentary-makers (Lindsay-Hogg and his crew), and the crises engendered *by* those relationships.

However, although *Get Back* makes visible the production context of the original *Let It Be* documentary – and Lindsay-Hogg's role in the proceedings – it is not explicitly self-referential about *Peter Jackson's* role in re-editing the material, and reshaping it to offer a competing (and more positive) version of the *Let It Be* sessions than the original film. This is not the case with *Mistaken for Strangers*, the final case study in this section, which positions the production of the documentary as its structuring framework. The film is directed by Tom Berninger, whose brother Matt is the lead singer of The National, a band composed of said singer and two sets of brothers (Aaron and Bryce Dessner; Bryan and Scott Devendorf). Tom is thus one of six brothers involved in the film, but the only one not in the band (for this reason, I will take the unusual step of using first names when referring to band members; any references to 'Berninger' relate to Tom as the documentary maker).

The basic narrative of the film concerns Berninger – an aspiring filmmaker – being invited on tour as a roadie, and using the opportunity to shoot material for a prospective documentary. However, it soon becomes clear that he is inept in both roles. He annoys the entourage, and especially tour manager Brandon Reid, by filming at the least appropriate moments, disabusing the notion of non-interference when he actively, but unintentionally, hinders Reid's attempts to fix an issue during a sound check, forcing him to stop his work to tell the filmmaker that 'I can't do this right now, dude. You gotta leave me alone'. Berninger is rarely where Reid has asked him to be, usually because he is preoccupied with recording footage ('it's not in your job description … stop taping') and he is eventually fired when he fails to return to the tour bus on time and is left behind.

The documentary approach is thus highly interventionist, not just in terms of the relationship between filmmaker and participants (which at first appears to be an accidental product of Berninger's ineptitude), but also in terms of the discernible presence of the filmmaker in the editing choices. John Ellis has suggested that when filming interviews for inclusion in a documentary there is usually a shift in the situation from 'the less formal activity' that precedes the interview, which might include checking sound levels or asking the interviewee if they are comfortable, to 'the formal activity of the interview itself', and that these preliminary activities 'are usually off-camera, and so unavailable for scrutiny' (2012: 55). However, by including some of these moments of informality a documentary maker can convey a sense of the unguarded subject outside of the 'highly constrained and unusual exchange' (Ellis 2012: 54) of the interview. Thus, the documentary backstage is partly indicated through the focus on the documentary subject prior to the call of 'action', avoiding the staginess of over-rehearsed anecdote or mannerism.

Documentaries that employ such a device have become increasingly common and include Sarah Polley's *Stories We Tell* (2012), Kirsten Johnson's *Cameraperson* (2016) and a number of Nick Broomfield's documentaries. *Mistaken for Strangers* takes this strategy to almost absurd limits, by prioritizing these moments over the interview material itself. This is highlighted in the opening scene where Berninger is unable to formulate a coherent and incisive question for his brother to answer. The scene takes place on the edge of a golf course, and begins with Matt expressing concerns that he might get sunburned, and using a boot to hammer a large golf umbrella into the ground so as to create shade. Tom, who as the filmmaker should be in control of the situation, complains that the noise is affecting his ability to think of suitable questions, his best attempt being:

> Do you ever get ... I mean, on tour its day in and day out...Um ... Do you ever get ... Does that ever make you sleepy on stage? ... Um ... Or tired? Tired on stage? That's my question. Question number one is that. Have you every woken up in a nightmare, on a bus? Because the movement ... What kind of nightmares have people talked about of having?

For obvious reasons, Matt is unable to respond in a meaningful way, and instead confronts his brother about his lack of preparation and professionalism, asking if he has a notebook with pre-prepared questions and even if he has 'any kind of organisation and plan for this film?'

Similarly, instead of including carefully composed and staged tableaus to introduce each band member, we see Berninger directing his subjects into these arrangements, which are then mostly omitted from the finished film. Bryce Dessner is directed to rise up from the bottom of the frame ('bend down and come up ... this is going to be perfect for your intro shot'), Scott Devendorf is seen in an underground car park moving furniture around, and Bryan Devendorf is filmed while showering backstage, concerned about how much of his body is visible to the camera. Both Matt Berninger and Aaron Dessner are asked to perform moments of contemplation, the former semi-naked while looking in a steamy bathroom mirror as he attempts multiple takes of the scripted (and absurdly clichéd) line 'The National belongs to everyone now'. The inclusion of these informal moments of direction at the expense of the formal and the polished acts as a constant indicator that what we are seeing is not the intended 'finished product', but an element of backstage preparation.

These interventionist moments create a tapestry of scenes which position the film far away from the formalized structures of the classic documentary approach to the musician; this is a far cry from the narrative discipline of Bendjelloul's work on *Searching for Sugar Man*, for instance. In place of direct observation and carefully composed interviews, the personalities of the band members are teased out through their interactions with the director and how they respond to these moments of directorial intervention. This off-kilter approach seems to have conveyed a sense of ineptitude that has the ironic effect of eliciting interesting contributions from Berninger's subjects, perhaps because – much like the 'elephant traps' (Wood 2018: ix, 126) sprung by Nick Broomfield's 'cameraman' persona – the participants in the documentary don't perceive the filmmaker as a credible threat to their public image. However, this approach also encourages an unusual process of information gathering. Berninger's askew approach to interviewing becomes familiar very quickly, and his questions are frequently unanswerable: 'How famous do you think you are?' 'Where do you see The National in fifty years?' 'What kind of drugs and how many drugs have you done?' However, this means that when Scott Devendorf is asked if he takes his wallet and ID on stage with him, he doesn't dismiss the question as ridiculous, and we are able to gain a highly personal sense of who Devendorf is as a person *through* his reaction, as well as a granular sense of his live performance practices.

Although the band members respond quizzically to Berninger's requests and questions, their sense that he is unthreatening means that they appear to play along, and in so doing create a sense of fraternal intimacy that feels more like a friend making a home movie than a legitimate documentary. Much as the footage shot by Billie Eilish's mother instils a direct sense of intimacy to the observational material that opens *The World's a Little Burry*, Tom's status as Matt's brother combines with his position within the road crew to give him privileged access not usually available to even the most trusted documentary maker. At its most extreme, this insider status results in a montage of highly voyeuristic footage of each of the band members asleep in the bunks on their tour bus.[18]

The other major aspect of the documentary that is established in the opening interview with Matt is that this is ultimately a very personal film about the relationship between two brothers that is articulated through this collision of their respective professions and personalities. Tom's curiosity about Matt's professional life as a rock star, and his attempts to gain some insight into their differences, rubs up against what Matt sees as Tom's unstructured and amateurish approach to filmmaking (and roadie-ing) that contrasts with his own personality and, crucially, turns out to be an attitude that reflects a much broader understanding of Tom as a 'quitter'. This dynamic between the two brothers is put on display across the first half of the film, especially when their personal and professional relationships become intertwined. Tom's frustration in his role as a roadie stems from his view that other members of the crew – especially the tour manager – think that he's only there because he is the singer's brother. This is a view confirmed by Matt on camera when he says:

> Here's the truth. The only reason you *are* here is because you're my brother … Or rather … you wouldn't be here if you weren't my brother. But we need you here and I'm glad you're here. You just have to make sure that all that other stuff is taken care of.

Elsewhere in the film, the pair argue about Tom losing the guest list for the New York show, whether he is allowed to film their friends backstage, and his domestic habits while on tour – spilling cereal in a hotel room and not mopping it up; hanging a wet bathing suit up on the tour bus – that moves the film out of the professional realm and well into a discussion of inter-personal domestic relationships. Nevertheless, Matt clearly advocates for Tom and it is evident that this is the only reason why he remains part of the crew for so long.

As the film progresses, the initial haphazard nature is shown to be part of a much more carefully crafted strategy to establish – almost covertly – the key narrative shift as it becomes clear that the film is actually about fraternal relationships, rather than the specificity of The National's story. Tom's struggle to give shape to his film is partly due to his initial inability to grasp this fact – though, of course, this is not just a concern of the footage-gathering aspect of the production but a deliberate narrative and thematic progression created during editing, once the end of the story is known.

This focus on brotherhood becomes a more central component of the pair's relationship once Berninger has been fired. This is a moment of personal crisis for the filmmaker, but is also – perhaps – the redemption of the documentary, as the filmmaker is forced to turn his attention inwards. This involves probing the brotherly relationship in a more rounded and direct way. This shift in focus also represents a transitional moment for Berninger's abilities as a filmmaker. His questioning becomes more direct, focused and insightful once he becomes the film's central subject: 'Growing up, how were Matt and I different from each other?' he asks his mother, and to his father he poses a similarly direct question, 'What other differences do you see between me and Matt?' In answer to these questions his mother makes it clear that unlike Matt, Tom was an uncertain child who did not like to be left at school and football practice, and who 'always wanted to quit things'. His father defines the key differences as being Matt's self-confidence and his moodiness compared to Tom's more casual attitude to life. These are, of course, the attitudes that we have seen on display in the film up to this point, from the earliest moment of Matt being concerned about sunburn and the film's mise en scène and Tom not having considered these aspects at all, which we are now asked to reread as examples of sibling relationships rather than simply of Tom's ineptitude. These are also almost uncomfortably personal insights into the lives and personalities of the central subjects, with the domestic and the familial once again providing the backstage framework of access and intimacy.

Having identified these personal aspects of their relationship through the intimacy of family engagement, the final act of the film focuses on Matt's encouragement of Tom to finish the film, an act of completion that now has greater symbolic weight. Matt invites Tom to New York to stay with his family as he edits (along with Carin Besser, Matt's wife, who is not shown editing, but played a key role in shaping the finished film and is evidently the person operating the camera on numerous occasions during this closing section). The process of editing the film that we are watching becomes the focus of the film, with both Besser's camera and a fixed rig capturing a different kind of creative process (filmmaking) than that examined so far in the film (music production and performance). We also see Matt's part in this process, as he offers constructive criticism and encouragement. This is primarily articulated through a series of interview extracts with Matt in which he recalls his own fears and anxieties early in The National's career, and the techniques used to overcome them. The relocation of Matt's role from primary subject to collaborator leads directly to more personal insight into his experience of starting a band.

This also leads to Tom restructuring the wall of Post-it notes that he has created to keep track of the footage so as to more directly write himself into the film, and he holds up notes to the fixed camera reading 'Tom fuck up', 'Tom gets fired', 'Tom failed screening'. Thus Matt's interview testimony about The

National's history, and his advice for how to overcome anxiety by not focusing 'on the wrong stuff' and '[leaning] towards the things that make you like yourself', becomes a source of encouragement for the filmmaker who is able to use the material both to convey his own struggle to finish the film that we are currently watching, but also as a meta-reassurance that enables him to continue in the first place. As a result, the discussions around Tom's ability to finish the documentary are the lens through which insight about the brothers' relationship – and the band's history – is conveyed, and this relationship ultimately drives the project to completion.

The film ends with two moments that characterize their relationship of complex, but mutual, support in a particularly substantive and emotional way. In the first, Matt – now behind the camera – sneaks up on his brother at the computer, ostensibly to 'check on the progress'. Tom's focused attention means that he doesn't hear Matt approaching, but when he does, he shields the screen, not wanting his brother to see, a gesture that seems to suggests real progress for the first time (Figure 2.7). 'I'm getting close,' Tom says, 'Just let me figure it out, OK?', a verbal reflection of his general state of mind throughout the whole film, but this time with a clear sense that for the first time there is a clear trajectory and that he is in the driving seat. These are the last spoken words of the film, but they are followed by a live sequence of The National performing the song 'Terrible Love'. As Matt strides into the crowd, Tom is seen dashing across the stage to support his brother's progress, freeing up the microphone cable and running it

Figure 2.7 Tom Berninger hides the screen as he edits the film that we are currently watching in *Mistaken for Strangers*.

through the crowd as the singer continues into the depths of the audience. Matt keeps going all the way to the back of the venue and out into the concourse, singing as he goes. He is clearly 'in the zone' that has been discussed elsewhere in the film, a state of mind – partly fuelled by wine – that enables him to 'get inside' the performance, but means that he is often in a trance-like state, and largely unaware of his surroundings. In the concourse, and away from the audience, the stark contrast between the two men is evident, but so is their connection; the physical practicality of Tom's 'cable-bashing' enabling his brother's visceral performance, in a final reversal of the dynamic of facilitation that has driven the latter half of the film (and demonstrating that Tom wasn't entirely terrible as a roadie).

This final moment offers insight into the practical and technical minutiae of live performance (something made even richer now we know that at least one band member has their wallet on their person). It also has a psychological dimension because of how it captures a close-up view of Matt's state of mind during live performance, and he seems entirely unaware that it is Tom aiding him at this point. It is a moment of dynamic, raw documentary-making in which the access and immediacy of the familiar 'going on stage' tracking shot that is a feature of direct cinema documentaries is deployed to capture the relationship between two people, as opposed to just the progress of one. In articulating both of these aspects it conveys the film's emotional centre, and shows the determination of both the driven rock star and 'the quitter', and demonstrates how it is the documentary itself that is able to convey their relationship in a profound way. The brothers return to the theatre for the song's conclusion, Tom helping Matt back on the stage and then standing with a gleeful expression on his face in the wings as the set continues and the credits roll.

As with *Sugar Man*, which occludes cultural nuance in order to maintain the streamlined storytelling, *Mistaken for Strangers* minimizes the involvement of other figures in the production of the documentary. Besser's role as co-editor is underplayed, and although the live sequences indicate that the filming process (of the live sequences at least) was a more formalized multi-camera affair, this is never acknowledged in order to keep the focus on Tom as the sole 'author' of a story about his relationship with his brother. To end this section where we began, then, the trajectory of Berninger's journey to make *Mistaken for Strangers* feeds back into itself and comes to determine the documentary's structure. Once the focus shifts to a direct interrogation of the brothers' relationship, and Matt's encouragement of his brother to finish the project, the rationale for the choices made throughout the earlier portions of the film becomes clear. The end of the journey structures the start of the documentary, but the process of discovering what the film is about is incorporated into the narrative structure, rather than being external to it. The inclusion of this process of self-reflexive discovery projects a documentary backstage through which intimate access emerges through the visibility of the production processes and the gradual (but increasingly deliberate) inscription of the filmmaker as a central subject.

Self-reflexivity

In the previous section, I noted how the filmmaker's own journey in producing the film introduces a self-reflexive dimension to the music documentary that allows for the projection of an almost literal documentary backstage in which the 'behind the scenes' process of making a documentary becomes the infrastructure through which intimate access to the pop star is asserted. In this final section, I want to take this sense of self-reflexivity further through an analysis of *20,000 Days on Earth* (2014), a film that functions almost as an anti-documentary that is almost indignantly non-conformist when it comes to following established conventions, and which deliberately destabilizes (though does not necessarily undermine) any claims of authenticity and truthfulness that the sounds and images might imply. As such, the documentary backstage that is projected here emerges through the assertion of a sense of truth and insight that comes into being through the collision of the real pop star – in this case, Nick Cave – and the series of loosely fabricated situations in which he is placed.

Anthony Kinik has noted that *20,000 Days on Earth* is 'a film that takes pains to alert its audience to its constructedness, and one that problematizes its status as a documentary, in any kind of "pure" sense, right from its opening seconds' (Kinik 2021: 199). Almost every moment of the film involves some artificial element that inflects the documentary investigation of the star. Nothing in the film is straightforward and even those sequences that appear to be more tangible than most – lunch with his long-time collaborator Warren Ellis; a trip to the Nick Cave Archive to talk through a range of photographs of his past exploits – are deceptively manipulative. There *is* a Nick Cave Archive, for example, but it isn't in Brighton where Cave lives. And although we see Ellis preparing a meal, neither man is seen to eat anything, and the location is not Ellis's actual home as is intimated, but instead a location that was chosen because it accords more closely with 'what things *should* look like' rather than the reality. 'Warren … has a functional place in Brighton', co-director Jane Pollard notes in a press interview, 'but it wasn't telling you enough about him. Warren *should* live on the edge of a cliff in the middle of nowhere. He looks like he should live there, his music sounds like that' (Lynch 2014). Such fabrications are plentiful in the film: the elaborate office where we first see Cave working, for example, is Cave's actual office, but as Pollard notes, 'it's completely dressed to create a space that the camera tunnels in to' (Lynch 2014).

The spine of the film involves Cave discussing his childhood memories and making key reflections on his early musical career and on the affective dimensions of being a rock star. These discussions are framed as taking place with a psychoanalyst. The psychoanalyst is real – he is the author Darian Leader – but almost everything else about these sequences are not; the set is elaborately stylized with chiaroscuro lighting and a television monitor facing the 'fourth wall', and the situation is not occurring for genuine therapeutic reasons, but as a means through which reflexive information can be conveyed in a more informal way than a talking-heads interview.

The hybridity of fact and fiction in these sequences imbues the reflections, anecdotes and observations with an aura of mystique so that Cave can convey (presumably factual) information about his life without the kind of gravitas being attached to them that would come from the directness associated with an interview. We understand them to be fictionalized in some way, and thus not to be taken as gospel; to a large extent, the Cave that the documentary is investigating here is a fiction created by the documentary infrastructure, and so we understand the anecdotes to belong to the character played by Nick Cave in the film as much as they do to the performer himself. To adopt the discursive manoeuvre employed by Stella Bruzzi to differentiate between Nick Broomfield's on- and off-screen personae (Bruzzi 2006: 208), throughout the film the subject is 'Nick Cave' as much as it is Nick Cave.

This, of course, has implications for any conceptualization of a 'backstage' within the film. This is not a documentary that suggests that it is stripping away layers of performance and persona to unveil a notional ideal of a 'real person'. Nor is it a film that attempts to show the impossibility of such a task, and thus – through its reflexivity – create an alternative conceptualization of access to 'the backstage' through the acknowledgement of the artifice of documentary conventions. Instead, *20,000 Days on Earth* offers an inversion of the 'backstage' approach that has been central to my analysis so far. In positioning Cave on a series of fabricated 'stages', a range of performative spaces are created which do not aim to maintain a façade of 'direct access'. Rather than stripping away layers of artifice, the film instead builds them up. But by doing so in such a deliberate and apparent way, a space is created for commentary on this process and its similarity with the process of public image management. In other words, the fabricated settings, scenarios and conversations offer a series of arenas in which Cave can reflect on the creative process – including his own self-performance – through which something truthful appears to emerge. We can see this clearly in Forsyth and Pollard's reflections on the fabricated settings as a means of conveying how something *should* be, rather than how it actually is, because what is suggested here is that the use of a fabrication – Warren Ellis's cliff-side cottage, for example – can tell us something truthful about a person and their character even if that involves a distortion of another aspect of their reality; knowledge and understanding emerge alongside myth.

This anti-documentary approach is reflected in the message, expressed by Cave repeatedly, that all aspects of the rock star's being – their star image, their mannerisms during live performance, their capacity for composition – are less interesting the more understood they are. These are all aspects that I discuss in more detail elsewhere in this book, and so it is appropriate to end this chapter by reflecting on a film that directly addresses the link between knowledge, understanding and documentary efficacy and which, in so-doing, asks questions of the role of the documentary within this sign-making system.

The documentary's representation of Cave's creative process oscillates between two extremes: observational footage of the writing and recording sessions for the 2013 album *Push the Sky Away* and highly stylized, almost hallucinatory, sequences in which Cave converses with significant collaborators, while driving them around Brighton (Figure 2.8). The soundscapes of these sequences are expressive, and each is underpinned by an off-kilter score (by Cave and Ellis) with a droning bass augmented by the irregular appearance of

Figure 2.8 Kylie Minogue appears in Nick Cave's car in *20,000 Days on Earth*.

tinkling chimes that together create an ethereal tone for the sequences. Added to this are the somnambulistic sounds of car engines, rhythmic windscreen wipers and ambient traffic noise that lull us into a dream-like state, but which are heightened at particular moments to punctuate the conversation and jar us awake. Cave's collaborators appear in the car as if by magic, and disappear just as mysteriously – sometimes mid-conversation – as if suggesting that Cave has summoned them from his imagination.

The first of these is Ray Winstone, star of the film *The Proposition* (2005), which was written by Cave. The pair discuss the question of public image and the separation of person from persona, with Cave's meditative voice-over initiating the sequence by suggesting that 'You turn it on. You turn it off. But then one day you find you can't and have become the thing you wished into existence.' Winstone reflects on feeling a need to reinvent himself within the film industry as he has aged, but Cave feels the opposite, suggesting that 'I can't reinvent myself ... I don't want to either.' This he links to the notion of the rock star as a deliberately indistinct figure: 'I think the rock star ... you've got to be able to see from a distance. It's something that you can draw in one line. And you can't have them changing ... every second week they're something different. Because they've got to be God-like. But it's all an invention.' Here Cave seems to be suggesting that the figure of the rock star can't be easily pinned down or understood in any great detail, either because to look too closely is to reveal the artifice or that the 'God-like' being will be shown to be ordinary. As Cave has noted in interviews about the film, the hybrid approach enables a delicate balance to be struck between offering insight into his own biography and psychology, while also maintaining the mystique which makes him an interesting documentary subject. This is most clearly articulated in Cave's aversion to the observational approach, which he views as merely offering 'a deconstruction of the people [the audience] think are special' and that in doing so those 'special' people are 'being made ordinary. And why would they want that to happen?' (Lynch 2014).

The Winstone sequence appears around 30 minutes into the film and picks up a thread already established by Cave about not looking at things too closely. The opening scene of the film includes Cave ruminating on his daily routine: 'Mostly I write. Tapping and scratching away; day and night sometimes. But if I ever stop for long enough to question what I'm actually doing – the *why* of it – I couldn't really tell you. I don't know.' This is picked up in the subsequent car interview sequence with Blixa Bargeld, former member of Nick Cave and the Bad Seeds. The subject of this conversation is collaboration and creativity, and again Cave's voice-over introduces the sequence with some observations about the creative process: 'For me, that's where collaboration comes in. To take an idea that is blind and unformed and that has been hatched largely in solitude and allow these strange collaborator creatures that I work with to morph it into something else; something better.' Although the discussion concerns the tensions within this collaborative process that ultimately led to Bargeld's decision to leave the band, the nub of the discussion concerns working on a song, of editing it into its final form, and ultimately on understanding it. As Cave says to Bargeld, the editing process changes songs and that 'you don't even know what the song really is until some time later ... because of the ramifications of the edit.' More pertinently, Cave suggests that 'Once you've understood the song, it's no longer of much interest.' This understanding needn't occur straight away, and he admits that 'in some of those great songs that you do you kind of become aware of new things over the years and that's the reason why you keep playing them.'

Cave's comments about stardom, about performance and about songwriting, all have a clear relationship with his approach to being documented. The stylized aesthetic of *20,000 Days on Earth* positions him as documentary subject in the same register as the line-drawn star viewed 'from a distance', and the unfinished song that isn't yet fully understood. When Cave extemporises in the voice-over following his discussion with Bargeld that he '[loves] the feeling of a song before you understand it', when it still feels 'wild and unbroken', it is not hard to make a link to his own self-presentation in *20,000 Days on Earth*, where the fabricated elements maintain a clear distance between the subject of the documentary and its audience. Cave contrasts this with a song that is finished and, ultimately, understood: 'soon it will become domesticated and we will drag it back to something familiar and compliant and we'll put it in the stable with all the other songs. But there is a moment when the song is still in charge and you're just clinging on for dear life.' Like the process of taming the song, the documentary impulse has the potential to get too close, to make the subject knowable and understandable, a potential that – for Cave – only diminishes the subject and makes it ordinary, uninteresting and no longer special. The aesthetic stylization of *20,000 Days on Earth* prevents this from happening by upholding the mythical and reenforcing the unknowable, even as it shows the mechanisms through which each of these characteristics is sustained. The documentary backstage, however, is projected through the acknowledgement of the impossibility of the documentary project being able to both understand the subject and maintain their status as mythical figures worthy of documentary attention. Instead it becomes a film about how these two positions are carefully balanced within the public image of the pop star, and this revelation may well be one of the most truthful and insightful observations worked through in all music documentaries, given that it takes a self-reflexive approach to working through – and placing at the centre of the documentary exploration – the tension between art and commercialism that I have argued is central to the music documentary's energy.

This is, of course, metonymic of the various 'documentary backstages' that I have examined across this chapter. The assertion of intimate access and proximity instils the documentary text with a sense of privileged engagement with the star, but it does so in a way that – for the most part – obscures the elements of 'cleaning up' that occur in order to project a preferred sense of insight and ordinariness. As Cave makes clear, this investigative strand needs to be counter-balanced by a continued sense of the star as indistinct and unknowable in order that they continue to function as mythical figures worthy of attention, and it is through the articulation of this tension – evident at a generic level – that the music documentary negotiates its position; bringing the star closer than they appear on the stage or in the press, while preserving the mystique by implying that despite the privileged access, there is always more to know.

3

Songwriting

It is perhaps the archetypal songwriting story. 'I used to live in this little flat up at the top of a house, in a little room I had, and I had a piano by the bed', the artist begins,

> and I just woke up one morning with this tune in my head. And I thought, 'I don't know this tune. Or do I? It's like an old jazz tune or something,' because my dad used to know a lot of old jazz stuff. 'Maybe I've just remembered it.' ... So I went to the piano, found the chords to it, ... made sure I remembered it and then I just hawked it round all my friends and said, 'What's this, you know, it's gotta be something? It's a good little tune. And I couldn't have written it.' 'cause I just dreamed it, you know. You don't get that lucky.

The raconteur is Paul McCartney, the song is 'Yesterday', and the account comes from the fourth episode of the 1995 documentary series *The Beatles Anthology* (1995).[1]

It is a televisual moment that embodies several key tensions at the centre of this chapter, and in the popular understanding of the songwriting process more generally. Jeff Tweedy, lead singer and songwriter of the American band Wilco, recognizes that 'we all sort of assume songs are more conjured than written' (2020: 2) and Paul Long and Simon Barber have argued that songwriting is often incorrectly considered to be 'romantic and ineffable' and 'a product of intuition, instinct or inspiration' (2017: 558). McCartney's account might be the most famous articulation of this position, and its notoriety acts to mystify songwriting more generally by positioning songs as products of genius rather than labour.[2] This chimes with Mike Jones's observation – made in 2002 – that the relative lack of scholarship in the area of songwriting (and particularly the multifaceted relationship between artist and industry) has meant that 'we know a great deal about our emotional attachment to the popular music we love, but, simultaneously, next to nothing about how such music is made' (2002: 148).

This chapter is not an attempt to fill this gap directly, and that work is being undertaken by other people better-placed than myself (Caves 2003; Clarke 1983; Jones 2002, 2005; Long and Barber 2015, 2017; McIntyre and Thompson 2021; Negus 1995; Thompson 2019). Rather, I want to explore some of the ways in which the process of song creation has been depicted in film and television documentaries, and how these representations contribute to (or challenge) the mythologizing of the music-making process.

Songwriting is a creative process that is located at the centre of a vast commercial and industrial enterprise of which the writer is only a small part. Thus, songwriters are both autonomous artists *and* employees of a record company required to produce product for profit, and Keith Negus has argued that the art versus commerce binary isn't particularly helpful when it comes to thinking about the actual process of songwriting, because 'the vast majority of recorded music that has been produced and consumed over the past fifty years has been manufactured and distributed by a small number of transnational entertainment companies' and so '*is* commercial in some way' regardless of its artistic status (1995: 316, 317). Long and Barber argue that 'the fact that professional songwriting involves remuneration serves as a reminder that while it might appear to be the result of "talent", "intuition" or indeed a passionate vocation, it is a job of work' (2015: 150). And Jones warns against 'too quickly [consigning] the effort involved in songwriting to the ineffable', suggesting that by doing so 'we put that activity beyond analytical reach' (2005: 223).

However, because songwriting is also a cornerstone of the recording artist's viability as a public figure (literally the source of their claims to artistry), it is the aspect of their work and public image that can be least explored if their position as 'greater' than the average person is to be maintained. Hence what Jones calls the proliferation of the 'myths of music-making' (2005: 224), and his assertion that much of the existing published literature around songwriting is located 'firmly within the ideological parameters of the constructed "artist"' (2005: 225). Those attempting to undertake a documentary exploration of this process are faced with a particular set of problems. The access given to the filmmaker places them within the industrial system they are investigating, and any demystification must be achieved in alignment with the strategies of image-management set out by the artist, their management and the record company. Configuring the songwriting process as labour (rather than talent alone) has the potential to shatter the illusion of the star as a 'genius'.

For Jones, accounts of songwriting 'rarely deal directly with creativity as a form of effort, not because it is ineffable but because the tendency is to settle with, or fail to see beyond, the terms in which creativity is socially constructed and debated' (2005: 225–6). How this relationship is managed in the world, and how it is depicted in documentaries about songwriting is significant, because how the recording artist is positioned by the documentary in relation to their work feeds into their wider public image, of which both the music and the documentaries are a part. At the centre of this discussion is a complex network of interconnected aesthetic challenges and conceptual tensions with which the documentary maker is confronted. These speak to the particularities of the subject matter and its industrial production context (the location of songwriting as both art creation and commodity production) and the relationship of the documentary text *to* this context (the extent to which the documentary attempts to demystify the writing process or uphold the status of the songwriter as a 'genius' who is worthy of sustained documentary attention).

Another complexity concerns the ways in which non-visual processes are depicted, made sense of, and examined in documentary texts more generally. Thomas Austin has noted that the inability to directly access human interiority 'presents a particular hermeneutic dilemma for documentary, one that complicates its conventional epistemology, centred as it is on representing and making sense of the profilmic world' (2016: 415). This is a particular problem for representations of creativity, and therefore songwriting, given that a significant portion of the work occurs within a songwriter's head or as part of a 'flow' of process (McIntyre and Thompson 2021: 118) that either leaves scant profilmic traces or else lacks explanatory insight. As a result, the documentary focus tends to be placed on 'exteriority' – on faces, bodies, verbal articulations and physical actions – that do not necessarily adequately speak *for* the interior processes that might be taking place. As Agnieszka Piotrowska suggests, 'the face can ... be perceived as a metaphor, or perhaps the metaphor, for the human' and that 'in documentary ... [a] close-up of the face ... often defines the meaning of the scene' (Piotrowska 2014: 150). Yet Piotrowska also acknowledges Sarah Cooper's point that 'the documentary subject is always more than his or her image' (Cooper 2006: 23) and that ultimately, 'the face takes us out of the very relation it simultaneously creates: the Other always exceeds the idea I have of it, escapes my grasp' (Cooper 2006: 18). We might, therefore, be able to watch someone thinking, but we can't know *what is being thought* without mediation. As I will also suggest, songwriting is an unpredictable activity, and capturing it on film is another significant challenge. Where documentaries *do* manage to offer revealing insights into the writing process, it is often achieved in a haphazard fashion (the observational camera happens to be present at a moment of inspiration) or as the result of consciously engineered situations.

The question of how documentary makers navigate these dilemmas, and which aspects of song creation are prioritized to do so, is central to this chapter. I am, therefore, also interested in how the song's concurrent status as a work of art and a commercial product creates tensions within the representational strategies available to documentary makers. In particular, there is a tension between the song as a product of genius (which upholds the status of the artist as exceptional, but is difficult to represent) and as a product of labour (some aspects of which are easier to show, but risks making the craft of songwriting appear ordinary). The various ways in which this tension is navigated provide the main structural thrust of the chapter, and I argue that an understanding of songwriting as 'process' is often occluded in favour of a focus on 'progress' for aesthetic, industrial and – often – pragmatic reasons. I also suggest that the labour of production is frequently emphasized over that of writing, and that where writing *is* observed it is often placed within discourses of authorship and ownership. The overall result of these choices is documentary texts that do offer insightful investigations into the creative process, but which also tend to preserve the mystique of songwriting as a creative act, and, by proxy, reinforce the artistic achievements and status of the artists under discussion.

These tensions are all apparent in my opening example, where the *mise-en-scène* suggests an attempt to enliven the visual imagery in order to match the spectacular nature of the story of 'Yesterday'; McCartney tells the story while piloting a boat. But just as important is the emphasis on the initial moment of inspiration, which occurred in November 1963, rather than the subsequent *work* needed to finish the song, which was not recorded until May 1965, thus prioritizing the magical paradigm of instant songwriting over an understanding of it as durational work.[3] Furthermore, McCartney's account is first and foremost about dreaming a melody. Simon Frith reminds us that 'popular music is a song form; words are a reason why people buy records' (1989: 90), and so it's reasonable to argue that 'Yesterday' did not become a song (as opposed to a tune) until its words were composed over the intervening months. Jones suggests that one aspect of the record company's involvement in the curation of a successful image for a pop act is the 'potential for stories to be told about how and why they make the sounds they do' (2002: 150). Documentaries about songwriting play an important part in the transmission of these stories and cannot be untangled from this commodification – even mythologizing – process. The rhetorical strategies through which narratives around songwriting are communicated form an important cornerstone of the pop artist's public persona, and the kinds of narratives that are prioritized in documentary accounts of *how* songs are written contribute to this. McCartney's recollections of writing 'Yesterday' in his sleep is just one example of the contribution that such stories can make to an artist's public persona; this chapter explores several others, though few that are presented as being quite so serendipitous.

Showing Writing

There are two significant challenges confronted by documentary-makers looking to capture an insight into the songwriting process. The first is that songwriting is not always a scheduled activity and so arranging for it to be captured on film is difficult. The second is that it is often a laborious, internalized process, and so the visible evidence produced is unlikely to do justice to the products of the act being observed or be that entertaining to watch. It is for these reasons that there are relatively few examples of documentaries that contain extended sequences of songs being written, despite the creation of music being a key part of many music documentaries. There are some notable exceptions: cameras catch Taylor Swift coming up with the idea for 'Only the Young' in *Miss Americana* (2020), Mick Jagger and Keith Richards are observed finalizing the lyrics for 'Sittin' on a Fence' in *Charlie Is My Darling* (1966), and Paul McCartney's unstructured bass playing gradually turning into the rhythm for 'Get Back' is a justifiably celebrated moment from Peter Jackson's *The Beatles: Get Back* (2021) series.[4] However, in general the depiction of the creative practice of musicians largely focuses on recording and production – a distinction that I will return to in the next section of this chapter – where examples are much more abundant, including entire documentary strands like *Classic Albums* (1992–2001) and *Song Exploder* (2020). In this section of the chapter, however, I want to consider in more detail the realities of songwriting as a creative practice, the challenges that this poses for documentary-makers and, through the example of *It All Begins with a Song* (2018) – one of the few documentaries explicitly dedicated to the process of song*writing* (rather than recording/production) – explore how these challenges are manifested in the film, as well as some of the ways in which the filmmaker attempts to overcome them. I suggest that the film mitigates the practical difficulties of filming songwriters at work by creating highly structured scenarios in which they can be observed in a controlled manner. However, it is less successful at dealing with the laborious nature of the work, frequently occluding the 'process' in favour of a focus on 'progress'.

A particular challenge faced by documentary-makers is the random and haphazard nature of songwriting as a creative practice, given that inspiration – and thus songwriting – can strike at any time. However, inspiration is often separated from focused work in accounts by professional songwriters. Tweedy articulates this tension as follows: 'You hear things like "I'm just a conduit" and "The universe wanted me to have this song." Whatever you say, man. I'm pretty sure it's still ME doing the work' (2020: 1). Long and Barber have suggested that routinized work is partly an attempt to mitigate the inherent risk present in any commercial system dependent on creative (and created) artefacts, and that regular engagement with the labour of songwriting ensures a constant stream of songs, a high proportion of which will never see the light of day (2017: 564–5). As Tom Robinson notes, 'if only one song in every ten is any good, unless you write the first nine, you never get to the tenth' (Long and Barber 2017: 567).

Although this might seem to be the antithesis of the popular characterization of songwriting as magical, it is not unrelated. Moments of serendipitous inspiration *do* occur, but rather than waiting for the 'muse' to strike, they are facilitated by the regularity of work. Tweedy recognizes that 'inspiration is rarely the first step' (2020: 17) and that:

> I've found that most people who have a fulfilling life in art are, like me, the people who work at it every day and put the tools of creation in their hands frequently, who not only invite inspiration in but also do it on a regular basis. Instead of waiting to be 'struck' by inspiration, they put themselves directly in its path. Pick up a guitar and you're much more likely to write a song. (2020: 19)

This might involve setting aside a certain amount of time every day to focus on writing, or blocking out days at a time for dedicated writing sessions, and it connects the extraordinary (dreaming one of the most successful songs of all time) with the ordinary (dreaming 'Yesterday' was the product of extended creative labour for which unconscious productivity was an intended outcome). Understood in these terms, just as you or I might dream about our jobs, it is unsurprising that professional songwriters might dream songs into existence from time to time. Tweedy makes this connection explicit, suggesting that the period after midnight is an ideal time to work on songs 'to have them in your head right before you go to bed', suggesting that 'I often wake up with the last musical puzzle I was contemplating completely solved' (2020: 47). However, the song doesn't emerge from nowhere as a marker of genius, but is the logical product of the work undertaken in the preceding hours, days and weeks.[5]

This is a difficult process to film, given that songwriting is both spontaneous (and so impossible to predict) and ever-present, ordinary and laborious (and so impractical and resource-heavy to film). Observing this process on film would produce a vast amount of material with no guarantee of seeing a successful song being written or of the footage captured being visually interesting. As Long and Barber note, once the vagaries of the magic of songwriting are stripped away, what remains are 'detailed diversions into the banal aspects of routine and process' (2017: 561). We see both aspects in the footage of Paul McCartney developing the idea for 'Get Back' in *Get Back*. His (initially) aimless strumming is only interesting because we know the results (a caption signals that we should be paying attention), and the regular mundanity of the situation is evident on the bored-looking faces of George Harrison and Ringo Starr (Figure 3.1) who are barely paying attention until something more structured begins to emerge. The sequence demonstrates clearly how the moment of inspiration emerges from a longer process of 'work', and that the transformation of this inspiration into a finished song is not quick.[6] Rather than conjuring the song 'out of thin air' or 'in just a few minutes', as some commentators have claimed (Irwin 2021; Marshall 2021), the series actually shows the dedicated work required to produce the moment of inspiration in the first place, McCartney's skill in recognizing the point when a solid idea begins to emerge from the 'noise', and the time needed to

Figure 3.1 The tedium of songwriting: George Harrison yawns as Paul McCartney (foreground) begins composing 'Get Back' in *Get Back*.

turn it from a rough sketch into the finished song we are familiar with. However, such moments are exceptional, and it is only because of the continuous nature of filming that this example was captured at all, and the lengthy running time of the series allows space to be given over to it (it is totally absent from *Let It Be*'s (1970) version of the same events).

Mike Jones has suggested that one reason why it is so difficult to get a sense of the labour of songwriting is because there is 'so little dedicated work on identifying how music is made *at the time of its making*' (2005: 231). While a documentary approach to this subject might seem like an ideal way of doing this work, to focus 'closer and systemic attention' on these routines 'in order to understand the specificity of this mode of production as work' (Long and Barber 2017: 569), the practical difficulties of capturing this labour on a day-by-day basis are significant. One solution is to find ways of placing restraints on both the songwriting process and the duration of filming, and this is the approach taken by both *It All Begins with a Song* (discussed here), where songwriting sessions are staged for the camera, and the Ed Sheeran documentary *Songwriter* (2018) (discussed later in this chapter), which concentrates on a handful of pre-scheduled multiday writing sessions during the production of his ÷ album. Both scenarios have a resonance with Stephen Mamber's conceptualization of the 'crisis structure' typical of 1960s direct cinema documentaries which had both practical and dramatic impetuses: 'a crisis moment appears to do no more than specify a period in which to film, providing in return a workable structure' (1972b: 116). This means that the filmmaker is not required to employ the 'diffuse and haphazard' method of 'filming every waking moment for months on end' (Mamber 1972b: 117) in the hope of capturing something. Instead, scenarios are selected (or constructed) which increase the likelihood of the filmmaker witnessing the creation of a song (if not an actual crisis).[7]

The centrepiece of *It All Begins with a Song* is a sequence of five scenes in which songwriters are shown working on songs. These are highly interventionist and (with one exception) have clearly been staged for the camera. The film does not try to hide the controlled nature of its production, and like *Mistaken for Strangers* (2013), which establishes a documentary backstage by including the informalities that are usually edited out of interview sequences (see Chapter 1), *It All Begins* opens with shots of the interviewees readying themselves: unpacking guitars, having lapel mics attached, being repositioned in the shot. The self-reflexive emphasis on fabrication and the prominence of the filmmaker within the songwriting sequences might seem like a counter-intuitive way of filming the creative process, given that it necessarily imposes an inauthentic framework upon the activities. However, this serves two purposes. The first is that it resolves the practical issue of how to observe songwriting happening. The second is that by eschewing a mode of documentary reliant on observation, situations are engineered in which interesting audiovisual material is produced *because of* the filmmaker's presence.

The validity of this approach is demonstrated as this central section *of It All Begins* unfolds, starting with talking-head interviews emphasizing the ethereal paradigm of songwriting and becoming more interventionist, and more work-focused, with each subsequent example. At the start of the sequence, the director's (Chusy) voice can be heard offering the prompt, 'writing a song is like what?', a question that elicits responses that largely conform to magical notions of songwriting. Shane McAnally offers several snappy responses: 'Writing a song is like a drug'; 'Writing a song is like flying'. John Hiatt describes it as being 'like hopping in a little spaceship and taking a trip … It's almost like I'm kinda steering, but not really'. Luke Bryan explores the inconsistency of songwriting by recognizing that 'You have your good days and you have your bad days and you have your days that it's almost you don't even remember feeling it come through your body and down on paper'. And Rodney Crowell makes the direct connection to the ethereal when he suggests that 'songwriting is prayer', in that

> you open yourself up to receive, and however you do that, whether you do that through a couple of joints or a shot of whiskey or if you do that by literally getting on your knees and praying for inspiration, that's what prayer is, it's opening yourself up to the possibility of something that doesn't exist. As a songwriter, it's like clairvoyance.

Here, the conduits to inspiration are not the kinds of routinized labour outlined by Long and Barber, Jones or Tweedy, but are divine (and/or chemical) in nature. This emphasis on the ethereal within the interviews also demonstrates Long and Barber's argument about the limited lexicon related to creativity:

> One of the challenges of investigating creative work is the degree to which individuals are able to articulate the essence of what they do *as* work. In so doing they themselves often rely upon the familiar notions of creativity *ex nihilo*, describing particular songs as a 'gift' whose origin need not be examined too closely, however fanciful its explanation. (2017: 562)

Tweedy extends this point by suggesting that this limited lexicon shapes the ways in which songwriting is depicted within culture more generally. 'Art is difficult to write about', he states, 'and the more difficult the art is to comprehend, the harder it gets to share our impressions in coherent and illuminating ways. That's at least part of the reason the artist becomes the story rather than the art' (2020: 38). It might also explain Simon Frith's observation that so little music television actually focuses on music and musicality (Frith 2002). This is exacerbated by the fact that, for the songwriter, the details of the work are unremarkable and ordinary and potentially understood as unworthy of sustained attention.

The inference of divine intervention expressed in the introductory interviews is further illustrated by the first example of songwriting process: Busbee's composition of the top-ten single 'Try', ultimately recorded by P!nk. This is another example of a song being dreamt and in an interview, he recalls waking up 'with that chorus in my head'.[8] The writing and recording sessions for the song were not filmed for *It All Begins*, but are represented by footage appropriated from a highly stylized promotional film, which condenses the creative process into a few minutes of work as we see the basic rhythm and chord structure being set out, the order of the verses discussed and new lines suggested, and finally the finished song being performed.[9] Busbee links this experience to ethereal paradigms of song creation, noting that 'people talk about … tapping into something, that there's something bigger than you', and emphasizing that 'it's like an act of God, man!' This replicates the clichéd narratives around song creation usually found in the limited lexicon of pre-packaged promo films, and acts as a benchmark against which the following scenes of songwriting 'work' are contrasted.

The first of these shows singer and songwriter Andrew Combs being asked by Chusy to compose a song using the 'cut-up' technique, where a selection of pre-existing text is used to generate lyrics (Tweedy 2020: 81–3). Combs draws a selection of phrases from a hat, reading them as he goes: 'a stranger you met on a plane'; 'a wrong number'; 'yesterday's beer'; 'a ring of keys and none of them work'. The interventionist nature of the sequence is gestured to when Combs asks, 'So I'm supposed to make a song out of this?' (Figure 3.2) and Chusy replies, 'Yeah', an exchange which suggests that the cut-up technique is not a regular part of Combs's practice. Nevertheless, the scene proceeds from this point to the performance of a complete verse and chorus, the fabricated scenario producing a song in a way that can be observed and, to some extent, understood through seven short sections:

1. Combs draws the phrases from the hat.
2. He begins trying out phrases along with some tentatively chosen chords.
3. He alters lyrics in a notebook, a close-up showing lines being scribbled out and new ones written in their place.

Figure 3.2 Andrew Combs writes a song based on Chusy's prompts in *It All Begins with a Song*.

4. Combs expresses hesitancy.
5. He arrives at a broad concept for the song: 'It just seems like trying to paint a picture of a missed connection, basically.'
6. Combs finalizes and performs a complete verse and chorus.
7. Combs reflects on his writing process.

There are two particularly interesting aspects of this sequence. The first concerns the moment of hesitancy (section 4), where Combs's statement of uncertainty – 'Yeah, I don't know where this is going, you know. It would take me a minute' – is clearly for the filmmaker's benefit, almost as an acknowledgement that what he is doing is not particularly interesting to look at. It suggests an incompatibility of process with situation, with the camera's presence creating an expectation of quick productivity at odds with the task at hand. Paradoxically, this awkward juxtaposition spurs Combs into action, and as if to avoid being filmed doing (apparently) very little he continues to vocalize. This centralizes the filmmaker as a constituent part of the writing process, supplying both the 'cut up' fragments that initiate it and the impetus to persevere. It is too much of a stretch to suggest that the pressure of the camera stands in for the kind of pressure that a songwriter might feel coming from a record company, but as Jones (2005: 244) has noted, there *is* often a requirement to produce material quickly, and so this feeling of being up against the clock is abstractly conveyed by Combs's motivation to fill the (audible *and* visual) silence.

The second significant aspect is how the temporality and velocity of the sequence sit in tension with the film's aim of communicating the details of creativity. The sections are short – the longest is section 6, where the final performance lasts around one minute; the shortest is section 3, lasting only four seconds – and are delineated by captions that indicate the time that has elapsed between them. For instance, after Combs says that 'it's going to take me a minute' (section 4), a caption reading 'A minute and a half later' appears, by which point he has arrived at the broad theme for the song (section 5). In total, Combs composes an initial version of the song in around fifteen minutes, but the editing makes it feel like an even more impressive achievement by condensing this – already sleek – quarter of an hour into two minutes of screen time. What remains are the moments that demonstrate that progress has been made; what is cut out is the work that went in to realizing those developments. These occlusions, then, place the emphasis on *progress* rather than *process* and are the primary way in which the aesthetic challenge of representing creativity remains unresolved in the film. This is something that Long and Barber identify in their own work, noting that when Paul Williams says that 'you just follow the pebbles of an idea and suddenly, magically, a song has appeared', he is 'too pragmatic … to suggest that his sense of magic is anything other than ellipses for the actual graft of songwriting' (2015: 151).[10]

Similar occlusions structure all but one of the other songwriting scenes, and suggest that even in such controlled conditions, the material qualities of the songwriting process do not lend themselves to inherently interesting visual material. This is most apparent in the middle sequence, which is both the longest and the most formally conservative, with Caitlyn Smith and Bob DiPiero filmed in an observational style co-writing in a cosy-looking practice space, which DiPiero identifies as his 'bunker'. Once again there is a general focus on progress rather than process and the scene is tightly edited. However, it also demonstrates the limitations of the observational approach which is not able, on its own, to adequately orientate the viewer to what they are seeing. Instead, the footage of Smith and DiPiero is intercut with interviews with other songwriters who provide context – and some explanation – for what we are seeing in the observational material. This creates a mutually supportive rhetorical strategy in which the observational footage illustrates the points being set out in the interviews, while the interviews make sense of what we are seeing when we watch Smith and DiPiero writing.

The scene begins by setting up the professionalized arrangements of songwriting in Nashville and particularly the practicalities of collaboration through a number of talking-head interviews. Barry Dean describes it thus: 'You go in. You write either with a friend that you know well or someone you've never met, and your job is to let your guard down and just be honest with them.' This statement frames the Smith/DiPiero sequence, and the early sections deal with the transition from initial chit-chat to the discussion of potential song ideas. We watch Smith looking at notes on her phone and DiPiero picking out some chords on his guitar. The sense of 'letting one's guard down' is emphasized by the presence of the camera – an unfamiliar participant in the writing process – and the trading of ideas has an element of self-consciousness about it. 'I love this line, I don't remember where I heard it', Smith says, as she selects an idea from her phone, 'Like a building with rooms I've never explored'. There is a cut to DiPiero sharing his own 'dumb idea' for a song called 'It Ain't A Lie If It's the Truth', which Smith riffs on for a few seconds over a basic guitar strum. At this point a short interview with Jessi Alexander provides a commentary on the process that we are seeing – 'it's just this ping-pong process of song idea, song idea, song idea' – that bridges the gap to the next point of progression: 'And then all of a sudden, someone says something that rings a bell.' At this point the image cuts to the camera jerkily reframing into a close up of Smith's face, eyes closed, half-covered by her hand and clearly deep in concentration as she tentatively sings the phrase, 'Baby, you're my lighthouse. La la la la lighthouse.' This clearly 'rings a bell' for DiPiero, 'Did you say, 'Baby, you're my lighthouse?' I love something like that!' This enthusiastic response gives Smith the space to work through the phrase with more confidence, though at this point she concedes that 'I don't know what it is.'

The interviews condense the intermediate action through description and explanation rather than simple omission, and another interview, this time with Ben Folds, addresses the development of a song from an initial idea, describing the process as 'truly a mess', but that after some trial and error 'suddenly you've got something that's great.' We don't *see* Smith and DiPiero's work from one stage to the next, instead we hear it from the interviewees, and when we return to the pair, they have clearly made progress with Smith's lighthouse idea, and she is able to articulate what the song is about and begin formalizing the practical and technical aspects of turning the sketches into a finished song. This is the subject of the next set of interviews, Lee Thomas Miller discussing the movement in the process from one in which the initial idea is being sought out to one in which direct and precise work is being done to shape that idea into a coherent piece of work: 'Now, we need a hit chorus, and we need two verses', he says matter-of-factly. 'It needs to be simple, but it needs to be profound,

Figure 3.3 Forest Glen Whitehead explains his process to the film crew in *It All Begins with a Song*.

you know ... But when you start getting into those things, this is a different part of your brain from the part of the heart that made you think of the idea in the first place.' As with Combs, the Smith/DiPiero sequence ends with a full performance of a verse and chorus, the lyrical and melodic finessing having been done largely off-screen.

This sequence emphasizes the limitations of observation as an investigative approach, given that the resultant footage requires further explication from the interviewees. This is countered in the penultimate songwriting sequence, in which Forest Glen Whitehead constructs a song layer-by-layer in his home studio while explaining his process to the filmmaker (Figure 3.3). It balances the approaches taken in the previous two sequences; it is not as straightforwardly fabricated as the Combs sequence, while also encouraging the kind of self-reflection absent from Smith/DiPiero. Once again, much of the actual work is removed, this time by frequent dissolves, though Whitehead's descriptions fill in the gaps. The sequence begins with Whitehead using a keyboard to add drum and percussion sounds to a track in a digital production programme. This is looped and (after the first dissolve) he adds a rhythmic keyboard and (after the second dissolve) an arpeggiated acoustic guitar. This looping backing track provides a sonic structure to the sequence with each dissolve timed so that the rhythm stays regular. Whitehead explains his process directly to the camera, 'Most of the time I hear the phrasing first, before an actual lyric', he says, demonstrating this by vocalizing a mumble track over the existing backing.[11] He quickly finds a phrasing that works, but – like Combs – becomes hesitant about finding a lyric idea under the glare of the camera. He half-says and half-sings the phrase, 'I don't know', as an indicator of mild frustration, before acknowledging that 'I don't know's not bad'. The line is then used as the starting point of a lyric that is sung spontaneously as the song loops round again: 'I don't know / Where the time has gone / But it sure goes / Quicker than a wrong word / I can't say / When you'll ever get it back / There ain't no way'. Whitehead breaks off and acknowledges that 'some of them make sense, some of it doesn't, but you just kind of blindly go in a direction that just feels right.'

In each of these four sequences we see a song develop from a basic idea to something more complete. However, we rarely get a sense of *why* certain choices are made. Combs's lyrics are suggested by the cuttings, but we have no insight into why he chooses the chord progression that he does. Furthermore, the occlusions hinder a full understanding of how these ideas evolve, even if the gaps are partly filled by interviews and self-commentary. The move from stimulus to output *is* evident, but what we are shown might more precisely be described as progress rather than process. In each sequence we see the products of creative work appearing in stages – a new instrument added to Whitehead's composition or Combs having worked out a better phrasing – but not much of the work that leads to these decisions, perhaps because those moments of thoughtfulness are too lengthy, visually uninteresting, or lack insight into what we are being shown. Much as how 'magic' comes to stand in for 'creative labour' in spoken accounts of songwriting, the visual ellipses in *It All Begins* achieve a similar effect, by giving a sense that *something* happened in the gaps, but not explicitly pinning that 'something' down as work.

This emphasis on songwriting as a product of labour rather than magic is also suggested by the ordering of the songwriting sequences, which stress a narrational movement from the mythical end of the spectrum (Crowell describing songwriting as 'prayer', Busbee dreaming the chorus of 'Try', Combs writing a song in fifteen minutes), through to the more labour intensive work undertaken by Smith and DiPiero's co-writing and Whitehead's digital layering which, in being done alone in the digital space of the computer, is some distance away from the romance of McCartney dreaming 'Yesterday'. In the latter sequences, this labour is made visible because there is an additional presence in the songwriting space. For Smith and DiPiero this figure is the songwriting partner to whom ideas are being presented. For Combs and Whitehead, it is the filmmaker himself, whose intervention provokes the creation of the songs we see being written and pushes the songwriter on by requiring Combs to fill an awkward silence, and by turning an interview response into a lyrical hook upon which Whitehead can hang the lyrics to a verse. Intervention is shown to be a useful approach to eliciting insightful and visually interesting documentary material.

The trajectory from romance to work is completed in the final songwriting sequence, where Amy Stroup and Trent Dabbs discuss the process of gathering material – ideas, phrases, titles – in notebooks as a way of initiating writing sessions. At first the scene unfolds in a similar vein to the others. Stroup scrolls through notes on her phone, illustrating the process we have just heard Caitlyn Smith describe in an interview, and she reads out some of them: 'She's been living in all of her junk. Going for the kill / Making thrills. Crying diamonds. I don't know what those would mean yet, but I'm sure they'll turn into something'. However, Stroup and Dabbs resist the encouragement by Chusy to try and compose a song on the spot. 'Come on, come on, sing it. Give me some of that "Crying Diamonds" action!', Chusy says after Dabbs makes a wry attempt to sing the song's title in an overly countrified manner. However, both Stroup and Dabbs are hesitant, quickly abandoning a tentative effort with Dabbs saying, 'Now we're like the TV show *Nashville* (2012–18). That doesn't happen', suggesting that the ability to conjure a song spontaneously is the purview of fictional representations of songwriting rather than the reality. Here, the interventionist method goes too far, and this final moment focuses both on the work that goes into preparing to write songs, and affirming that songs cannot – generally – be conjured out of thin air, not even (or, perhaps, especially not) when under the watching eye of a documentary camera. The fictional representation of songwriting seen in *Nashville* is used as a reference point, in part, because such implied spontaneity obfuscates the actual labour that goes into writing songs, propagating the myth that songs arrive out of the blue.

It All Begins with a Song offers a self-aware examination of songwriting through a performative mode of filmmaking that stresses its own part in the songwriting process and emphasizes that what we are seeing are not the day-to-day activities of the songwriters who are their focus. These moments provide an insightful exploration of how songs are written by constructing environments that can be easily controlled and filmed, even if they produce only an approximation of the reality of songwriting. They also challeng some of the grand narratives that drive the popular conceptualization of songwriting as a magical process that upholds the songwriter's status as an artist. It is to this aspect of representation that I now turn.

Production Stories: Making *Sgt. Pepper's Lonely Hearts Club Band*

So far, this chapter has proceeded under the assumption that demystification of the writing process is a key aim of music documentaries that focus on song creation, and that overcoming the practical and representational difficulties is a primary concern. In the previous section, I examined a documentary approach which addressed the practical issue of how to film songwriting happening by staging scenarios over which the filmmaker has some element of control. However, this approach is less successful at overcoming the representational question of how to capture informative material that is also visually interesting. In this section I want to continue this discussion by suggesting another approach to representing songwriting that achieves the opposite effect: it produces a range of interesting audiovisual material but does so by shifting the focus towards production and recording practices.

Alan Williams has argued that 'if one accepts the premise that popular musicians are artists, then the sound recordings that serve as the lasting artifact of the music they create are the works of art' (2010: 167). Given that the emphasis of programmes like *Classic Albums* and *Song Exploder* is on the creation of albums and songs as art objects, one might think that there would be a strong emphasis on the process of songwriting itself, but this is not always the case, and raises wider discursive questions about the relationship between art and commerce in the music industry. If the central section of *It All Begins with a Song* was able to refocus the analytical paradigm of songwriting from the ethereal to the laborious, the focus on production tends to do, if not the opposite, then something equally complex. I suggest here that the 'ethereal genius' dimension of songwriting is preserved by repositioning the laborious aspect of song creation in the field of production, which also happens to be rich in audiovisual material. This has an ideological impetus that challenges the underlying assumption that such documentaries are primarily interested in demystification. Claims of artistry are made via stories of complex musical performances and technological achievement, which complement a series of inspiration stories that pull focus and leave the actual writing process largely undisturbed.

In order to demonstrate how this works in practice, I examine how programmes that explore the production of The Beatles' 1967 album *Sgt. Pepper's Lonely Hearts Club Band* position the artistry of Paul McCartney and John Lennon within a production-focused paradigm as a means of solving the practical and aesthetic difficulties inherent in depicting songwriting, while also preserving the pair's status as artistic geniuses, rather than as labourers within a commercial ecosystem. Two television programmes will be examined here, a 1992 episode of *The South Bank Show* (1978–) called 'The Making of Sgt. Pepper' (hereafter 'Making of ...') and the 2017 documentary *Sgt. Pepper's Musical Revolution with Howard Goodall* (hereafter *Musical Revolution*). The former programmes has been described by Alan Williams as a 'template' for the *Classic Albums* television series (2010: 167) and 'one of the first films to both demystify recording practice and mythologize the recording process' (2010: 168). In 'Making of ...' and *Musical Revolution* songwriting is frequently overshadowed by counter-narratives that emphasize the importance of groundbraking production to the album's ongoing cultural status. This is done in such a way as to place the artistic vision of the band members (and specifically Paul McCartney and John Lennon) as the creative drivers of production innovation. Furthermore, this centralization of the production process speaks to the tension within documentary production about what aspects of the creative process can be conveyed on screen in a visually engaging way. That both programmes are made for television is also important, because the solutions are particularly televisual in nature.

The Form of Production Narratives

John Corner reminds us that 'the conditions of documentary production within television established an aesthetic order different from that of cinema', in part because documentary programmes 'were frequently made within a series format' and that 'along with this went the use of regularly scheduled spots, a named reporter/presenter who appeared (and often 'featured') within the programme, a style of more personalised, intimate address and a recognition of the fact that most viewers were sitting at home' (1995: 84). Both 'Making of ...' and *Musical Revolution* are structured around a presenter. In *Musical Revolution*, composer Howard Goodall acts as an expert guide who analyses the album's music in meticulous detail, explaining what is significant about it from a perspective grounded in music history and theory.[12] Although 'Making of ...' features interviews with the three (at the time) living Beatles, it is their producer George Martin who takes on the role of presenter. Taking a similarly expert role to Goodall, Martin spends much of his on-screen moments either at a piano discussing particular compositional elements (such as the five-note verse of 'With a Little Help from My Friends' needed to accommodate Ringo's limited

Figure 3.4 George Martin (left) and Paul McCartney (right) interrogate the multitrack tapes in *The South Bank Show*: 'The Making of Sgt. Pepper'.

vocal range) or else sat at a mixing desk (occasionally alongside McCartney) (Figure 3.4), guiding the viewer through the album's production via a 'forensic analysis' (Williams 2010: 168) of the original multitrack tapes. Pioneered by 'Making of …', the producer-at-the-mixing-desk device would subsequently provide *Classic Albums* with a signature framework that compensates for a general lack of illustrative archival footage by providing a suitably dynamic visual accompaniment to the historical evidence, which is largely aural in nature. The device is now so familiar that it has been subjected to popular criticism and parody (Figure 3.5), as well as being widely reworked, including in the 2021 Hulu series *McCartney 3,2,1* with Rick Rubin taking the George Martin role in a much more stylized and self-reflexive performance space (Figure 3.6).[13]

Williams suggests that deconstructing the multitrack tapes 'creates unique artifacts wherein stages of process are preserved in the elements of the completed work' (2010: 167). These sequences direct the programme's focus onto production, and the use of the multitrack tapes creates an effect that is not dissimilar to Karen Lury's arguments about the close-up in television documentary and Corner's discussion of how television documentary often works by ' "making strange" that which may have come to be familiar' (Corner

Figure 3.5 Parodying the 'producer-at-the-mixing-desk' trope in *The Life of Rock with Brian Pern*.

Figure 3.6 The 'producer-at-the-mixing-desk' trope is reformulated by McCartney (right) and Rick Rubin (left) in *McCartney 3,2,1*.

2003: 96–7). Lury argues that the moving close-ups of still photographs in documentary texts, sometimes referred to as the Ken Burns effect (Edgerton 1997: 14) 'allows the image to be 'pored over', pulled closer to view' (2003: 103). The deconstruction of the multitrack tapes produces an engagement with a song that is similar to this, but in the aural register of the programme; an audio close-up. This requirement to 'listen closer' and to pay attention to the contents of the audiotape is signalled visually by close-ups of tape machines starting and the prominence in the image of the carriers of the informational content of the documentary (the tape, the desk, the producer's hands) in a way that 'relates to the tactile, sensual approach television has to such material' (Lury 2003: 103).

Lury's argument about the close-up also gestures towards television's propensity to 'make strange', when she argues that

> the audience is pulled in different directions. On the one hand, getting closer indicates that we should indulge in greater scrutiny, look for missed details that we had not noticed before, and asks that we perform an active and penetrating gaze. On the other hand, we may find that we are not seeing more, but seeing less, as the image blurs at close quarters, or confronted with a fragment, we see only the unremarkable. (2003: 103)

By isolating layers of sound, we are brought closer to the individual components of a song, the constituent parts that make up the familiar whole. But the breaking down of the multitrack tapes or the presentation of earlier (and thus unfinished, unfamiliar and 'not quite right') versions of a song makes them strange and encourages us to hear the songs on *Sgt. Pepper* from a new perspective. We can hear individual ingredients more clearly, but must lose sight of the final mixture to do so, a process that results in a 're-seeing' (Corner 2003: 96–7) – or 're-hearing' – the next time we encounter the finished song (which we invariably do later in the programme).

This 'making strange' through the audio close-up doesn't just occur for the television viewer, and an important part of these documentaries can be the moments when those who were themselves involved in the production hear something that surprises them. Martin expresses some curiosity when playing back an early take of 'Strawberry Fields Forever' as to why a guitar part played by George Harrison may have been recorded on the same track as the vocals, and McCartney points out the absence of his bass on an early take of 'Lucy in the Sky with Diamonds', which surprises him at first, but leads to a discussion of how multitrack recording allowed him to add more complex and melodic bass lines later in the process. Such moments help to draw further attention to 'missed details' of the song that, as Lury suggests of the visual image, 'we had not noticed before'.

In each case, however, the structural reliance on the mixing desk positions the finished record as the central component of attention because its inherent artistry (available to hear in the unpicked multitrack tapes) can be demonstrated in an audiovisual way, and then explored through a discussion of its production.

In relation to *Classic Albums*, Williams argues that such an approach works to 'establish a canon of practices' (Williams 2010: 175) central to the production of landmark popular music. In demonstrating rather than describing, Martin's contribution is to instil a clear sense of televisual dynamism into the proceedings which also acts to pull focus away from writing and onto production. Likewise, Goodall starts with the finished songs and works backwards to demonstrate what we can hear, how we have come to hear it, and why that matters within considerations of its artistry.

Omitting the Writing

Although my general focus in this section will be on how these programmes represent the creation of one specific song, John Lennon's 'Strawberry Fields Forever', I want to begin this analysis by looking at the ways in which songwriting in general is addressed in each programme.[14] The only direct discussion of songwriting practices in 'Making of …' occurs within the context of a broader section on the influence of drug-taking to The Beatles' music, when McCartney says in an interview that

> We mainly wrote in the afternoons. I'd either go to John's house or he'd come to mine. So, I'd sort-of drive out to Weybridge; now you don't want to be stoned doing that, you know. So we'd go out and we'd have an afternoon of it. And it would be later, listening in the evening that a little wine might come out and this and that might come out.

This is a slight overview that only conveys the vaguest sense of Lennon and McCartney's songwriting routine (though there clearly *was* a routine). More prominent in both documentaries are inspiration stories; anecdotes about the source of a song idea. Examples from 'Making of …' include: 'Lucy in the Sky with Diamonds' being influenced by a picture painted by John's young son Julian; 'Being for the Benefit of Mr. Kite' being based on a poster that Lennon had stumbled across in a Kentish antique shop, which we see via a photograph of the poster hanging in Lennon's hallway, and which George Harrison suggests 'contained nearly all the lyrics to that song'; the 'grabbed-from-the-headlines' source material for 'A Day in the Life' is inferred through the inclusion of newspaper cuttings of the events referred to in Lennon's lyrics (notably, the death in a car accident of Tara Browne, Guinness heir and friend to The Beatles, in December 1966).[15]

Both programmes contain some discussion of the inspiration for 'Strawberry Fields', which connects the song to 'Penny Lane', its counterpart on the eventual double A-side single. In *Musical Revolution*, Goodall suggests that the two songs were integral to the album in terms of musical complexity and establishing a central theme of childhood. He acknowledges the inspiration for the title as coming 'from a Salvation Army children's home near to where John Lennon grew up' and that the song 'draws on his childhood memories of its annual garden parties, complete with Salvation Army band, and playing – away from adult supervision – in its overgrown grounds.' In 'Making of …', an interview with McCartney frames the two songs in terms of the instinctive, at times competitive, relationship between the two songwriters:

> Penny Lane was a place that John knew about, so, you know, for me to just say, 'I've got a song called "Penny Lane"', he knew exactly what I was doing. Similarly, 'Strawberry Fields' I knew about … from when I used to go and visit him when we were kids. It was the place right opposite him where he used to go and play in the garden … so it was a magical childhood place for him. And we transformed it into the sort of psychedelic dream, like everybody's magic place instead of just ours. We took them from being little localised things and made them more global.

Although we get a clear, though retrospective, sense of the inspiration and intensions behind the songs, and also an idea of how some of the universalizing effects were created in the studio, there is little tangible discussion of how these points of inspiration were transformed into lyrics and music.

This is true of all the songs discussed in the programmes, with the exception of 'Mr. Kite' where the lyrics are a broad transcription of the poster. The progression from these stories of inspiration to the point at which the songs were presented at the studio ready for recording is an unaddressed gap. Although Harrison does dwell briefly on the kind of observational songwriting process found on 'Mr. Kite' – 'that's how you do it, you know. You get ideas, you hear people say stuff, or you hear a phrase that sounds good and you write it down and remember it' – the work required to turn the idea into a song is not addressed, as the focus transitions quickly into the production process.[16] This mirrors the 'Yesterday' narrative, where the story of dreamt inspiration is emphasized over the work required to develop it into a song and this is a general rhetorical tendency within McCartney's accounts of his own work. Diana Erickson and Duncan Driver have suggested that the stories that McCartney tells about inspiration '[don't] really explain' how these ideas *become* songs, nor do then give any insight into 'the emotional centre of the song' (Erickson n.d.). This also, of course, has the discursive benefit of 'perpetuating the myth of the mystically inspired freely expressive artist' (McIntyre and Thompson 2021: 101).

The occlusion of the intermediate steps between inspiration and recording is apparent in 'Making of …'s treatment of 'Strawberry Fields'. George Martin begins his discussion of the song's development in the studio by describing the recording of an initial version that was both 'virtually complete' and 'the way I first heard it when John sang it to me', indicating that the song itself had been largely written – if not entirely arranged – prior to its arrival in the studio.[17] This speaks to a broader, almost philosophical, question about when a song *becomes* a song. Long and Barber argue that 'a song is not reduceable to a recording, although many songs are indeed formulated in the studio as part of that process' (2017: 557). Although both documentaries make it clear that the final form of 'Strawberry Fields' was shaped in the studio, and thus there is an interesting story to tell about its production, the central elements of the song were clearly in place prior to 24 November 1966 when Martin first heard it.

This offers another rationale for the tendency to focus on production rather than writing. Bennett and Baker suggest that a key strategy in the 'discursive positioning of rock music as distinct from pop' was the centralizing of the album as 'a sonic tapestry on which the [rock artist's] more invested interest in music as a form of creative expression could be fully exercised' (2016: 43). This also emphasized an 'aesthetic separation of studio and live performance', with the complexities of the former underpinning rock's position within emerging cultural hierarchies of popular music (Bennett and Baker 2016: 42–3). This focus on *the recording* as the valuable art object means that it makes sense to focus attention on the production of that work, rather than on the writing of the songs more generally, especially given that the song and the recording are not synonymous.

Although the spoken accounts of the writing process are limited, there is some attempt made within *Musical Revolution* to express it visually through a highly stylized *mise-en-scène*, particularly evident during the portions of the programme where Goodall is exploring the non-musical elements of the *Sgt. Pepper* story. This includes the sequence where the presenter examines the thematic continuities between 'Strawberry Fields', 'Penny Lane' and *Sgt. Pepper* as a whole, and Goodall is either superimposed over footage from the 'Strawberry Fields' music video or else standing within a darkly-lit studio set, complete with a mellotron, photo-enlargements (of Lennon as a child and then of the real Strawberry Field childrens' home), and an oversized Salvation Army badge, all shot through the red-painted framework of what Goodall tells us are '[the house's] original iron gates' (Figure 3.7). This arrangement – and it is the first of many similar ones in the programme – places Goodall within the

Songwriting 133

Figure 3.7 Howard Goodall stands amidst the expressive mise-en-scène of the 'Strawberry Fields Forever' sequence of *Sgt. Pepper's Musical Revolution with Howard Goodall*.

psychedelic world of the song, and it is not entirely clear which elements of the *mise-en-scène* are genuine physical objects and which are the result of digital manipulation.

The dream-like quality of the mise en scène point towards a less formalized and didactic approach to capturing creativity than is evident elsewhere in the two documentaries, which are more direct in their approach (as I will discuss shortly). Here, however, *Musical Revolution* deploys a flamboyant documentary style where, to turn to John Corner's work on television documentary aesthetics, 'the impact and attractiveness of the picture' is presented 'not simply to be looked through, but also to be looked at' (2003: 96).[18] Corner suggests that many documentaries deploy 'an intermittent aesthetics', whereby a programme shifts between different stylistic registers, with some moments which 'retain referential integrity' and are to be 'looked through', and others – those to be 'looked at' – which 'may also involve indirect engagement with the subject through the use of metaphor, which usually requires to be read as a discourse about the world rather than a depiction of it' (2003: 96). The slightly surreal imagery of *Musical Revolution* shifts our engagement away from a literal visual interpretation of the factual content to a space that feels more imaginary. The programme exhibits an 'opaque' stylistic tendency when the inspiration and the meaning of the songs are being discussed, 'temporarily transferring viewers into a deeper imaginative space (and perhaps also further into themselves) without breaking engagement with [the] theme' (Corner 2003: 97–8) of the documentary.

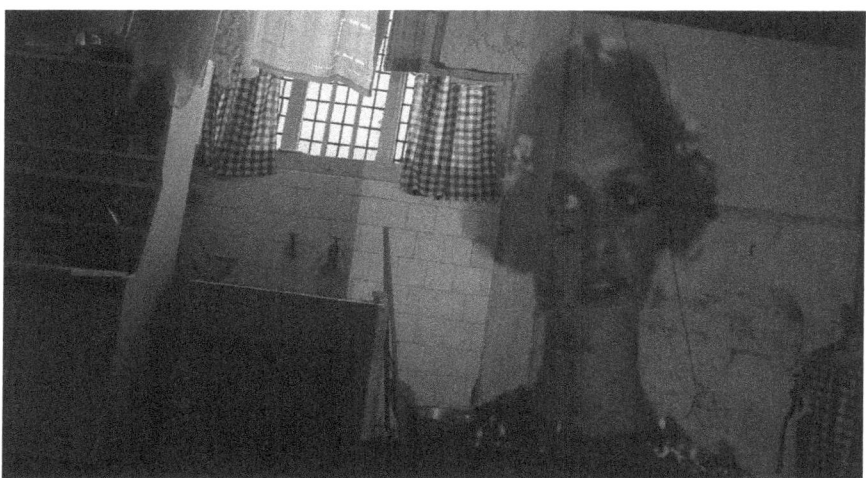

Figure 3.8 Inter-generational conflict and the 'kitchen sink' inspirations of 'She's Leaving Home' are combined in the mise-en-scène of *Sgt. Pepper's Musical Revolution*.

Similarly stylized sequences accompany the inspiration stories for other songs on the album. The *mise-en-scène* of the 'Mr Kite' segment replicates the nightmarish world of a circus hall-of-mirrors. The treatment of inter-generational discontent in 'She's Leaving Home' is established through a shot of a dingy kitchen space, that would be stereotypically 'kitchen sink' were it not for the cracked white tiles being used as a screen on which footage of Twiggy dancing and publicity material from the *Wednesday Play* (1964–70) 'Cathy Come Home' (1966) is projected (Figure 3.8). Perhaps most effective is the sequence which traces the inspiration for 'Lucy in the Sky with Diamonds' not just to Julian's painting but also to the imagery of Lewis Carroll's *Alice in Wonderland* which had re-entered the zeitgeist of the mid-1960s as part of a more general revival of Victoriana within British culture (Guerrier 2017: 44–7; Sandbrook 2009: 447–9). As in the other sequences discussed here, 'referential integrity' is maintained through Goodall's detailed and knowledgeable factual discussion, but the mise en scène and editing foster a genuinely dislocating sense of space, which at its most extreme finds Goodall being pursued through the corridors of a Victorian mansion by Anne-Marie Malik's version of Alice from Jonathan Miller's television adaptation, shown by the BBC 1 in December 1966 (two months prior to the song being recorded).

Although it can be argued that these moments continue the programme's overall focus on the finished album by visualizing the finished songs in a thematic way, that these moments tend to occur during discussions of a song's influences means that they depict a 'state of mind' evident in the song, and by implication, in the imagination of the song's writers. This visual exhibitionism contrasts with the sobriety of Goodall's analysis and the fragments of archival studio discussion, creating an 'intermittent aesthetic' that seems to focus on both the atmosphere of the finished songs while also looking backwards, through the mise en scène, to their inspirational reference points. Although not directly relaying the process by which these songs came to be written, in its superimposition of often indeterminate visual layers, the style gestures towards the kinds of transformational process required to turn a moment of inspiration into a song in a 'suggestive and associative' (Corner 2003: 96–7) way. These sequences could, then, be said to represent a conceptual sense of the creative process of songwriting as much as they depict the atmosphere of the finished song.

These moments of stylistic exuberance also speak to the medium-specific qualities of these documentaries. Corner suggests that the casual encounter that a viewer might have with a television documentary within the flow of the daily schedule means that they 'might be pleased to see [a] topic treated in a 'lively' way as well as informatively' (1995: 84). Bennett and Baker emphasize this point more generally, suggesting that because it is on television, the *Classic Album* series 'has the potential to garner a much larger and more diverse audience' (2016: 45) than that of classic rock magazines where detailed technical information would be received with enthusiasm, and that this results in an approach designed 'to tell the story of the classic album in a way that will appeal to a wide audience' (2016: 53). This can have a material influence on the aesthetics of the finished programme. For instance, Bennett and Baker suggest that the selection of albums chosen for *Classic Albums* is 'dependent on the availability of compelling archival footage' and 'access to the album's contributors' as much as it is down to a particular album's cultural status (2016: 46). This is a pragmatic aspect of documentary production also addressed by Keith Beattie who suggests that compilation films, in general, 'are produced within a context that involves issues of availability of, and access to, source footage' and that 'in the absence of relevant footage to illustrate a subject important topics may go unaddressed' (2004: 126). The focus on production can be partially explained by these practical considerations, given that the opportunities for visual material of historic writing sessions to be accessible are relatively low, even if pre-studio demo tapes might exist, as they do for 'Strawberry Fields' (Thompson 2019: 126–7).

However, the focus on a documentary subject that has a compelling story attached to it is also important in keeping the programme 'lively'. This emphasis on visual interest sits in contrast with the 'routine' and 'banal' (Long and Barber 2017: 569) aesthetic qualities of songwriting practice itself. Furthermore, as Mike Jones suggests, 'no one wants to know the reality, it is too mundane ... and, crucially, it would break the spell that promises the magical transformation that drove the music's creation' (2005: 247). The need for an interesting story that fulfils both a dramatic and aesthetic function, while also upholding the status of the artist or artwork under discussion, goes some way towards explaining the selection of songs covered by both 'Making of ...' and *Musical Revolution*. It is striking how Lennon-centric both programmes are, especially given how evenly matched the two lead-songwriters' contributions to the album are and the fact that McCartney was available to both documentary crews (and appears on camera throughout 'Making of ...'). All of Lennon's contributions ('Strawberry Fields', 'Lucy in the Sky With Diamonds', 'Mr. Kite', 'Good Morning, Good Morning', 'A Day in the Life') are discussed in detail in 'Making of ...' compared to just two of McCartney's ('Penny Lane' and 'Sgt. Pepper's Lonely Hearts Club Band'). McCartney's other contributions ('Getting Better', 'Fixing a Hole', 'She's Leaving Home', 'When I'm Sixty-Four' and 'Lovely Rita') are passed over quickly or not mentioned at all. This is marginally rebalanced in *Musical Revolution* which *does* include 'She's Leaving Home' (though it leaves out the title track), and which pays more attention to McCartney's musical contributions to Lennon's compositions than 'Making of ...' does, such as the importance of Paul's bass and lowry organ parts to 'Lucy', and his mellotron introduction to 'Strawberry Fields'.

These choices speak very strongly towards the prioritization of production narratives, and in his book about the making of the album, producer George Martin explains how a key difference between Lennon and McCartney as practitioners was that the latter quite often arrived at the studio with a song already well-formed, and with very clear ideas of what he wanted it to sound like, and how to achieve that sound. By contrast, Lennon 'would always have a pretty good idea of where he wanted to get to with a song ... but he would not necessarily have a very good idea of how to get there, in practical terms' (Martin and Pearson 1995: 87). With the work of arranging and realizing largely done in-studio, Lennon's compositions offer a greater space for stories to be told about their experimental character than McCartney's, where the conceptual elements of both writing *and production* had often been decided at home, and thus exhibit the kinds of inaccessible working practices already discussed at length in this chapter. As Martin says of 'Fixing a Hole', 'Paul knew exactly where he was going' and that 'as a result, it was one of the fastest tracks we recorded' (1995: 85).[19]

This is not a particularly exciting recipe for television entertainment, and so it is hardly surprising that those songs where there is an interesting and accessible story to tell about both the inspiration and realization are those that become the focus of the programme. This discursive technique of giving a brief insight into the inspiration for a song before jumping straight to the in-studio production process and omitting any intermediate writing stage(s) helps to maintain interest and satisfies television documentary's requirement to present 'an engaging story that will draw an audience' (Bennett and Baker 2016: 45-6).

Producing 'Strawberry Fields Forever'

For Williams, a key aspect of the *Classic Albums* series is the way it provides the television viewer with access to the 'previously rarefied worlds' of 'commercial recording studios' (2010: 166), and to the 'crucial contributions of behind-the-scenes collaborators' who are largely invisible from the public discourses around popular music (2010: 167). The tendency is for the programme to deploy the narrative trajectory of 'the triumphs of technicians over technological limitations' (2010: 168-9), and that 'the all-knowing genius of the artist is supplanted by the mastery of machine and environment exhibited by the engineers and producers' (2010: 169). This doesn't fully apply to 'Making of …' and *Musical Revolution*, because in neither case are The Beatles displaced as the central 'geniuses'. Instead, their totemic status is reinforced by positioning them as the driving force of the creative work in the studio for whom technological limitations pose no creative obstacle, and at whose behest the technicians are working. Technical 'wizardry' *is* often emphasised, but the technicians are usually shown to be innovative so as to fulfil the recording artist's creative vision.

This is particularly apparent in 'Making of …' where despite George Martin's authoritative position, the studio technicians involved in 'Strawberry Fields's' production play almost no part in the specific narratives that are forwarded. Martin's analysis of 'Strawberry Fields' focuses on three stages of the song's development. He begins with an initial version (Take 1), recorded on '24 November 1966 – a Thursday' – which he plays through the mixing desk and describes as 'quite charming'.[20] This version was deemed unsatisfactory and was tackled again after Lennon and McCartney had both 'thought about it' over the weekend (Take 7). Again, Martin picks out salient features from the multitrack tapes to show clear progression: a signature mellotron introduction, the song now opening with the chorus, and being in a lower key. Still deemed unsatisfactory, a third version (Take 26) is presented as a response to Lennon suggesting that 'I want a bit more bite in it; brass, strings'. This third version is the most familiar, and is presented by the programme as if it is the final version, Martin deconstructing the track – 'double-tracked vocals on [tracks] three and four, but with percussion as well on three'; 'backwards cymbal on track one' – and concluding the sequence by suggesting that Take 26 'showed the way that *Pepper* was going to be. This was the first psychedelic track'.

Despite showing a progressive evolution in response to the desires of the songwriting team, the role of the technicians is minimized in this account. Lennon's request for brass and strings is met with a simple 'let's give it a whirl', which occludes the orchestration and arranging that was within Martin's purview as well as removing the players themselves from the story.[21] These vital additions are depicted instead via a black-and-white photograph of Lennon blowing into a French horn, which has the potential to give the impression that he recorded these brass parts himself.[22] Although we do get a very clear sense of the song's development in the studio, the contributions of Martin and his team are minimized, and the song's artistic achievements are drawn out through a discussion of the transformations that changed the 'simple' initial version into something much more ground-breaking and complex, each of which is attributed to Lennon or McCartney.

The removal of the production personnel in this account also obscures the fact that the final version of the song that Martin presents is not, in fact, the version released to the public, which was a composite of Takes 7 and 26. The account in 'Making of …' suggests quite a rapid process: a Thursday night (Take 1); a Monday-morning rework (Take 7); a third and final go with brass and strings shortly after (Take 26). However, *Musical Revolution* is altogether more detailed about the technical achievements of 'Strawberry Fields', and the labour involved in completing it, and in his contextualization of the song, Goodall frames the sessions thus:

> 'Strawberry Fields Forever' took 55 hours of studio time to create. Nowadays many of the techniques it employs are routine. Back then, though, they had to be painstakingly developed, often from scratch, by producer George Martin and his Abbey Road engineers.

This moment marks an aesthetic shift in the programme, from the stylized sequence already described which focuses on the inspiration for the song, to the kind of 'quiet' style (Corner 2003: 96) that is illustrative in nature and characterizes the sections focusing on production. The shift between the two occurs via a montage of analogue recording technologies – two-inch tape running through the play-head of a tape machine, a four-track mixing desk superimposed over shots of a revolving tape spool, a black-and-white photograph of McCartney and Martin at another mixing desk during the *Sgt. Pepper* sessions – and Goodall himself is framed differently, superimposed over a split screen, with further images of analogue recording technologies occupying the left portion and a digitized waveform of the song appearing on the right, providing an almost over-literal visualization of the portion of the song being discussed.

Now in the more illustrative mode, Goodall turns to the 'remarkable example of … ingenuity' that occurred 'when John decided he wanted to combine the dreamy opening mood of one take, with the energetic groove of another, the two performances having been recorded ten days apart.' These are the aforementioned takes 7 and 26 heard in 'Making of …'. However, whereas Martin made no mention of the challenges involved in combining the two, or even that the two were combined at all, Goodall uses the edit in *Musical Revolution* as a representative demonstration of the technical achievements of Martin and his team across the album as a whole. 'The two takes are not only made up of different instruments playing at different volumes,' he notes, 'but they're in different keys. And, most inconveniently, performed at different speeds too.' He demonstrates what a simple cut between the two takes would have sounded like, a sonic disruption that is visualized within the split-screen, and which Goodall describes – with dramatically raised eyebrows – as 'awkward' (Figure 3.9).

Figure 3.9 The more literal mise en scène of the production-focused sequences of *Sgt. Pepper's Musical Revolution*.

The technical stakes are raised even further when Goodall suggests that although this edit could now be done using a phone app, 'in December 1966 it had never even been tried'. The proposed solution was to alter the speed of the tapes, so that the tempo and pitch could be matched. However, this only presented a further dilemma: 'In those days, magnetic tape recorders didn't have a variable speed function', and so could not be slowed down or sped up by a regulated amount. Goodall attributes the solution to EMI engineer Ken Townsend, who 'effectively invented just such a function by cunningly manipulating the electricity supply feeding the playback machine'. The place where the join is located on the final track is then played back, with Goodall's 'awkward' now transformed into a more appreciative 'awesome', as the image cuts back to the 'Strawberry Fields' music video, the less literal visual image returning the focus back to the band and the cultural product rather than the technical processes.

That the inventive solution to the musical problem was a technical one demonstrates Martin's creativity and Townsend's individual mastery of the electronic studio, and the sequence aligns the ingenuity of 'Strawberry Fields' with the technical achievements of the EMI engineers. However, it is fundamental to the programme's positioning of 'Strawberry Fields' as a work of art that this feat of engineering is framed as being driven by John Lennon's creative aims in wanting the two takes to be stitched together in the first place. This kind of delegatory relationship is explored in both programmes. In 'Making of ...', Martin suggests that in the early days of his relationship with The Beatles he took on the role of 'an organiser – to get them into some kind of shape and make sure they were tidy in the studio, musically', but that by the *Sgt. Pepper* sessions he 'was a realiser of their ideas.' Rather than sidelining Lennon from the narrative, as Williams suggests is frequently the case in episodes of *Classic Albums*, he and the other Beatles are positioned as the creative drivers of technological ingenuity at EMI – and across popular music culture more generally – retaining their central position as boundary-pushing artists.[23]

Ultimately, the aim of accounts like those articulated in these programmes is to reinforce the cultural status of the *Sgt. Pepper* album as a landmark in popular music. Songs are used as a springboard to tell stories that uphold the status of the artist or artefact under discussion – an unsurprising aim given that such validation renders the subject as being worthy of attention in the first place. However, the stories told here about song creation tend to erase the labour involved in song writing and relocate it in the spaces of production, where myths about artistic credibility are perpetuated through narratives of boundary-pushing creativity that centre on overcoming technical limitations. As Long and Barber argue, narrative motifs such as the story of McCartney dreaming 'Yesterday', 'inform powerful structuring stories for both creative workers and consumers and have a normative role explaining distinctions between writers in terms of concepts of talent and the hierarchy it enables' (2017: 562). This can be extended to the stories about how production technologies were revolutionized to realize The Beatles' creative ideas. Such stories might appear to demystify the process, but they remain partial, occluding key elements vital to the success of the final album. Perhaps the most obvious omission in these documentaries is the detailed focus on the writing process itself, which *is* gestured towards, but not in a way that gives any real sense of how a song comes into being. Instead, the labour that is made visible is that required to overcome the obstacles of production, and this work is framed as being in the service of artistic genius. By focusing so intently and in such detail on the specificities of the song *as a recording*, attention is diverted away from the process of its composition, and the mundane aspects of creative labour – the ordinary (for the songwriter), daily labour of songwriting – remain mysterious and ineffable.

Ownership and Control

In the previous sections of this chapter, I have focused on some of the practical solutions to the challenges of representing creativity in a feasible and interesting way. Controlling the scenarios in which songwriting happens in *It All Begins with a Song* means that we are able to see songs emerging, but the documentary maker still has to omit large portions of the process in order to maintain interest. Conversely, *Sgt. Pepper* documentaries solve this issue – and the added complication of the need to uphold the status of the artist – by focusing on inspiration stories and depictions of the production process that uphold the magical ethos that circulates around songwriting as an artistic craft, but do not provide any real insight into the labour of writing. This final section extends the discussion of the interface between artist and industry further by considering how documentary representation can help to uphold the status of an artist as the author of their creative works. This is particularly the case for artists working within pop, where, as Frith argues, songwriters tend to be understood as *metteurs en scene* when compared with the *auteurs* of rock (Frith 1989: 92–3), and 'the mechanized nature of production pushes even the artist to the background of a song's identity' (McNutt 2020: 74).[24] By showing the artist at work and exploring how they write songs, and by demystifying the co-writing and co-producing practices of modern musicmaking, the artist is able to demonstrate their ownership and authorship of their work.

The focus of this discussion is an analysis of the Ed Sheeran documentary *Songwriter*, which centralizes his role in the creative process by emphasizing the control that he has over his creative choices, which are contrasted with various other figures, both seen (representatives of his record company) and unseen (artists who have recorded the songs we see being composed). This is especially important for an artist like Sheeran who is hugely successful, but has – through accusations of plagiarism – had the authorship of his work repeatedly questioned (Seabrook 2023).[25] Nevertheless, the demystification of Sheeran's broader process preserves his 'magical' status, because the documentary tends to focus on lesser-known material in his oeuvre, or well-known songs written for other artists; we see very little material that focuses on the writing of his most successful hits.

The film's structure is critical in emphasizing Sheeran's creative control and propensity for work. It opens with an inversion of the 'going-on-stage' tracking shot that I have talked about elsewhere (2019: 83–4, 2021: 201–5), as Sheeran *leaves* an unspecified arena stage and returns to his dressing room to find his co-producer and co-writer Benny Blanco working at a mobile recording studio. The lengthy shot connects two of the main forms of creative labour undertaken by pop stars (songwriting and live performance), and emphasizes that songwriting is an on-going process, and especially so when technology allows for recording to occur in a peripatetic manner. The choice to open the film with Sheeran leaving the stage eager to get back to the business of songwriting, even before showering and changing, places the emphasis on him as the titular 'songwriter', rather than as a performer.

This short opening is followed by a substantial observational sequence on Sheeran's tour bus (which also contains a portable recording studio), where he and Blanco write and record a demo of the song 'Love Yourself', later a number one record for Justin Bieber. The underlying beat of the song is already in place when the sequence begins, as is the recognizable and sparse guitar part, but over the course of the seven-minute scene, the pair work the song into a finished demo. The 'ping pong' of ideas is evident, with Blanco suggesting that 'it should be about some real shit … Is there any relationship shit right now?' Sheeran responds that although there is, and that this *could* be a source of inspiration, 'I don't really want to write a song about it.' This comment is itself picked up by Blanco, 'So why don't you write it about that?', and after a series of cuts (again, occlusions remove much of the process in favour of progress) the pair have finished an opening verse that is a self-reflexive meditation about not wanting to write songs about relationship difficulties. Sheeran acknowledges that it's going to be 'quite harsh', and this is taken to its limits with the inclusion of the lyric, 'If you love the way you look that much / Oh baby, you should just fuck yourself'. Blanco advises that 'It instantly becomes a classic if you say "love yourself"'. However, when the finished recording is played back at the end of the scene, the 'fuck yourself' is still in place, suggesting the 'harsh' version remains Sheeran's preference.

'Love Yourself' is not an obscure record, and this demonstration of authorship of a song more closely associated with another artist neutralizes any pre-conceived notions that Sheeran might not write *his own* songs. The sequence also adds to the public narrative around that particular song, as it implies that Justin Bieber's contributions are not as substantial as have previously been claimed. Bieber has an equal writing credit alongside Sheeran and Blanco, but in media interviews the Sheeran/Bieber collaboration was played up over the Sheeran/Blanco work. This is a rhetorical device that Joshua Wolf Shenk has suggested is common within successful partnerships more generally, with the question of who contributed what being deliberately unclear in order to preserve the dynamic and creative integrity of the writing team, and which also acts as 'an impediment to any outsider telling its story' (Shenk 2014: 41–2).

In an interview for Capital FM, Bieber recalled that 'we wrote a song together … It's just me and a guitar', intertwining the aesthetics of the track – which we now know were Sheeran's choices – with his own personal narrative: 'that's how I started, playing on the street with a guitar.' Sheeran's role is positioned as secondary, with Bieber noting that it was important 'just to have his input and his stories and our stories and match them up together' (Capital FM 2015). In a rhetorical dance which speaks to ways in which an enticing story can help sell records, the idea that the song was about various of Bieber's ex-girlfriends – most notably Selena Gomez – helped to create a buzz around the song when it was released in 2015 (Bassett 2016; CalHx 2017). Indeed, the conversation around Gomez's subsequent single 'Lose You to Love Me' also played up the idea that *her* song was a response to 'Love Yourself' (Bailey 2019), though this has subsequenly been challenged by Gomez in *My Mind and Me*, where she suggests it is about her struggles with bipolar disorder.

The opening of *Songwriter* corrects these broader narratives, offering an alternative that places Sheeran at the creative centre. The film was released with enough temporal distance from the song's release that reframing the narrative in this way could not hinder its commercial success. Although we don't see the song being performed in its entirety, and so the possibility remains that Bieber made considerable alterations to the sections we don't hear, the lyrics that we *do* hear in the demo accord almost exactly with those on Bieber's finished record. The only exception is Sheeran's 'fuck yourself' ending, which had been softened to Blanco's preferred 'love yourself' by the time of Bieber's recording. Nevertheless, the retention of the harsher lyric for the demo represents an example of Sheeran taking control of the creative process, proceeding with *his* version and vetoing Blanco's moderating voice. By ending the sequence with a fade to black as this lyric is played back, director Murray Cummings (who is, not insignificantly, Sheeran's cousin) underscores this point, leaving the viewer to compare Sheeran's version with Bieber's, and creating the implicit suggestion that Sheeran has an 'edge' that Bieber lacks.[26]

The sequence also gives us a clear sense of Sheeran's process, and especially that there is little distinction between writing and recording. What we observe is an iterative process where compositional elements (lyrics, musical phrases) are recorded to the computer by Blanco as they occur, and are then altered, re-recorded or augmented as new ideas develop and the work progresses. Blanco's co-writer/producer role is made apparent as he works on the recorded material digitally as Sheeran contemplates the next section. We also see how Sheeran develops vocal melodies and lyrics, and that like Forest Glen Whitehead in *It All Begins with a Song*, mumbled vocal lines start to suggest lyrical ideas through repetition. We see this in the way the resolution of the second line in the 'Well I didn't wanna write a song / Cause I didn't want anyone…' phrase develops from an incomplete mumbled melody into something more concrete, though we don't hear the final lyric – "Cause I didn't want anyone thinking I still care' – in its entirety during the sequence.

This level of detail could act against the arguments made in the first half of this chapter about how demystifying the songwriting process has the potential to diminish the aura of the pop star. However, this is another reason why the song choice is important, as it separates Sheeran's process from his best-known work. By opening the film in this way, *Songwriter* undertakes a similar project to that seen in *It All Begins with a Song*, locating Sheeran's process *as a songwriter* within a broader commercial and artistic system in which many professional songwriters are employed to write songs for others to 'cut', playing up a separation of songwriter and performer that is related to the separation of a song and its recording. As Brett James notes towards the start of *It All Begins*, 'I've had about 500 of my songs recorded. I've had 42 top 20 singles. And 25 of those songs ended up being number ones. Which means nobody knows who the fuck I am.' It is also significant that the songs that we see being composed in that film are not well-known compositions, but musical products of the documentary infrastructure. Thus, the demystification process is constrained by the relative public anonymity of the subjects compared to the artists recording their songs (even though these are songwriters who have written a great number of hits). For Sheeran, there is relatively little to lose by demonstrating his songwriting credentials – and thus his authorship – of hit records recorded by others, while continuing to conceal the 'magic' that underpins his own material.

This balancing act between upholding the artistic mystique and depicting the details of the process is maintained throughout the film and it is striking that many of the tracks that we see being written are not songs that ended up on Sheeran's ÷ album. We see Sheeran on a multiday writing retreat in Malibu, working with a range of collaborators, including Blanco, Johnny McDaid, Julia Michaels, Foy Vance and Amy Wadge. In this section of the film we see work being done on a number of songs which remain unreleased ('When My Dad Cried'; 'Brother's Blood') or which were eventually made available on the extended version of the album ('Barcelona'; 'Nancy Mulligan'), but only fragments of more well-known material ('Dive'). This preponderance of non-album and unreleased songs maintains a sense of distance between writer and performer. The main exceptions to this in the film are 'Happier' and 'Galway Girl', which we also see being worked on in a second group writing session at Decoy Studios, and 'Perfect', where the focus is on the recording of orchestral arrangements at Abbey Road. What each of these sequences highlights is Sheeran's central position within a large network of collaborators, and whether the songs being written are ultimately released by him or by another artist (or not at all), it is he who is positioned as the orchestrator of these processes and responsible for their fate.

There are, then, two points of interest here. The first concerns the autonomy of a songwriter in control of their artistic material within a commercial system. The second concerns the balance between emphasizing this autonomy through an exploration of their creative process, while maintaining their totemic status within the popular imagination. In *Songwriter* these two positions are addressed through the oscillation between showing in detail how some songs (usually those not directly associated with Sheeran as a performer) are written, while shifting the focus of those that *are* very strongly associated with Sheeran away from the writing process and towards narratives of production and creative control. The most notable example of this is the final section of the film which deals with Sheeran's most popular song, 'Shape of You'.

'Shape of You' only takes centre stage at the very end of the film, once Sheeran has delivered what he considers to be the finished album to his record label. At a meeting with executives at Warner Music Group, we hear, but do not see, a discussion between Sheeran and an unnamed executive who is concerned about the 'shape' of the planned promotional campaign. The executive makes it clear that while they like the album, they foresee that the absence of 'a rhythmic record' for the second single makes it harder to 'move the campaign on' and that 'trying to go from ballad to ballad would be really difficult'. Sheeran clarifies the position: 'Just so I'm not worrying myself to death, you guys think the album's there? But if I write a song between now and Christmas you won't complain?' To which the executive responds: 'I won't complain if you write a massive single.'

The stylistic incongruity of the sequence draws attention to its significance. The camera does not have access to the meeting, and instead an audio recording is accompanied by shots taken around the Warner Music Group offices, including a large portrait of Sheeran. The comments from the record company pick up threads sewn earlier in the film where Sheeran reflects on his relationship with the industry. After casually strumming through the song 'Happier', Sheeran turns to Blanco and ironically says, 'Can you hear that? Can you hear the sound of 4,000 label executives coming to you and being like, "Yo! We need another one of those Benny!"?' Blanco makes it clear that this does happen 'a lot' and airs his frustration about being asked to repeat himself, rather than tread new creative ground. Drawing on work by Antoine Hennion, Keith Negus suggests that 'music industry personnel act as mediators, continually connecting artists and audiences' and that this operates 'not only during the most obvious marketing and promotion activities, but also when 'introducing' the idea of an imagined audience into the writing, producing and recording of songs in the studio' (Negus 1999: 18). This is what we see being reflected on in these discussions, but is also an aspect of music creation that is usually obfuscated within public discussions of creativity in the music industry. As Jones suggests, 'the intermediary figures [absolve] themselves of their controlling and intrusive management, their impacts on "creativity". In this way, popular music "creativity" is concealed as the composite activity it is, one driven by the over-arching need to achieve sales in the marketplace, to which end creative management, as any management, is directed' (2005: 247).

Sheeran's meeting at Warner provides a concrete example of a record company directly asking the songwriter to produce a 'hit' record – if not quite 'more of the same' – to improve the prospects of the larger marketing campaign rather than, necessarily, to improve the artistic merits of the album. The sequence also sets up the context in which 'Shape of You' is located as both an artistic and commercial product. Following the meeting, we see a shot of Sheeran looking pensive and thoughtful at the wheel of his car, admitting to Cummings that 'I've got an idea of a song in my head, that I think will sort it out. … That's my one little thing that I'm clinging onto'. An audio dissolve indicates that this idea is 'Shape of You' as the song begins playing over the scene of Sheeran driving before the image track follows to show a close-up of a mixing desk strewn with handwritten notes. In the scene that follows we see Sheeran and record producer Mark "Spike" Stent mix the song which – from a writing and recording standpoint – has already been completed.

The sequence functions as a satisfying denouement for the film by stressing Sheeran's artistic (and commercial) instincts, in contrast to those of his record company. We see the kind of nuanced relationship between corporation and artist that Jones (2002), Negus (Negus 1995, 1999) and Toynbee (2000) identify, in which the artist has neither outright autonomy nor are they entirely controlled by the commercial system. Sheeran is strongly encouraged to produce a new song to make the marketing campaign viable, but he is also able to overrule the executives about the final shape of his song. Although supposedly a straightforward mixing session, Sheeran expresses distaste with the way an alternative mix has been completed without his input, to emphasize the 'hooky' elements. Much of the sequence involves Sheeran removing these unauthorized musical elements against the wishes of his management, to preserve the stripped back quality of the verse and chorus and emphasize the 'Oh I' refrain that makes up the song's post-chorus. Sheeran takes control of the session by asking the record company representative, Ed Howard, to 'Just let me do it, it'll sound good, I promise you' and arguing that 'If you want it to lift and drop, and do all of that, then keep it the way it was.' The new additions mean that the song 'doesn't lift' in the way that both he and the executive want it to, and Sheeran is unequivocal that his way 'is the best way, though'.

Sheeran completes 'Shape of You' by reverting to his original mix (or so the film suggests), altering the balance of some of the existing elements (a 'really high jangly guitar' needs to come down in the mix) and correcting some of the vocal harmonies. Once again, music *production* is the focus and neither of Sheeran's two co-writers on the song, Steve Mac and Johnny McDaid, appear in the scene (McDaid has featured heavily elsewhere in the film). The sequence is emblematic of how songwriting tends to be occluded within the music documentary in the service of the wider structural need to enhance the image of the artist. It is significant that how Sheeran's most successful song came to be written remains a mystery in a film which purports to place the songwriting process at its centre. This might be for innumerable practical reasons; Cummings may have simply not been present when the song was written, a strong possibility given that it was written during a session with Mac and McDaid where the focus was on producing material for other artists to sing.[27] It is also possible that the session *was* filmed by Cummins, but that this material was omitted from the film for another reason: the co-writers may not have wished to participate, perhaps, or the shared authorship would have upset the aims of the *Songwriter* project.[28] Instead, we move straight from Sheeran's acknowledgement that he has an idea in his back pocket to the mixing of a finished record, with no account given of the intervening activity. This serves several functions. In the film's rapid movement from 'an idea' to a finished record it gives the impression that the writing process was fast and easy and that Sheeran is an artist that can write hit songs to order, something established in the 'Love Yourself' sequence at the top of the film. It also gives the impression that Sheeran is the sole creative force behind the song; his co-writers are not mentioned and the work of intermediaries is presented as a hindrance to commercial and critical success. Finally, in focusing on the battle for creative control of the mix, it plays up the artist versus label / art versus commerciality dynamic that has been an undercurrent within the film, but is also typical of the kinds of opposition that we have already seen to be at play within the popular discourses around songwriting more generally.

Much as Jane Feuer notes that the effort required to achieve the final masterful performances in the backstage musical remains mysterious, even as the rehearsal process is demystified (1977: 315), so it is here that Sheeran's craft is only explored in detail for those songs that have a lesser presence within the popular consciousness. The film occludes the songwriting process on 'Shape of You' to frame Sheeran as the creative lead, producing a best-selling hit to order under pressure from his record company and doing so via a creative tussle with an executive about the minutia of the mix. 'Shape of You' *belongs* to Sheeran at every step. Despite the film's overall focus on songwriting, we are given no sense of how the smash hit came into being, and the division of labour within its creation – the 'who contributed what' – is obfuscated. McDaid and Mac's contributions are glossed over entirely, and it is unclear whether 'Shape of You' existed only as an idea or as a completed demo intended for another artist at the point at which Sheeran's meeting at Warners takes place. In the final moments of the film, then, we see Sheeran and Cummins undertaking a similar approach to constructing a narrative around the song's creation as that found in Justin Bieber's public claims of authorship over 'Love Yourself'; the collaborators must fade into the background in order that the artist maintains public autonomy over the work of art.

Overall, then, this chapter has argued that although there are ways of capturing the process of songwriting on film, almost all are compromised in some way. Interventionist approaches do not quite capture the haphazard qualities of songwriting. Observational approaches require additional explication. Most result in a need to condense the process of songwriting in order to maintain visual interest, and do so by focusing on progress instead of process. There is also a tendency in work that focuses on either significant musical productions (*Sgt. Pepper*, 'Shape of You') or particular stars (The Beatles, Sheeran) to relocate the work involved in song creation to the realm of production, a move that has both a practical dimension – visual material is more abundant – and an ideological one: the status of the artist is maintained despite focusing on labour. These aspects feed back into the public image of the star through a fine balance that reveals certain elements of their process without diminishing their 'extraordinary' status.

Conclusion

The first three chapters of this book have exhibited a gradual shift in the discourses of access evident between the documentary crew (and thus the documentary audience) and the pop star, from the distance of the on-stage figure who is also most obviously 'performing' to the interiority of the songwriter, via a varied regime of backstage access to the star's personal and professional life. Each of these aspects is tightly controlled by the star, their management team and their record company as a means of projecting an image that is congruent with broader commercial imperatives. This is achieved through the careful regulation of access (and/or the projection of certain kinds of implied access). These depictions are not always clean, and there are instances where the documentary imperative to gain insight and understanding clash with the carefully curated public image – this is perhaps most apparent in the documentaries about songwriting, where any attention on the labour of the process has the potential to reconfigure the star from being understood as an exceptional 'genius' into an ordinary worker. In each case, however, they play an important role in the projection of the star's public image and in the preferred way in which the individual and the commercial system wishes them to be understood. The final chapter in this book shifts this framing to explore documentary subjects (and thus also documentary texts) that act beyond the reach of these controlling commercial influences. This final chapter examines what happens once the musical product – the song, the live performance, the star themself – comes into contact with the fans who are the intended recipient of these products and how this determines their meanings.

4

Fans

In previous chapters, I have considered three aspects of the pop star that are central to their identity as creative figures, and which play a key role in the production and projection of that public identity, both within and beyond documentary representation. All three of these aspects of the music documentary – onstage performance, the public projection of a backstage/private identity, and the act of songwriting – are under the tight control of the artists (or their PR representatives and record labels) and can be manipulated for the public in any number of ways to address the malleable needs of the central star. This final chapter moves beyond those tightly controlled aspects of star-making to consider the place of the fan within this structural schema; a figure who is central to the star's commercial and cultural success, but who can act beyond the grasp of the artist and their management.

Work on fandom in general, and music fans in particular, is extensive and has largely evolved from foundational scholarship on audiences of popular cultural forms such as soap operas (Ang 1985; Brunsdon 1981; Modleski 1979) and romance novels (Radway 1994). Fan Studies has been a thriving – if often under-appreciated – area of academic interest since the early 1990s, when the intellectual case was made for taking the participatory activities of fan audiences seriously, and methods were proposing for doing so.[1] In terms of popular music, Barbara Ehrenreich, Elizabeth Hess and Gloria Jacobs' (1987: 10–38) work to place the response of adolescent girls to The Beatles (and in turn, the response of the media and cultural theorists *to those responses*) within a regendering of the sexual revolution was pioneering, and has been followed by numerous studies of fans of specific musicians and musical genres including Elvis Presley (Doss 1999; Joyrich 1993), Bruce Springsteen (Cavicchi 1998; Häkkänen-Nyholm 2021), Kate Bush (Bennett 2020; Vroomen 2004), Avril Lavigne (Vannini 2004), K-pop (Choi and Maliangkay 2014; Kim 2018), punk (Bennett 2006) and boy bands and 'teenybop' (Coates 2003; Duffett 2013; Gregory 2019).

However, there is a relatively limited body of literature to draw on that directly addresses the representation of music fans within documentaries. The most prominent piece of scholarship remains Matt Hills's 2007 article on the depiction of Michael Jackson fans in the controversial Channel 4 documentary *Wacko About Jacko* (2005), which considers the intersection of production logics, documentary ethics, and fan representation to argue for a careful and nuanced analysis of texts which represent fan communities. More recently, Paul Booth and Lucy Bennett's edited collection *Seeing Fans* (2016a) has contributed work on the representation of fans in *Mission to Lars* (2012) (Duffett 2016), *Pulp: A Film About Life, Death & Supermarkets* (2014) (Williams 2016) and *Crazy About One Direction* (2013) (Asquith 2016; Jones 2016; Proctor 2016). These contributions focus on specific documentary texts, and I wish to extend this scholarship by looking at documentary depictions of music fans more generally.

As with the representation of song creation, fans are a pervasive presence in music documentaries, but are rarely given direct attention, except at moments where they are encountered by the central subject. In this chapter, I want to consider some of the ways in which music documentaries have negotiated the complex position of the fan as both a vital component of an artist's commercial success, but also as a potential rogue agent that can influence how an artist is understood by the public at large. In the first half of the chapter, I examine some of the ways in which the image of the fan has been managed in music documentaries. This discussion necessarily draws on scholarship concerning the pathologizing of fans, but I also want to attend to Hills's argument – summarized by Duffett – that it is 'too simple to frame contemporary representations as either wholly positive or wholly negative' (2016: 14–15). Instead, I want to suggest some of the ways in which fan representations can serve an instrumental purpose. Fan adoration emphasizes the status of the star, but the depiction of 'bad' behaviour can also serve a pedagogical function by giving the star the opportunity to forward preferred modes of fan engagement.

This connects to broader arguments about *how* fans are represented and especially Joli Jensen's (1992) argument that fans are often represented negatively as either a mob or as strange loners.[2] As well as arguing that there is a pedagogical imperative, the first half of this chapter confronts some of the representational and ethical issues that are raised when fans are presented as a homogenous 'mob', and I argue that one particular stereotype – the screaming, female, teenage pop fan – has been repeatedly and problematically deployed as a foundational image in the discourses around rock culture being positioned as a teleological advancement over pop.

The second half of the chapter challenges Jensen's assertions about the 'strange loner' figure by arguing that films made about individual fans (or small groups of fans) can offer sensitive and insightful engagement in the phenomenon of music fandom because they challenge narratives of homogeneity bound up in the fans-as-mob discourse. The final section of this chapter – and of the book itself – offers an alternative to this, by considering the ways in which the negative stereotypes of mass fan activity are less pervasive once the focus is drawn towards individual fan articulations of their passion. *I Used to Be Normal* (2018), *Sound It Out* (2011) and *Our Hobby Is Depeche Mode A.K.A. The Posters Came From the Walls* (2007) demonstrate how the musical products explored elsewhere in the book (the live performance, the artist as public image, the music itself) only gains meaning once they interact with an audience.[3] In so doing, they suggest that fan identities are complex, nuanced and ever-changing, and provide a central way of understanding pop music as a significant cultural form.

Fan Representation as Pathology and Pedagogy

As numerous Fan Studies scholars have noted, the long-standing image of the fan in popular culture is not a positive one. Matt Hills captures this succinctly when he suggests that fans are often represented 'as obsessive, freakish, hysterical, infantile and regressive social subjects' and that 'pop culture's take on fandom has typically been one of distaste and critique, with fans' emotional attachments to media texts and celebrities being viewed as "irrational"' (2007: 459–60). But just as Raymond Williams (2014) argued that culture was not an elite activity, but a part of everybody's daily life and therefore 'ordinary', Joli Jensen points out that many of the behaviours and enthusiasms that underpin fandom are also central to the social and cultural life of 'ordinary' people too and that 'while my particular affinities may be somewhat idiosyncratic, everyone I've ever met has comparable ones' (1992: 23). As Britta Lundin suggests, 'fans are everywhere and they look just like regular people, because they ARE regular people' (Askwith, Lundin and Romano 2017: 366).

However, rather than take these similarities as a means of forging connections, Jensen argues that the 'images of deviance' that 'haunt' (1992: 9) popular cultural representations of fandom are the result of discursive processes designed to reinforce the identity of the self-appointed non-fan:

> Fandom, it seems, is not readily conceptualized as a general or shared trait, as a form of loyalty or attachment, as a mode of 'enacted affinity'. Fandom,

instead, is what 'they' do; 'we,' on the other hand, have tastes and preferences, and select worthy people, beliefs and activities for our admiration and esteem. Furthermore, what 'they' do is deviant, and therefore dangerous, while what 'we' do is normal, and therefore safe. (1992: 19)

The 'othering' of fans, therefore, occurs along socially-constructed lines and 'supports the celebration of particular values – the rational over the emotional, the educated over the uneducated, the subdued over the passionate, the elite over the popular, the mainstream over the margin, the status quo over the alternative' (Jensen 1992: 25). One way in which this is achieved is through an attempt to legitimate one object of enthusiasm above others; collecting records (which is usually coded as a masculine activity) is positioned as more acceptable than following a boy band (which is usually coded as feminine), for instance. By defining one's own behaviour as somehow above that of the fan other, a power dynamic is created in which the non-fan assumes an implied position of superiority.

This process of othering is not limited to the relationship between fans and non-fans (or even between fans of different cultural objects), but also occurs *within* fan communities. As Jenkins suggests, 'fandom is a conflicted space and does not speak with a single voice; there are also diverse fan communities, not simply because of different tastes and interests, but also because of different norms, values, ideologies, and practices' (2018: 21). Discussing her experience of making *Crazy About One Direction*, Daisy Asquith argues that 'fans vary wildly and it is the interaction between them that constitutes fandom. The One Direction fandom is perpetually writing their communal rulebook and trying to pin down the territory and own it' (2016: 87), and this lack of homogeneity is central to the performance of fandom.[4] Bethan Jones (2016) argues that this is a key aspect of intra-fandom relationships, and Kristina Busse describes such practices as 'border policing', and that the impetus for such activities 'is a clear sense of protecting one's own sense of fan community and ascribing positive values to it while trying to exclude others' (2013: 75). The lack of agreement within fan groups about how to correctly perform their fan identity can cause issues when brought into proximity with the objects of fan adoration, and such encounters are where fans are most commonly found in music documentaries.

The star's encounter with their fans is a key site where this work is undertaken. Kerry O. Ferris and Scott R. Harris argue that in large part, 'the meaning of celebrity' emerges most clearly in 'real-word interactional practices' (2010: 8). This is because the outcomes of the star-making process only truly come to fruition when they encounter an audience, an event that also represents the realization of the desire for access and proximity that I have been arguing also underpins the documentary engagement with music stars. As Ferris and Harris suggest in relation to Hollywood actors, 'direct contact provides something closer to an authentic interactional encounter than does merely viewing an actor portraying a character on-screen' (2010: 13). The concert space offers one means of spatial and temporal access to the music star, and as Bernard, a David Bowie fan interviewed by Fred and Judy Vermorel, suggests, 'the clamor for tickets for the '83 concerts was so immense because you are sharing two hours of your life with him' (2007: 488). However, a face-to-face meeting is even more exciting, because 'fans can feel intimate, if only momentarily, with an individual who is important in their lives' (Duffett 2016: 20). Duffett suggests that the dramatic potential of the 'dream coming true' narrative that underpins such on-camera meetings is mutually beneficial because it is associated with the sense of 'the celebrity doing a good deed, sometimes in the name of charity' (2016: 20).[5]

Representations of such encounters can make a positive contribution to the public image of the central star in a way that accords with carefully controlled PR strategies. Both Billie Eilish and Taylor Swift have cultivated public personas built around discourses of access and connection between themselves and their fans and this is emphasized in documentaries about them. It is clearly a priority in *The World's a Little Blurry* (2021) where – intertwined with the emphasis on domesticity described in Chapter 2 – the film opens with images of Eilish greeting her fans before and after a show in Salt Lake City, accepting gifts, taking photographs and hugging them, while asserting that 'I don't think of them as fans, ever. They're not my fans, they're like, part of me.' In *Journey to Fearless* (2010), Swift shows great enthusiasm for encouraging an intimacy between herself and her fans, promoting a particular mode of authenticity through access that has been a longstanding aspect of her star persona (Wilkinson 2019: 442). Large sections of the second episode of the programme are given over to exploring how this sense of intimacy and access is created through a backstage tour (see Chapter 2), a post-show tea party, and the mid-concert use of a small 'B-stage' located within the audience – or on occasion simply on the stadium steps – that all indicate a lack of separation between fan and artist. These are all carefully controlled, carefully planned and highly staged scenarios where Swift's image of authenticity through proximity can be put on display for both her fans and the documentary cameras.[6]

However, the deployment of images of fan-celebrity encounters as a discursive tool in documentaries is rarely so straightforward, as can be seen in the filmic career of The Rolling Stones (James 2016: 310–11). *Charlie Is My Darling* (1966), for instance, addresses the fan violence at early concerts and includes a startling sequence in which the stage is invaded and the performance destroyed in a wave of feedback. On the one hand, this demonstrates a breaching of the expected conventions of the performer-audience relationship (Auslander 2006a: 107), but it also acts to support the public positioning of the band as 'dangerous' in comparison to their closest peers. Conversely, *Gimme Shelter* (1970) shows the consequences of getting the balance disastrously wrong, especially once the actions of the Altamont crowd pass beyond Jagger's ability to control it as part of the performance.

Fan behaviour reflects upon the fan object with which they are associated and just as Dyer (2004: 4) argues that a star's image is not completely controlled by the media industries in which they operate but is also shaped by external factors, Hills has suggested that fans can be understood as 'extensions' of a star text (2007: 465). This can take a tangible form, such as how the reputation of certain football teams have been tarnished by their association with 'hooliganism' (Hopkins and Treadwell 2014; Kossakowski 2021; Murphy, Williams and Dunning 1990; Perryman 2002), where – as Jenson argues – extreme fan behaviour can inflect the public's view of both the majority of the fan group and the object of fandom itself (Jensen 1992: 13). Alternatively, an audience can shape a star's image in a discursive or interpretive way, especially if a negotiated reading runs counter to the intentions of the media industries, something Dyer suggests 'is tantamount to sabotage' (2004: 5) in relation to counter-readings of stars like John Wayne and Judy Garland.[7]

How the relationship between the star and the fan is managed in music documentaries is important, then, as it is a site on which questions of appropriate fan behaviour can be worked through directly. This is especially the case if the film is produced in collaboration with the star, where the power disparity between them and their fan operates in two dimensions: the artist has the power to control the fan's access in the pro-filmic world, and they also have some element of control over the representation of their fans in the finished documentary, and especially in cases like *Homecoming* (2019) or *Folklore: The Long Pond Sessions* (2020) where the star is also the director. At the most extreme, this can involve the withdrawal or withholding of films from circulation, as was the case with Jeremy Deller and Nicholas Abrahams's film *Our Hobby Is Depeche Mode* which was commissioned by the titular band, but remains officially unreleased because of sensitivities about how fan activities depicted in the film might chafe against the band's public image. As Deller states, 'the band have been so carefully branded and marketed that the fans' behaviour sometimes disrupts this carefully crafted image. The fans appropriate the band, they do their own thing and have a laugh; it's not clean, it's messy and it's chaotic' (Deller n.d.). The presence of fans in films made in collaboration with a central star tend to serve a strategic function, upholding their popularity through images of fan worship or forwarding a sense of accessibility, or else by defining a model of acceptable fan activities that meet the artist's approval (and conversely a set of behaviours that do not).

Most often, extreme fan behaviour is positioned in a negative light. Perhaps the most notorious fan-focused documentaries – *Wacko About Jacko* and *Crazy about One Direction* – were both heavily criticized for treating fans as a spectacle (Asquith 2016; Hills 2007). Elsewhere, the man hanging from the bonnet of Bob Dylan's car and the drunken (and possibly stoned) glass thrower in *Dont Look Back* (1967) stand in for an unacceptable mode of fannish appreciation, and are expelled from the entourage (and the film). Similarly, though far less dramatic, are those fans who express a dislike for Dylan's transition away from acoustic folk music. The most prominent of these is Carol, the starstruck teenage girl that Dylan meets in Liverpool, who dislikes the electric 'Subterranean Homesick Blues' because 'it doesn't sound like you at all'. He categorizes the girl as 'that kind' of fan and takes the opportunity to propose his preferred reading of his work, eschewing the criticism that he has become too commercial by saying to the fan, in a somewhat patronizing way, that 'You know different, though, right?' This is, of course, the same outlook that the film as a whole is projecting, and Dylan is more sympathetic towards the band that he meets backstage in Leicester who perform full-band covers of his acoustic songs. This is a prominent example of an artist navigating a period of transition by training their audience in how to follow their shifting musical styles, and this occurs through the direct encounter between artist and fan, where the young female fan is (politely) informed of the preferred reading of his music, as well as in the recirculation of that encounter – and that reading – to other fans via its inclusion in the documentary.

The co-existence of different modes of fan-engagement offers a reflection on the 'correct' way to be a Dylan fan in the mid-1960s, and Hills (2016) has argued that intra-fan activity more generally can be understood as a mode of pedagogy that is often imposed from above, but is internalized and propagated within a fandom to teach what Booth and Bennett call '"proper" fan behaviours by highlighting particular fan practices and identities as more valid than others' (2016: 4). It is significant, for example, that although the fans chosen to attend Swift's tea party are designated 'the craziest fans', they are also those who most closely accord with an enthusiastic, but non-threatening iteration of fan behaviour. This has become and increasingly visible part of the discourse around the conditions of (especially female) pop stardom, with artists such as Lily Allen and Chappell Roan speaking very publicly about their experiences of fan entitlement, public harassment and being stalked (Cain 2024; McVeigh 2016; Soteriou 2024).

Another instructive instance appears in *Miss Americana* (2020) where Swift and Brendon Urie, lead singer of Panic! At the Disco are observed during a break in a recording session discussing the difficulty of living securely while in the public eye. Urie describes being forced out of his home because of excessive fan attention: 'They would jump the gate and, like, try to open our front door and I was like, "This is not okay."' Swift responds 'Yeah, let's not do that', before recounting her own experience of housebreaking: 'I had a crazy dude break into my apartment and sleep in my bed a couple of months ago. I didn't like it.' This conversation is unequivocal about the unacceptability of these actions and Swift explicitly delineates acceptable and expected behaviour from its opposite when she suggests that 'There's a difference between "I really connect with your lyrics" and "I'm going to break in."' As well as conveying a sense of what it is like to live their lives, the moment also functions as an instructional statement for their fans, drawing lines of acceptable behaviour and using the documentary framework to broadcast those rules in a direct and unambiguous way.

The formalized 'meet-and-greet' is, perhaps, the site at which the 'rules of engagement' for fan-celebrity encounters are most rigorously upheld. Ferris and Harris define meet-and-greets as 'pre-staged encounters' where 'producers or other groups organize circumscribed opportunities for face-to-face encounters (such as conventions, luncheons, personal appearances, book signings and golf tournaments). At these events, fans can ask questions or request autographs from celebrities, but only within tightly orchestrated limits' (2010: 18). Such events have a set of literal or social rules and conventions with which the participants (both the fans *and* the artist) will abide, including a carefully organized queue, a restriction on the time spent with the star, and a well-defined set of restrictions on physical interaction. Although 'a fan may feel that she has received a bit of personal attention … she has done so only under the watchful eye of security personnel – an unusual type of interaction, in which the power relations between the interactants are clearly unequal and, therefore, protect the [celebrity] while constraining the fan' (Ferris and Harris 2010: 20). It is significant that the imagined 'fan', here, is gendered as female, in a similar way to the how Stalh (2013: 2–3) genders the commercialized pop star as female (see Introduction), and how the general discourses around music replicate this discursive device in order to uphold masculine practices.

The conflicting (and gendered) dynamics of the staged 'meet-and-greet' can be seen in Kyoko Miyake's 2017 film *Tokyo Idols*, which examines the 'idol' culture prominent in East Asian countries, where adolescent teenagers acting as 'lifestyle role models ... sing melodramatic love songs, dance to peppy electronic tunes, act in dramas, and strike poses in commercials' (Aoyagi 2005: 3–4) as part of a wider consumer culture formed around the self.[8] The film follows a small number of female teenage idols and some of their fans, most of whom are middle-aged men. The question of appropriate fan behaviour is central to the film, given the clearly troubling gender and age disparity between the fans (older men) and their fan object (younger women) – a reversal of the fan gendering noted above, that – ironically – acts to position the female teenage fan as more acceptable in comparison. The contemporary idol industry is contextualized in the film in relation to the Asian financial crisis of the late 1990s, which stimulated idol culture as a response to economic hardship (Kang 2014: 60), but also saw a reformulation of social roles, with Japanese men seeking financial security in professional roles that according to Koji, one of the fans featured, are 'totally devoid of excitement' and which are no longer conducive to a fulfilling family life. For Koji, idol fandom is understood as a way of countering a keen sense of identity loss due to his unrewarding work as a salaryman and his inability to attract and support a partner, by offering a space for connection with both his favourite idol – Rio – and her other fans. Indeed, Koji suggests that part of his attachment to Rio is that she embodies the ambition that he feels has been lost from his own life.

There is, then, a reasonably nuanced approach to the idol and her fans in the film, which configures the relationship between the two as transactional and, therefore, mutually predatory. Drawing on Jenkins's notion of 'affective economics', Patrick W. Galbraith argues that idol culture depends on 'building, developing and maintaining relationships to shape desires and impact purchasing decisions' and that in particular, 'it markets and sells direct experiences, or embodied encounters' (2021: 70). The handshake events that are seen in the film are an experience of intimacy offered for the price of a ticket or a CD, where 'the main content is the direct experience and the CD is merely a vehicle to gain access to it' (Galbraith 2021: 70). There is, therefore, a complex relationship, here, where the idols explcit the men's fantasies as a lure to ensure their own economic stability. The timing and physicality of the 'handshake' events that Rio holds are carefully regulated, and although the policing of fan behaviour is socially inscribed, it is also enforced by security. As Rio says, 'when fans take pictures with me, there are rules about where they can touch'.

The transactional nature of the encounter is made clear through the repeated motif of the physical action of the handshake, which is often placed in proximity to images of money-changing hands. Such images accompany an interview with economic and industrial analyst Masayoshi Sakai, who frames the history of the handshake in Japanese culture as 'a very sexual gesture' which plays into the promise of intimacy offered by such events. But it also stresses the disparity in power dynamics given that the idol has control over the encounter and knows that this is the extent of their physical engagement with the fan. While the idol gives out dozens of handshakes at a time, few of which have any significance to them, the fan receives only one, which might mean a great deal (Figure 4.1). The fans in the film recognize this fact, with one – Mitacchi – acknowledging of his favourite idol Yuka, that 'I'm rational enough to know that nothing will happen with her in reality. She's only nice to me as an idol.' This acknowledgement of the constructed world of intimacy demonstrates a clear understanding of the limits of acceptable behaviour, and while Sakai suggests that the sexual dimension of the encounter represents 'a legal grey zone', the reiteration of accepted social behaviour – and its repetition in the film – acts as a tool to convey the 'correct' way to behave at such events. Each of these examples retains the power dynamics that place the star in control of the encounter, but they also provide an experience of intimacy (and sometimes spontaneity) for the fan. Where access

Figure 4.1 The intimacy of the handshake in *Tokyo Idols*.

to the intimate space is determined by some pre-defined criteria – best costume, good behaviour, having bought a CD – the documentary becomes a means of demonstrating that fans might be rewarded for correct behaviour.

The Mob and the Individual

In her seminal work on fandom as pathology, Joli Jensen argues that there are two primary ways in which fans are understood (and pathologized) within wider popular culture: 'the obsessed individual' and 'the hysterical crowd' (1992: 9). These images are 'iconic' (Jensen 1992: 13) and each articulate different anxieties over modernity: 'the obsessed loner invokes the image of the alienated, atomized "mass man"; the frenzied crowd member invokes the image of the vulnerable, irrational victim of mass persuasion' (1992: 14). Although Duffett suggests that 'even documentaries about dedicated music audiences have tended to interpret their subject matter by focusing on fandom as a mass "phenomenon" (exploring communities of like-minded followers or the travails of celebrities on tour), or by dwelling on the lives of smaller cohorts of "extreme" fans' (2016: 14), this section of the chapter argues for a more nuanced examination of this delineation. While the depictions of fans as 'a mob' might tend to present a pathologized image of fandom, it has also come to serve a range of discursive functions in telling the history of popular music. In the first half of this section I focus on how the image of young, screaming women has been used in music documentaries as an anchoring point to tell a teleological story of music history. In these narratives, the 'mob' comes to stand in for a primitive 'pastness' against which more recent trends are favourably compared. In the latter part of this section, however, I want to suggest that one way in which such narratives are challenged is through a more sensitive focus on individual music fans, some of whom are also constituent parts of the 'mob'. Rather than appearing as straightforwardly 'obsessed individuals', this focus on individuality allows an exploration of the place of fandom within a broader sense of identity, and especially how this might change across a lifetime. In doing so, this breaks down the notion that 'the mass' is homogenous in its views and attitudes.

Screaming

The image of the teenage girl – usually in black and white – screaming at the top of their lungs, weeping in their seat or pressed against crash barriers is one of the most enduring pop music images. Duffett describes it as 'the *sine qua non* of celebrity fandom' (2017: 143), and Jensen argues that 'this image of the frenzied fan predominates in discussions of music fans' (1992: 11–12). Diane Railton recognizes the collective nature of this representation, arguing that the image 'is not usually of one girl but of a heaving, screaming "mass" of femininity' (Railton 2001: 328).

The music documentary is one of the key spaces where such images are (re-)circulated and kept buoyant within mainstream popular culture. Fans and screaming are often presented as synonymous, as can be seen in the opening moments of the 2017 BBC4 documentary *When Pop Ruled My Life: The Fan's Story*. The programme begins by offering a definition of the word 'fan' – **Fan (n): Fr. Latin: fanaticus, meaning *'insanely and divinely inspired'*** – followed immediately by a short but striking montage of screaming music fans that is so ferocious that the closed captions for the version of the sequence that I have access to simply says: 'SCREAMING' (Figure 4.2). Screaming is thus positioned as *the definition* of music fandom.

This is not the only place where screaming fans are positioned as the anchoring image of a documentary. The *All You Need Is Love* (1977) and *The Beatles Anthology* (1995) television series both incorporate 'the mass' of screaming fans within their title sequences. The first proper episode of the former series, 'God's Children: The Beginnings', starts with a three-minute sequence that is largely formed of shots within a moving car as a mass of young fans press themselves

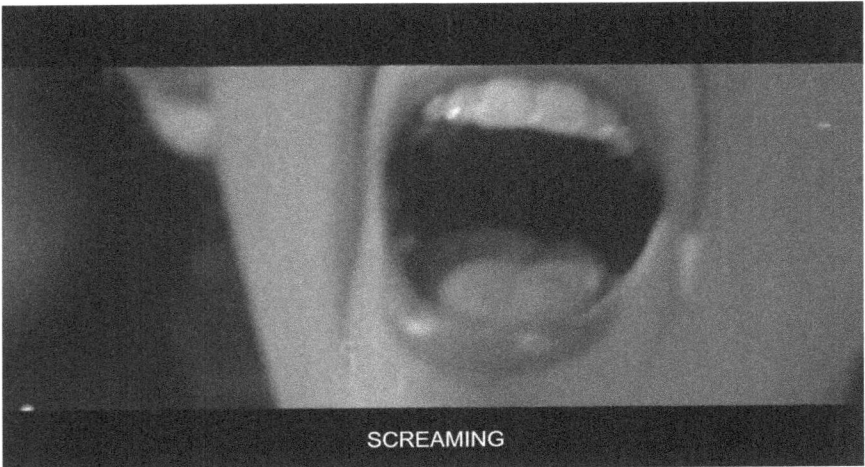

Figure 4.2 Part of the archival montage of screaming fans – complete with expressive subtitles – in *When Pop Ruled My Life: The Fan's Story*.

against the windows in an attempt to catch a glimpse of their (unidentified) idol.⁹ *The Beatles Anthology* plays on the familiarity of the image of the screaming mob in a different way, using the noise of screaming fans to overpower the sound of the band performing the song 'Help!', a device that contributes to the larger meaning of the sequence which indicates a sense of The Beatles' story becoming overshadowed by their own legend (the visual elements of the sequence shows the performing band being dwarfed by a giant version of their logo as the screaming intensifies). Both series are, then, established through images of the ambivalent connotations of mass fandom.

The sonic dimensions of *The Beatles Anthology* title sequence also speak to the wider positioning of screaming as pathological, and concert audiences screaming at The Beatles are particularly noted for their capacity to overshadow the performance of music itself. Describing the film footage of The Beatles' 1965 concert at Shae Stadium, Phillip Auslander recalls that

> it was nearly impossible to hear the Beatles play: the soundtrack was completely dominated by a barrage of nonstop screaming from the audience ... I can think of no examples outside the world of popular music in which it is conventional for audiences to behave in such a way as to make it basically impossible for the performers to perform. (2006b: 262)

Again, the parameters of acceptable behaviour are at stake here. Duffett notes that 'screaming is ... often dismissed as a form of "noise" – something that interferes with rather than contributes to "the music"' (2017: 146). However, this is not always straightforward – some level of crowd reaction is clearly desirable at a rock concert – and there is often an ambivalent relationship evident in music documentaries when it comes to the place of the crowd. A contrast can be drawn, for instance, between a sequence in the opening episode of *Ed Sheeran: The Sum of It All* (2023) where Sheeran is playing in a small club and has to ask the audience to stop their conversations so that his acoustic performance can be heard, and the following episode, where the noise of a sell-out crowd at Wembley is shown to be a powerful part of the experience of performing.

Nevertheless, the notion of screaming as disruptive has played an important role in upholding the hierarchical value structures of popular music, and especially the delineation between rock and pop. Diane Railton (2001: 321–22) has argued that evaluative discourses around music in the late 1960s instituted a cultural hierarchy that replicated the formation of the 'bourgeois public sphere' that Habermas theorized as emerging in the eighteenth and nineteenth centuries and occupying a cultural and social position that sat between the aristocratic culture of church and state and the low cultural forms of the circus and the carnival. For Railton, rock occupies a similar middle-ground, separated from both elitist regimes of classical music and the plebian associations of pop. The similarities between the two are exacted in a range of ways, including their 'inherent masculinity' (Railton 2001: 322), and for rock music 'by introducing a particular way of enjoying music that eschewed the feminine, emotional and physical response of early 1960s pop fans in favour of cool, laid-back and thoughtful appreciation' (2001: 323–4). This replicates the coffee house culture of the eighteenth and nineteenth centuries which Railton suggests excluded women as participants, based as it was 'on what are traditionally considered masculine values (reason, objectivity, the mind), and eschewed the traditionally feminine (emotion, the home, the body)' (2001: 322).[10]

I wish to argue, here, that more than just appearing as a symbol (or symptom) of the 'bad object' (pop) against which rock is often positioned, the deployment of the figure of the screaming adolescent girl has played an important role in shaping and entrenching the discourses that Railton set out. The characterization of screaming as a disruptive act has taken on a rhetorical function in both the development and upholding of music hierarchies and the (re-)positioning of certain groups within those same hierarchies. This is especially true of the way that footage of fans from the 1960s has been reused in documentaries produced in the last thirty years to historicize that period.

We can see this very clearly in the framing of The Beatles' album *Sgt. Pepper's Lonely Hearts Club Band*, which as I noted in Chapter 3, is often understood as instigating a shift in both the technical and conceptual capabilities of mainstream popular music, with 'the album' as a work of art being central to the establishment of 'rock' as a generic space apart from the 'pop'. Alongside discussion of the technological affordances of the studio, the invasive nature of the fan is regularly invoked as being responsible for this generic repositioning of the Beatles. In particular, the decision to stop touring in 1966 is usually framed as *the* key context for the album and of The Beatles' trajectory from pop to rock. Howard Goodall's introduction to the documentary *Sgt. Pepper's Musical Revolution with Howard Goodall* (2017) is indicative of this:

> Let's start the *Sgt. Pepper* story at the beginning; a momentous decision taken in August 1966. The Beatles had been touring the world for three years and the fun had drained away, along with the audibility of their music. They'd had enough, so they decided to give up touring altogether. This looked like madness. Pop group success depended on playing their music live so the audience would buy the records which were made quickly and cheaply ... Work began at Abbey

Road in November '66. The Beatles would be there for an unprecedented five months. Having given up touring, they didn't need to make music that could be played live. Instead, with producer George Martin, they could turn the studio into an audio laboratory, pushing the possibilities of recording technology to new limits.

The causal relationship is clearly set out and replicates – though more succinctly – similar narratives that can be found in *The South Bank Show*: 'The Making of Sgt. Pepper' (1992), *The Beatles Anthology* and *The Beatles: Eight Days a Week – The Touring Years* (2016).

Fatigue and inaudibility are gestured to by Goodall as reasons for the decision,[11] however, a more concrete explanation is provided via a clip from an archival interview that McCartney gave to ITN shortly after the start of the *Sgt. Pepper* recording sessions, and which is edited into Goodall's narration at the point represented by the ellipsis:

> performance for us ... see it's gone downhill performance, because we can't develop when no one can hear us. Know what I mean? So for us to perform is ... it's difficult ... gets difficult each time ... We wanna do it but if we're not listened to then ... and we can't even hear ourselves then we can't improve, you know. We can't get any better. So we ... we're trying to get better with things like recording.

A direct link is made between screaming fans and a lack of musical progress and, by proxy, between an attempt to swap human interference with the technical freedom of the recording studio. Even before *Sgt. Pepper*'s release, the ITN footage was acting to establish a narrative of intellectual change that has been upheld through its reuse in subsequent decades.

The narrative that the flourishing of The Beatles' creativity depended on a move away from screaming audiences towards technical and artistic experimentation has become calcified over time and the frequent reuse of the McCartney ITN footage has been central to this. The interview appears in *The Beatles Anthology*, preceding a sequence in which McCartney, George Harrison and Ringo Starr reminisce about the period in a group interview, and McCartney suggests that the end of touring 'meant we could get into the studio and do 'Strawberry Fields' and 'Penny Lane', and then *Pepper* ... and saying at the time "Now our performance *is* that record."' *When Pop Ruled My Life* incorporates the ITN extract as a means of contextualizing presenter Kate Mossman's claim that 'when the Beatles stopped touring in 1966 and cocooned themselves in the studio, they stopped being pop stars and started to think of themselves as artists'.

What is gestured to here, but largely unsaid, is the gendered dimension of this transformation, with the object of creative restriction embodied as a mass feminine scream and that of creative emancipation being represented by the masculinized world of the studio as 'laboratory'. By deploying such rhetoric, the move into the studio is figured as an escape from unrestrained femininity and as a shift from vapid to intellectual. No such hesitancy is apparent in a later sequence of *When Pop Ruled My Life*, when Rick Wakeman makes claims about the cultural status of his band Yes, and progressive rock in general, through the gendered nature of the band's audience. For Wakeman, the masculine audience is one explicit signifier of the shift away from pop, and he emphasizes the rhetorical division between male audiences and thoughtfulness/connoisseurship and women and emotion central to the maintenance of the evaluative hierarchies thus:

> We were just coming out of the screaming era, you know, with The Beatles and other pop bands, where basically girls went along to scream. Bit embarrassing for a guy to scream, unless he's been hit by a car or something like that. And so what it needed was something, really, for them, that they could go, 'Ah! Now we can relate to that and we don't have to scream.'

This is emphasized when Mossman identifies the centrality of the album to prog's critical status and re-enforces the point about musical experimentation being central to rock music's critical elevation. In doing so, it embodies Georgina Gregory's argument that 'virtuoso musicianship can only be acknowledged once an artist jettisons a teen female following' (2019: 102). *When Pop Ruled My Life* deploys such rhetorical strategies in an uncritical way, arguing that the 'elaborate artwork and intricate sleeve notes' of the LP 'released the inner collector in every greatcoated young disciple' and that prog in particular gained critical cache for 'its sophisticated instrumentation and complex time signatures'. By arguing for the shift in popular music from the pop of the early Beatles through to the rock and prog of the 1970s to be understood as a teleology, the programme continues the entrenchment of the kind of masculine perspectives of cultural value that has been central to popular musical discourse since the arrival of *Rolling Stone* magazine in November 1967.

The frequent reuse of the footage of screaming women as a means of othering those same women, in the service of the critical sustenance of masculine cultural spaces poses a number of ethical questions, and is not unlike Hannah Andrews's concern that the use of paparazzi images in Asif Kapadia's *Amy* (2015) 'is ethically questionable, inasmuch as it exploits the very images ...

whose production it critiques' (2017: 352). Although pop fans are nearly always presented as a screaming mob, this is often a construction of the soundtrack; the images themselves tend to focus on recognizable individuals within the larger mass. It is, then, particularly problematic when we see footage of individual screaming Beatles fans being recontextualized to make an argument about the primitive 'mob' mentality of early pop fans within a wider process of 'othering'.

Bill Nichols argues that 'the difference in the power' between a documentary maker and their subject

> can often be best measured by their relative access to the means of representation. Do subjects have the means to represent themselves; do they have alternative access to the media apart from that provided by a given filmmaker? To the extent the answer is 'No', the filmmaker's ethical obligation to avoid misrepresentation, exploitation, and abuse rises correspondingly. (2016: 159)

The fans in the archival footage are relatively powerless when it comes to their agency over the reuse of their image. Those filmed as part of large crowds may well have been unaware that they were being filmed in the first place, and the tendency for close-up framing means that although they remain anonymous, insofar as their names are rarely given on screen, they are not unidentifiable. Even if permission had been granted either explicitly (by signing a release form, for example) or implicitly (by being part of the audience at a television recording), and the legalities of such reuse were straightforward – a filmmaker can license the footage from the copyright holder, for instance – the ethics around the informed consent of individuals appearing in the footage becomes increasingly suspect as the level of 'intentional disparity' (Baron 2012) increases between the original purpose for which the footage was captured and its reuse. By including the footage in service of a teleology of music fandom, the women seen in these images become unwitting (and unwilling?) agents in their own pathologizations. Their position within the broader framework of 'the mob' acts to remove individual agency and the ability to speak up about their individualized experience, yet the images also fail to ensure anonymity.

A less ethically problematic approach to documenting fan engagement is to challenge the homogeneity of the mob in favour of a consideration of individuals' experiences *within* that mob. Such an approach can be glimpsed in one short moment in *When Pop Ruled My Life*. The programme contains an interview with Lillian Adams, a Beatles fan who recounts her experiences of being one of 'the screamers'. Early in the interview, she conveys the stereotypical – and pathological – viewpoint that the screaming was mindless: 'I've got absolutely no idea [why you had to scream at a Beatles gig], you just did.' Examining the reviews of the programme, Duffett notes that each journalist seemed to latch on to Adam's statement as 'the last word' on Beatles fandom and as such 'found an opportunity to stereotype' (2017: 144). Although Duffett himself is eager to argue that such stereotyping constitutes a 'misunderstanding' of the screams that circulated during Beatlemania and subsequent waves of pop phenomena, he is also somewhat guilty of failing to notice that this is not the extent of Lillian's reflections on her time as a screaming Beatles fan.

In fact, Lillian *does* articulate some reasons for screaming that go beyond being caught up in the 'mass hysteria' that the narrator describes, and which positions her alongside feminist scholarship around the significance of Beatlemania. Setting out a key context to the female sexual revolution of the 1960s, Ehrenreich, Hess, and Jacobs argue that:

> A girl had to learn to offer enough, sexually, to get dates, and at the same time to withhold enough to maintain a boy's interest through the long preliminaries from dating and going steady to engagement and finally marriage … the pedagogical burden of high school was a four-year lesson in how to use sex instrumentally: doling out just enough to be popular with boys and never enough to lose the esteem of the 'right kind of kids'. (1987: 20–1)

Furthermore, 'teen and preteen girls were expected … to be the enforcers of purity within their teen society – drawing the line for overeager boys and ostracizing girls who failed in this responsibility' (1987: 11). In this context, screaming can be understood not necessarily as a 'riot *for* anything' but as a means 'to protest the sexual repressiveness, the rigid double standard of female teen culture' (1987: 11). Placed in a broader discussion of the disparagement of feminine activities more generally, Gregory argues that 'rather than mindless hysteria, [the behaviour of female pop fans] could be interpreted as a meaningful response to the experience of subordination' (2019: 103).

Screaming en masse with other similar-aged and similar-minded girls also provided a safe space for an articulation of sexuality. This has two complimentary frames. The first is the act of lusting after a figure such as Paul McCartney, who represented the 'perfect' potential partner, and Ehrenreich, Hess and Jacobs suggest that the arrival of rock 'n roll 'offered an unprecedented vision of men, not as beaux or breadwinner but as sex object for *women*' (1987: 6–7), a reversal of the standard order of looks which positioned women as passive subjects of a male gaze, and as something to be looked *at*. As the authors suggest:

It was rebellious (especially for the very young fans) to lay claim to sexual feelings. It was even more rebellious to lay claim to the active, desiring side of a sexual attraction: The Beatles were the objects; the girls were their pursuers. The Beatles were sexy; the girls were the ones who perceived them as sexy and acknowledged the force of an ungovernable, if somewhat disembodied, lust. To assert an active, powerful sexuality by the tens of thousands and to do so in a way calculated to attract maximum attention was more than rebellious. It was, in its own unformulated, dizzy way, revolutionary. (1987: 18–19)

It is, perhaps, unsurprising that similar expressions of teenage sexual desire erupt with a frequency that equates to each new generation of teenage girls (see, for example, the adoration aimed at The Bay City Rollers, Take That and One Direction). Significantly, the form taken by these acts of teenage sexual expression was one in which the contradictions of the teenage girls' ordinary negotiation of sex did not apply. As Beatrice Verhoeven notes,

Part of the appeal of the male star – whether it was James Dean or Elvis Presley or Paul McCartney – was that you would never marry him ... The star could be loved noninstrumentally, for his own sake, and with complete abandon. To publicly advertise this hopeless love was to protest the calculated, pragmatic sexual repression of teenage life. (2021: 27)

Or as Sheryl Garratt suggests, the scream 'is a safe focus for all that newly discovered sexual energy' (2007: 401).

In *When Pop Ruled My Life* these points are bound up in Lillian Adam's comments about screaming as a means of expressing her desire for Paul McCartney:

Unlike going to a dance or a club or what-have-you, where there were real teenage boys who might have had real expectations, it was perfectly safe. You could pour out all your love and affection to this wonderful idol. This person that you are in love with is utterly perfect. So, it is a good start. Because later you meet real blokes who are not like that.

Lillian *does*, in fact, 'have an idea' as to why she was screaming, and – although easily missed by (re)viewers – it plays into a much more intricate social and cultural history of screaming that challenges the 'unthinking mass hysteria' stereotype that dominates the representation of fan engagement.

Rather than screaming being understood as a progressive or transgressive act, these aspects are pushed out of sight, veiled by the repetition of the same images of the emotional, irrational and anonymous mob, who are compared unfavourably with the thoughtful (male) connoisseur who enjoyed prog and rock. This argument is pithily condensed into Mossman's narration in *When Pop Ruled My World* that 'It seemed that, by the early '70s, collecting had become the new screaming.' In making such arguments, documentaries that focus on the mass audience instead of the individual re-enact the same denials of female agency, sexuality and transgression as the politicians and commentators of the early 1960s that Ehrenreich, Hess, and Jacobs describe, pathologizing the screaming teenage girls as a means of removing her potential power.

This also speaks to the wider derision received by female pop fans, even though their pathologized actions can be understood as both essential to the commercial interests of the music industry or transgressive in other less obvious ways. In this respect, Garratt suggests that 'even with the sickeningly wholesome Osmonds or the [Bay City] Rollers ... the feeling of going against normal society, of rebellion, persisted. One of the most important points about most teeny groups is that almost everyone else hates them' (2007: 403). Furthermore

> no matter how bad the music, what the press or any of the self-appointed analysts of 'popular culture' fail to reflect is that the whole pop structure rests on the backs of these 'silly, screaming girls'. They bought the records in millions and made a massive contribution to the early success of Elvis, the Beatles, the Stones, Marc Bolan, Michael Jackson, and many of the others who have since been accepted by the grownups and become monuments. (2007: 400)

These are notions that cannot emerge without the (former) teenage girl fan being given a voice, and this short sequence demonstrates the potential insight that can be gained by documentary makers breaking the mass audience apart and considering the varied, situated experiences of the individuals who are the constituent components of such groups.

In the final section of this chapter, I want to examine three documentaries that focus on individual fans as a means of teasing out the meaning and importance of music and music cultures. I want to suggest that these films express the meaning that music has once it – and the discourses around it – leaves the control of the artist and their commercial infrastructure and comes into contact with an audience. In *I Used to Be Normal* the focus on four individual boyband fans encourages the consideration of ongoing fan engagement through a life-course framework. *Sound It Out* is discussed in relation to the place of record collecting within fan identities. Finally, an analysis of *Our Hobby Is Depeche Mode* examines the social, cultural and political potential of fan engagement which is articulated by a culturally and geographically diverse collection of Depeche Mode fans.

Ultimately, this chapter – and the book – ends by considering the ways in which rather than perpetuating the kinds of pathological approach to music fandom often seen in musician-focused documentaries, films that place individual fan experiences as their focus can speak more profoundly to the meaning and impact of music and its surrounding industries and infrastructures to the lives of its fans, which, as I have already noted, is all of us.

A Life-course Approach to Fandom: *I Used to Be Normal*

I Used to Be Normal: A Boyband Fangirl Story (2018) is an Australian film directed by Jessica Leski which intertwines the stories of four boyband 'fangirls' from different geographical regions, each of whose enthusiasms relate to a different 'boyband', and began in different time periods. The women, in descending order of age, are:

- Susan, aged 64, a Beatles fan from Melbourne
- Dara, aged 33, a Take That fan from Sydney
- Sadia, aged 25, a Backstreet Boys fan from San Francisco
- Elif, aged 16–18, a One Direction Fan from Long Island

This focus on four separate fans allows the similarities and differences between the fan experience to be clearly articulated, and although there are numerous aspects of this that could be the focus of my discussion, such as the emphasis on fan behaviours such as collecting, creating fan artworks or developing parasocial relationships with celebrities they have never met, I want to emphasize how the film compares these women in terms of the place of fandom within their quite different life stages.

A central concern of the film is the suggestion that one's fan identity evolves over a lifetime. Paul Hodkinson has suggested that the idea that intense fan engagement should be understood as an adolescent phase has 'become so universal ... in popular consciousness as to be a cliché' (2013: 13). Similarly, Matt Hills argues that the '"hysterical" tweenage or teenage female fan' has become the archetypal image of a 'commonsense notion of fandom as an "all-consuming" stage in the life course that will later be abandoned' (2005: 804). This was an idea regularly articulated in relation to early Beatles fandom, where 'there appeared to be no cure except for age', and as Ehrenreich et al. note 'the media pundits were fond of reassuring adults that the girls who had screamed for Frank Sinatra had grown up to be responsible, settled housewives' (1987: 15). It is largely true that fan attachments begin during adolescence. Janet Wolff has argued, for instance, that 'the music of your teens is *your* music' (1995: 26), and given that teenage fandom is generally more publicly visible – in *I Used to Be Normal* Elif describes her younger fan self as 'an explosion' – it is understandable that these moments are prioritized in scholarship and on film. However, Nedim Hassan (2015: 58) suggests that the relative invisibility of older music fans within scholarship is not due to their non-existence, but that – drawing on Laura Vroomen's work on female Kate Bush fans – older women engage in 'relatively mundane expressions of fandom that agree with the women's lifestyles' (Vroomen 2004: 243).

Fandom is not isolated to a short, energetic moment of physiological and emotional transition, but should be understood as a long-lasting and mutable element of a person's ordinary life, hence why contributors to programmes such as the BBC's nostalgia-tinged *The People's History of Pop* (2016) have retained possession of musical artefacts that have personal significance to them, often over many decades. Ross Garner argues that 'attachments to fan objects endure over time, but that these affective investments rarely remain consistent' (2018: 91) and recognizes the 'affective fluctuations which form a normative part of long-term fan attachments' (2018: 94). There are many reasons why this might be the case including transformations of the fan object such as a favourite band changing musical styles (Garner 2018: 99–102; Harrington and Bielby 2010: 442–4), competing life circumstances reducing the opportunities for fan participation (Garner 2018: 98), aging bodies reducing the ability to participate physically (Bennett 2006; Harrington and Bielby 2010: 438–40), as well as adherence to age-appropriate social conventions (Harrington and Bielby 2010: 440–2; Hodkinson 2013: 16). Hodkinson suggests that recent work on older fans 'has started to illuminate the detailed ways in which older enthusiasts negotiate and adapt their participation in the context of lives increasingly focused to one degree or another upon adult priorities, orientations and responsibilities' (2013: 14).

C. Lee Harrington and Denise D. Bielby argue that rather than being something that people grow out of as they get older, 'fan objects serve as touchstones or "lifelines" as fans age' (2010: 445). Similarly, Hodkinson recognizes that shifting performances of fan identity over time 'ought not to be interpreted as a simple attempt to cling onto adolescence or refuse to come to terms with age but, rather, a particular approach to growing older and negotiating adulthood' (2013: 18). Persistent attachment to a fan object, in regularly modified fashion, can, then, be understood as a mechanism for resilience and *I Used to Be Normal* makes this focus on life-stage central to its meaning-making strategy. The four women do not just represent different generations of music fandom, but also the kinds of 'affective fluctuations' with their fan objects that can characterize different life-stages.

Within the film's structure, these fluctuations are most apparent in the different temporalities embodied in the documentary's encounters with its subjects. As adult women, Susan, Dara and Sadia are all reflecting retrospectively on the initial moments of fan engagement that took place several years (even decades) before their interviews. In doing so, they reflect on their ongoing fan identities and examine how they have both shaped their lives and been shaped by their shifting life-stages. Discussing the role that fandom played in her negotiation of adolescence, Dara places the teenage urge to 'be with' Gary Barlow within a discussion of her developing sexuality, recognizing the incongruity between her attraction to a male pop singer and her burgeoning queerness. Dara's fandom is a site through which her sense of self is worked through, the incongruity being resolved by her recollecting her realization that 'I don't *love* Gary Barlow. I want *to be* Gary Barlow ... I want that adoration of a million girls!', a revelation that enabled her to 'be gay now', and which is communicated in the film through a split-screen image that invites a comparison between Dara's personal style and Barlow's mid-1990s blonde hair (Figure 4.3).

Sadia describes a similar process of her Backstreet Boys fandom providing a means of working through her identity as a second-generation Pakistani immigrant living in America. Sadia's love for Nick Carter remains a source of inter-cultural tensions, and a symbol of more universal inter-generational conflict between a father and his adolescent daughter. An interview with Sadia

Figure 4.3 Dara wanting 'to be' Gary Barlow is depicted in *I Used to Be Normal*.

is intercut with footage of her searching through a box of old posters as she recalls that:

> when I had posters up, [my Dad] tore them down because it was such ... well it was an affront to his cultural sensitivity too ... but the thing that was happening to me, which was that I was starting to have feelings for men, was so ... I was so outward about it and that was offensive to him.

She also describes the whiteness of Nick Carter as being 'the antithesis of my Dad'. Sadia's mother describes an internal familial 'battle', which intensified as Sadia and her brother got older and more integrated with American life, and which left their mother feeling caught between 'my culture and our kids'.

As well as reflecting on their pasts, Dara and Sadia are also shown in the present day renegotiating their fan relationships as they navigate shifting personal circumstances commensurate with their respective life-stage, including living away from home (Sadia), being in a long-term relationship (Dara) and negotiating their fan and professional identities (both women). Sadia and Dara both belong to a life-stage described by Harrington and Bielby as 'early adulthood', where 'the challenge ... is to forge intimate bonds or risk isolation' (Harrington and Bielby 2010: 439), and this requires a reprioritization of fan engagement. In a review of the film for *The Guardian*, Adrian Horton suggests that the 'breezy' tone of the film means that 'uncomfortable images of gawking or obsession – no-longer-teenage fans, for example, following Nick Carter on a Backstreet Boys cruise like camera-laden hyenas to a gazelle – are unprocessed, as Leski never presses into discomfort or shame harder than the subjects themselves' (2021). While Horton is right that the film is not particularly interested in pathologizing fan behaviours, the sequence that Horton describes (and other moments where pathological fandom is hinted at) is central to the film's exploration of the relationship between fandom and life-stage. The amateur camcorder shots of Carter swimming away from pursuing fans, are unequivocally positioned as being uncomfortable for both Carter *and* for Sadia who witnessed it (and may have filmed it). This represents a rare moment of intra-fan tension in the film, as Sadia recalls the feeling of witnessing the 'mob' mentality as being like 'an observer to my own insanity. I was watching other people think like me and I was like, I don't know if I like that'.

Ironically, this outsider's perspective is only afforded to Sadia because of her inability to swim, a residual, but tangible, aspect of her teenage fantasy of being married to Carter and having *him* teach her (a dream visualized in the film using rudimentary animation). The cruise is positioned as a transitional moment in

Sadia's fan identity, and rather than going 'unprocessed', as Horton suggests, it is a catalyst for personal change; 'Is this who I want to be? Does this align with my values and my ideal self?' she asks. This sense of personal transition – of moving from one life-stage to another – is symbolized by a concluding sequence in which the camera accompanies Sadia as she goes swimming (with no support from Nick Carter) and reflects on the 'craziness' of having her life choices swayed by her intense boyband fandom. The pathologized image of mass Backstreet Boys fandom is included as a means of facilitating a narrative of personal transition, from the infatuation of youth into a more mature engagement with a fan object from a perspective that is temporally distant from the transitional moment. We also see this with Dara's negotiation of her fan identity in the workplace which parallels her negotiation of her gayness as she becomes more open about her previously closeted boyband fandom.

In contrast to Dara and Sadia, Elif and Susan occupy opposite ends of the life-course spectrum. Given that the production of the film was more-or-less contemporaneous with the height of her own fan identity, Elif's engagement with the documentary is slightly different to the other three participants. We first encounter her as a sixteen-year-old, but the filmmakers returned to interview her over a two-year period, and so we see Elif's present-tense engagement with One Direction develop over the course of the film. Like Sadia's family, Elif's are also immigrants to America, and her Turkish family will not countenance her dream to study music at college, despite gaining admission with a partial scholarship. Their pessimistic views of Elif's chances of musical success are intertwined with One Direction's association with *The X Factor* (2004–18) which is presented as a symbol of their daughter's immaturity; a transitional – and transient – phase not unlike her appreciation of One Direction, that her parents are protecting her from. There is a nuanced treatment of pop fandom, here, as when the film catches up with Elif several years later, she reflects on the fact that she has become less attached to the band and is now more interested in jazz. It is a bitter-sweet moment because although the transience of her intense One Direction fandom can be seen to legitimate her parents' worries, her love of music has clearly diversified (some would say matured), and being cut-off from this potential career path is clearly a source of great pain. She describes music as now 'more of just a hobby', but gives a tearful interview where it is clear that hers and her parent's wishes remain at odds. Indeed, it is indicated that Elif's lessening enthusiasm with One Direction is not due to a decline in interest, but because of painful associations between the band and a loss of her own artistic potential. This is symbolized by a lingering shot of her guitar; always previously seen being played, but now leaning against a wall, it's headstock snapped from the fretboard, a forlorn image that reflects Elif's 'broken' dreams of a musical career and which also indicates a violent act of destruction (or frustration).

The intercutting of the four women represent a constant shuttling backwards and forwards between life-stages. This editing encourages connections to be made between the quartet (who are never shown to have met) as one person's self-reflection about their present experience is brought into relief by being shown to resonate with another woman's past. As the eldest, Susan has a more fixed perspective on her persistent fandom, and has already undergone the personal transitions being faced by the other three participants in the documentary. Similar to Elif, she was not allowed to go to college despite being strong academically because as a young woman in the 1960s her father felt it was a waste of time. She has also experienced the kinds of personal struggles articulated by Sadia and Dara, and the ways in which fan engagement has to be negotiated within interpersonal relationships that is a key part of both Sadia and Dara's 'present'. The documentary concludes by offering a comparison between Elif, the youngest participant, and Susan, the oldest, when the former – still only eighteen and finding her place in the world outside the family home for the first time – anticipates sharing stories of her One Direction fandom with her (at this point hypothetical) children. Leski cuts from a close-up of Elif's smiling face to a similar scale shot of Susan, who embraces her own adult daughter, Kate. This cut between the youngest and the oldest women emphasizes that we have already seen Susan engaging in exactly the kind of inter-generational story-telling that Elif imagines for herself, in a sequence where Susan and Kate are observed looking through Susan's Beatles scrapbook.

Susan embodies 'older adulthood', a period in which 'the challenge … is to come to terms with life's accomplishments and thus achieve wisdom ' (Harrington and Bielby 2010: 439). Given this, she is shown taking the pragmatic position of recognizing the importance of the initial moment of fan engagement within a person's overall biography as well as the longevity and shifting form that fandom takes over the course of a lifetime. 'Nothing in your life is wasted', she notes. 'It's an era and you'll have it and everyone has it. It's not that it's your *only* time, but it is *a* time and it's before things happen in your life when you take on responsibility. Some people call it growing up and if you're lucky (and I'm very lucky) you can always be in touch with your inner child.' Reflecting Jensen's arguments about the ordinariness of fandom, Susan challenges the pathological implication of the film's title by arguing that it is entirely normal to have some form of fan connection in one's life that may persist, but will evolve and change. As such 'normality' – when defined as a life without an enthusiastic attachment to a cultural object of some kind – is not only elusive but distinctly undesirable (even 'abnormal'). As Dara describes it, 'a *normal* life to me sounds like a life without choruses. And who wants that?' These points are emphasized in the closing credits, which features archival scrapbook photographs of boyband fans alongside newly shot footage of their present-day selves. This creates a powerful visual articulation of the film's overall project of inscribing the individual and the personal back into the collective experience of boyband fandom (and the archive), and positions Elif, Sadia, Dara and Susan alongside numerous other like-minded individuals of all-ages, emphasizing that they are part of a much larger community whose stories are both deeply personal and also universal.

Collecting: *Sound It Out*

One aspect of *I Used to Be Normal* that I have only briefly touched upon is the sense of fans as collectors, and all four women in that film demonstrate clear collecting instincts. In this section of the chapter, I want to consider the ways in which the focus on individual music fans can shape the representation of the music collector that challenges (or at least complicates) some of the negative stereotypes of music collecting, through a discussion of Jeanie Finlay's film *Sound It Out* which centres on the eponymous record shop, located in Stockton town centre and framed by the film as 'the very last record shop in Teesside'. Although the spaces in which fandom takes place are multiple and, as Cressida Miles (1998) argues, often discursive and social rather than purely physical, *Sound It Out* connects the social and cultural space of the shop with the wider (mis)fortunes of the general locality (Stockton and Teesside) and the domestic spaces of the music buyers who are Sound It Out's customers. This allows Finlay to explore a complex network of interactions that place the act of music consumption as a key site of meaning-making for the people at the centre of the documentary, as well as a way of navigating the relative economic and social desolation of their local area.

Sound It Out's status as the only local record shop means that it is a hub for Stockton's music enthusiasts, but it is clear that it also serves an important function within the locality more generally. The opening words heard in the film are Tom Butchart's – the shop's owner – who sets out the stakes of the film: 'Sound it Out is the only record shop in Teesside, which is a massive area in the North

East of England. It's quite disturbing, to tell you the truth. I mean, I remember loads of shops when I was growing up and now there's none left at all.' The area's economic misfortunes are shown to have influenced both the genres of music that are popular in the area and the general engagement with music as a social activity. Butchart notes in interview footage that the popularity of heavy metal and dance reflect Stockton's identity as 'a hard town', and two of Sound It Out's customers, Frankey and John-Boy, are explicit that their productive relationship with Makina music – a kind of 'cheesy trance' which 'only exists from Newcastle to Middlesbrough' – is largely an outcome of having little else to do given the lack of dedicated youth services, and that it 'keeps us out of trouble'.

Sound It Out is a hub for Stockton's music consumers, and as John Doran has recognized, in a tribute to Butchart written after his untimely passing in June 2023, 'the owner of a record shop – certainly in the way that Tom fulfilled the role – acts as the social glue in a community ... they are the creator of a safe, friendly space often for people who have nowhere else to go; the provider of affordable dreams; the guardian of sacred knowledge' (Doran and Finlay 2023). Heavy metal fan Gareth describes Sound It Out as 'a safe home for everyone, really', and the shop's community-facing role is emphasized by the repeated appearance of a late middle-aged man who often comes into the shop to buy copies of songs that he has heard on the juke box of the neighbouring pub (we first see him buying a copy of Dire Straits's 'Sultans of Swing'), and Butchart's (and Finlay's) connection of the record shop with the nearby pubs and the local job centre runs throughout the film.

Butchart himself is also framed as just as much a destination for music fans as the shop itself. David, an employee in the shop, explains to the camera that 'people come in and they want to speak to Tom ... He knows what they like and they know that he will find them something that they like.' This establishes a tension in the film between the masculinized space of the shop, the activity of record collecting and of Butchart's customers (we see very few women), and the affective and emotional attributes which reposition these stereotypically masculine practices within an evaluative framework that is overwhelmingly feminine. Although Butchart's general musical knowledge is repeatedly shown to be exceptional, Finlay shows that it is the affective and emotional knowledge of his customers and their tastes that has ensured the shop's continued survival. In another interview, David describes Butchart as someone who 'feeds people with what they need', and compares him to a drug dealer, a metaphor that is extended by Finlay cutting to a lingering close-up of an 'authorized dealer' sticker affixed to one of the racks of vinyls. Shane, a regular customer who collects Status Quo records, is reliant on Butchart's ability to source rare and/or misprinted copies of the band's records, and John-Boy describes the excitement surrounding the acquisition of a long-awaited discovery: 'When you go to Tom's and find a tune you've been wanting for ages, it's like a little buzz and it's a relief as well isn't it? Like you've finally found it! 'Yes, I've finally got it after all this looking, it's *my* tune now.' Butchart also has a collection of plastic bags that he holds for customers while awaiting payment, or into which he places records that he thinks they will like. This human connection with record buying and taste curation is emphasized by Chris (an insurance auditor), who Finlay introduces to the film as he is putting £100 into his credit account at the shop, and who suggests with enthusiasm that 'you never know what's going to be in [the bag]. He sends me texts, "I've got these records."'

Because of this focus on collecting, the space of the record shop is intertwined with the domestic spaces in which those collections – and the enjoyment of them – are situated. Shane is first seen in the shop explaining Butchart's essential role in sourcing rare Status Quo records, but this is followed by a more focused discussion of the specificities of his record collection which takes place at his home. The representation of the customers who we see within domestic space (Shane, Chris, Frankey and John-Boy, heavy metal fans Sam and Gareth, and DJ Weedy D who DJs online from his shed) are considered in a nuanced way that positions them as exhibiting neither a highly masculinized performance of displaying cultural capital nor as 'obsessed loners'. This accords with Finlay's self-description as 'more a fan of people than music', and who is most interested in telling 'small shy stories' about 'people who have never been on camera before and might see themselves as unlikely contributors' (Bennett and Booth 2016b: 264). The Criterion Collection's 2023 retrospective of Finlay's work was titled 'People Person', and Finlay's films play on the balance between the small and personal and the universal, with the filmmaking process itself acting as a sort of magnifying glass. 'A film can make a very small and intimate story accessible by thousands, but without the need for shouting' Finlay has argued (Bennett and Booth 2016b: 264). This accords with Elizabeth Marquis's point that even the quietest documentary moments 'acquire a particular semiotic intensity' when they are 'held up and displayed for an audience' (2014: 49) and Finlay suggests that 'a quiet moment or a look can occupy as much real estate on-screen as someone who is used to amplifying [themselves]' (Hans 2023). Finlay is less interested, then, in the knowledge accrued by the Makina, Dire Straits or Status Quo consumers than she is in exploring the individuals' connections to the music that they love. This is why Shane's enthusiasm for Status Quo is treated similarly to Chris's framed set of Nick Cave lyrics, despite the two performers being popularly perceived as occupying different positions within the evaluative hierarchies of popular music.[12]

By shuttling between the bedroom, the shop and the region, Finlay encourages the nuances of individuality to emerge that speak to the profound importance of music to our daily lives. Filming in people's homes and leisure spaces demonstrates the reach of the public space of the record shop into the customer's private domains as collections talked about in the shop acquire physical form. From a filmmaking perspective, this is also a useful strategy to encourage more intimate reflections that is not unlike how domestic settings are used to convey intimacy in the music documentary more generally (see Chapter 2). Filming in domestic settings encourages a more nuanced exploration of fan performance to take place, and Daisy Asquith observed that participants in her documentary *Crazy about One Direction* 'were more complex in their performed identities when in the familiar safe space of their own bedrooms, whereas outside in the street, in large groups, they performed more stereotypical fan identities' (2016: 84).[13]

The bedroom, in particular, is often viewed as a sacred and privileged space within teenage fan identities. Christina Williams, writing about teenagers' everyday engagement with music has noted that 'both boys and girls talked about the importance of their "room" and about the time they spent in that room accompanied by music' (2001: 239), and this combination plays a key role in identity formation. 'Young people ... have limited access to spaces which they can control', she argues, and 'music is used in [the bedroom], perhaps as a way of marking it and controlling it' (2001: 240). The importance of the bedroom is clearly evident in *Teenland* (2007), Finlay's first film, which explores the detailed mise en scène of the teenage bedroom, and also in *I Used to Be Normal*, where Dara describes her teenage bedroom as her 'domain', and her collections of posters are emblematic of the mechanisms through which control over personal space is realized.[14] The alternative title of *Our Hobby is Depeche Mode*, *The Posters Came from the Walls*, also speaks to the centrality of domestic space to fandom, and that film opens with a camcorder shot of a bedroom crammed with Depeche Mode memorabilia, accompanied by the band's single 'In Your Room'.

This approach also means that the record collectors that we see are neither pathologized as 'weird' nor positioned as cultural snobs, even when Finlay probes some of the more unusual aspects of their collecting lives. To some extent, the collectors in *Sound It Out* are aligned with an approach to collecting that John Fiske describes as 'inclusive rather than exclusive' in that it operates on an 'as many as possible' (1992: 44) principle, with male collectors figured as 'completists, looking for rare artifacts and "completing" their collections' (Bennett and Booth 2016b: 265). Finlay herself aligns this with particularly masculine sensibilities, noting that 'the men in *Sound It Out* and *Orion* were usually completists' (Bennett and Booth 2016b: 265) whereas the women she encountered while making *Orion: The Man Who Would Be King* (2015) – a film about Jimmy Ellis, an Elvis impersonator – 'had more personalized collections – locks of hair, handmade t-shirts, signed and personalized memorabilia' (Bennett and Booth 2016b: 265). Finlay does not shrink away from some of the potentially negative stereotypes associated with the male collector. Chris is shown to have two variants of *The World of David Bowie*, and Shane's search for rare Status Quo records stems from a desire to go beyond the easily accessible back-catalogue: 'I am a person who will collect seven or eight versions of [a] record because of misspellings on the label or different coloured labels.' Both men appear to live alone (Shane is explicit about this), and so there is the potential to read the continuation of such engagement as symbolic of a failure to 'grow up'.[15]

Yet Finlay offers counter positions for how Shane, in particular, engages in music cultures that are not primarily about infantilization or loneliness. Shane's self-disclaimed Status Quo 'addiction' is partly an act of resilience. When he is first introduced in the film he describes his regular Quo marathons, stating that 'there's nothing like doing six solid nights, one after the other, of Quo' and that although people think him 'mad', this is offset by his view that his enjoyment of his record collection is no less problematic than any other common vice: 'I don't smoke, I don't drink, I don't have a woman, so what more do you want?' Furthermore, towards the end of the film Shane describes being diagnosed at an early age with cerebral palsy, epilepsy and hydrocephalus, and spending his childhood being bullied for attending a 'spastic school'. While being interviewed by Finlay in a semi-furnished and only half-painted room (Figure 4.4) – presumably an area of his home – Shane suggests that this background is 'part of the reason why I became sort of a bit reclusive and started this', he says, indicating his record collection, and he suggests that his music consumption acts as a counter-balance to working night shifts at B&Q: 'I go in, clock on, do the job, clock off, go home. This is my release.' Collecting and listening to records is neither a cause nor a symptom of Shane's isolation, but is instead a means through with he is able to connect to the wider social world through the shop and by attending gigs. This moment of self-revelation is dependent on Finlay's careful approach and on the domestic space as a site for the interview, and it unsettles any assumptions we might have had about Shane up to this

Figure 4.4 Shane listening to music in his semi-furnished home in *Sound It Out*.

point. It emphasizes his record collection as a 'lifeline', and this changes our understanding of the more extreme aspects of Shane's engagement with music, such as his consideration of having his collection melted down and turned into a coffin to be able to '[take] it with me'.

It is for this reason that Shane considers Finlay's hypothetical question about the closure of Sound It Out as an impossible thought: 'Don't even go there. I know what you're gonna say, aren't you? If he had to go? If he disappeared? I would literally, physically cry.'[16] That the entanglement between the shop, the customers and the music is fundamentally an emotional one is drawn out by Finlay's combining of Shane's words with an emotional version of Joy Division's 'Love Will Tear Us Apart' performed live in the shop by Saint Saviour. The centrality of emotion – rather than more masculinized values – is repeatedly emphasized as important to the act of record collecting. Throwing up the spectre of the life-stage approach to fandom outlined in the previous section, Chris describes his collection as part of his biographical self: 'It's a collection of like the last twenty years of my music listening life. It's, you know, I can remember where I was when I bought the records. The first time I listened to the records. There are like some records here that are just ... really important'. The objects in the collection are not exclusively positioned as important for their rarity or their collectability value, but for the emotional and biographical meaning that they hold as objects and when played. This is mirrored by Butchart's view that records are 'all about emotions ... Emotions and memories. I can tell you exactly what

I was doing when I play a record. Where I was, who I was going out with, it's all about memories. Records hold memories.'

Music collections thus become associated with life, something heavy metal fan Gareth makes explicit when he tells Finlay that 'without music I don't honestly think I'd still be here, really', recalling having made attempts to end his life, and crediting the support of the music community around him – including Sam, with whom he is always seen in the film – for still being alive. Chris also recognizes that 'record collections are never finished. They'll only be finished when they stop selling records. And I don't think that's going to happen. So it'll never be completed'. The collection is therefore synonymous with a life lived. Just as Tom Butchart displays a sensitive engagement with his customers on an emotional level, in *Sound It Out* Finlay uses the individuality of her subjects to challenge some of the gendered stereotypes related to collecting, by foregrounding the emotional and affective importance that music holds for a series of individual lives in a way that neither pathologizes these activities, nor does it shy away from exploring some of the more extreme aspects of record collecting.

Music and Meaning: *Our Hobby Is Depeche Mode*

As the previous sections of this chapter have shown, focusing on individual fans outside of 'the mob' encourages a nuanced set of personal stories to emerge. Although this neutralizes some of the ethical concerns associated with characterizing fans as a homogenous group, it raises a different set of issues around representativeness, especially how well individual fans can be understood to 'stand-in' for an entire fanbase. Paring down 'the mob' to its constituent individuals does not, in itself, guarantee that fans will be treated with sensitivity, and we can see the negative effects of what happens when the focus on individuals goes wrong, as is the case in *Wacko About Jacko* and *Crazy about One Direction*. Writing about the former, Hills argues that 'the documentary is able to mobilize a range of negative fan stereotypes even while appearing to "positively" portray fandom in part' (2007: 462), and in both cases the documentaries were criticized because the individual fans who were the focus were felt to have been misrepresented as individuals and to be unrepresentative of the fandom more generally. Jackson fans – including some of those who participated in the programme – felt that the documentary over-emphasized the place of Jackson within their lives:

I said [on camera] that ppl think that MJ fans are weird cos they have no lives outside MJ but the reality is that MJ is a part of our lives but not our entire lives. … Stuff like that cld have been kept in I think. (Hills 2007: 466)

Jealousy can also be an underlying consideration here, and Daisy Asquith, director of *Crazy about One Direction*, suggests that 'having your identity represented on television is a powerful form of recognition' that implies an elevation 'from "just another fan" into a significant fan' (2016: 81). This is not unfounded, and one of Dara's first contributions in *I Used to Be Normal* is to acknowledge that she occasionally makes life choices based on whether they will help bring about her dream of appearing on stage with Gary Barlow, and that participating in the film is one of those decisions.[17] Nevertheless, exploitative selectivity can have a pathological effect on the larger fandom. For example, the inclusion in the One Direction documentary of *Larry Stylinson* 'shippers' (fans who hypothesize and create fan works based upon the notion of a gay relationship between Harry Styles and Louis Tomlinson) led those opposed to the practice to '[accuse] *Larry* shippers of making the fandom look bad by recirculating notions of (young, female) fans as crazy' (Jones 2016: 61).

Both cases also speak to the position of both documentaries as television documentaries vying for viewing figures. Both *Wacko* and *Crazy* fit within the 'shock-doc' model that became a hallmark of Channel 4's documentary output in the 2000s, including one-off documentaries such as *The Boy Whose Skin Fell Off* (2004) and sensationalist series like *Benefits Street* (2014–15), *15 Kids and Counting* (2012) and *Big Fat Gypsy Weddings* (2010–15).[18] Both documentaries had their titles changed after shooting had finished (from *Michael Jackson's Biggest Fans* and *I Heart One Direction*) (Asquith 2016: 82; Hills 2007: 463) in order to attract a bigger audience, and this has clear ethical implications for the participants whose framing as 'exceptional' shifted from celebratory ('I Heart' / 'The Biggest') to something pathological ('crazy' and 'wacko').[19] Ultimately, Asquith recognizes that 'it is of course impossible to represent all fans at once' (2016: 87) and Jeanie Finlay suggests that the filmmaker is accountable, first and foremost, to the individual, arguing that 'I rarely think about the wider "fan" community, e.g., Shane in *Sound It Out* is a Quo fan but his experience is personal and that is what he reflects in the film' (Bennett and Booth 2016b: 265).

This final section explores some of the ways in which the balance between individuality of experience and collective representation is navigated in Jeremy Deller and Nick Abraham's documentary *Our Hobby Is Depeche Mode*. Unlike the previous two films where individual fans represent larger fandoms (Dara as a

Take That fan, Shane as a Status Quo fan, for instance), *Our Hobby* takes a closer look at the multiplicity of experiences and meanings found within Depeche Mode fandom more broadly through a series of individualized perspectives. This allows individuality to be expressed without it carrying the burden of wider representation. Again, the title is important, but unlike the exceptionalist implications of 'wacko' and 'crazy', here, the '*Our*' communicates communality, even as the images span a wide range of global, social, cultural and political contexts, and '*Hobby*' suggests a side-interest, rather than an all-encompassing obsession.

On the surface, the documentary examines some of the more extreme fan practices that are often pathologized in popular culture: a young Russian woman displays her self-drawn comic book in which she imagines herself and her friends being married to the members of Depeche Mode and all living in the same house; a German family recreate Depeche Mode music videos, costuming themselves and their young son in meticulously detailed replica attire; St. Edward's church in Cambridge mirrors its gothic architecture in its services, which includes music from a range of alternative bands. However, these activities speak to a broader political aim of the film which examines the meaning of a band to groups of people who find themselves on the margins of society, as outcasts, or positioned in (sometimes literal) borderlands. The film does not understand this outsider status as pertaining solely to the fan practices it depicts, which are often explained in terms of identity formation and companionship. Instead, it places them in combination with a broader set of political and social contexts where government policies have caused division and oppression, but where Depeche Mode's music is shown to have enabled fans to overcome – or at least challenge – the conditions that force them into roles as social or political outsiders in the first place.

This is established right at the start of the film when images of the rain-soaked concrete high street of Basildon, a brutalist 'new town' of the 1940s and the band's home town, are contrasted with the voices of fans from the United States, Mexico and Russia who imagine the town as a rural utopia, with 'a friendly atmosphere', 'quiet streets and small houses', 'a pub, a castle and green mountains'. Basildon resident Peter Burton highlights the band's own outsider status when he suggests that within the town, the members of Depeche Mode are 'not seen as big stars. There's no statue of [lead singer] Dave Gahan or [principal songwriter] Martin Gore. You would never know that Depeche Mode came from Basildon.' Although Depeche Mode might play a limited role in Basildon's identity, the opposite is not the case, and Burton notes that 'if anyone speaks about Depeche

Mode they speak about Basildon'. The documentary presents Depeche Mode as being both intimately connected with their hometown and entirely divorced from it. Similarly, the band has a much greater cultural impact outside of the UK than they do within it, where they are largely associated with a handful of hit singles ('Just Can't Get Enough', 'Personal Jesus', 'Enjoy the Silence'). In the United States and across central Europe, however, they are much more culturally significant.

The film's focus on central and eastern Europe is significant, and the documentary is a testament to the importance of the band to many ordinary (young) people during the final years of the USSR, and groups of fans in Berlin, St. Petersburg, Moscow and Bucharest position the band within narratives of oppression and freedom. Francisca, a Russian fan, talks of the emotional content of the band's music being sympathetic to a particular kind of Russian mentality forged through decades of oppressive politics. 'You see, in Depeche Mode's songs, there is always tragedy, in both lyrics and music', she notes. 'There is a kind of despair' that resonates with the Russian character, and an attempt to '[address] the transcendental nature of existence' that 'for a Russian is like the alpha and omega' and that 'really appeals to … the Russian soul'.

This affinity with Eastern Europe is neither imagined, nor accidental. Depeche Mode's album artwork, which includes Brian Griffin's striking photographs of a peasant woman cutting grain with a sickle (*A Broken Frame*) and a muscular man wielding a sledgehammer (*Construction Time Again*), 'used symbols and signs that were derived from … socialist realist art with the worker … as the central motif' (Burmeister and Lange 2017: 376). There is also a clear link between the brutalist architecture that characterized both Basildon and many of Europe's former-Communist cities as well as the band's musical style, which tends to supplement (and in some cases eschew entirely) acoustic instruments with synthesizers, tape samples and percussive, industrial sounds sourced by 'going off to derelict areas armed with a hammer and a tape recorder' (Miller 2008: 159).[20] As Peter Burton notes in the introduction to the film, Basildon's brutalist architecture is reflected in the industrial sound of the band's music, quoting Basildon musician Robert Marlow's claim that 'the music came from the bricks'.

In this combination of the synthetic and the industrial, the band was also taking cues from German groups such as electronic pioneers Kraftwerk and industrial metal bands like Einstürzende Neubauten, as well as composers of the musique concrète school such as Pierre Schaeffer and Karlheinz Stockhausen (Miller 2008: 157). At one point in *Our Hobby Is Depeche Mode,* fans are seen in an archival recording of a pirate TV broadcast from the early 1990s making connections between style and functionality, with one suggesting that 'it's technology, the sounds of life, of reality. It's not like musical instruments, guitars and stuff', and another asking 'Can you tell me what other music is as emotional? What other music has the sounds of forks, railway ties and scissors?' There is, then, a sympathy between the form and the content of the band's music (and its packaging) and the architectural, cultural, and political milieu of the Eastern European audience. Martin Gore – the band's principal songwriter – was living in West Berlin during the mid-1980s and the band recorded and/or mixed a number of albums (including *Construction Time Again*) at Berlin's Hansa Tonstudios, sharing the view of the neighbouring Berlin Wall that David Bowie allegedly used as inspiration for the final verse of 'Heroes', recorded in the same studio a decade earlier (Rüther, Matthews and Rüther 2014: 121–2).

Francisca argues that this cultural affinity explains why the band remains so popular across Europe, where the post-war traumas of oppression and division were being materially felt in the late 1980s and early 1990s alongside the band's rise to fame.[21] Albert, another Russian fan who has a large tattoo of lead singer Dave Gahan on his back, makes this connection between the music and the politics explicit, noting that 'this music coincided with the fall of the Soviet Union so I see it as having been the music of freedom'. This combination of the somewhat extreme – the giant tattoo – with the more perceptive political point is emblematic of the film's positioning of fan cultures as operating in parallel with larger processes of marginalization. Another example is Depeche Mode fans co-opting Russia's national Victory Day military parade, marked each year on 9 May, by coincidence also Dave Gahan's birthday. Fans in Moscow and St. Petersburg are seen holding a counter-celebration called 'Dave Day', gathering to sing and socialize before spending the evening at Depeche Mode themed club nights. Like other moments in the film, these events gain a sense of political purpose that extends beyond the simple meeting of like-minded people. Sergey, a fan from Moscow, explains that 'Dave Day' evolved in parallel with changes in Russian social policy, especially that of Perestroika, an approach to government most associated with Mikhail Gorbachev, in which public criticism of the regime was no longer expressly forbidden. At the same time, the continuation of the Communist regime meant that 'there were few clubs, none really, so there was nowhere for people to meet'. The 'Dave Day' celebrations represent the fan response to changing social and economic policies, while also embodying an underlying political dimension as it can be understood as constituting a kind of protest of the regime without appearing as an actively

Figure 4.5 Depeche Mode fans (left) and Russian military supporters (right) take part in their respective 9 May celebrations in St. Petersburg.

hostile demonstration on the part of those who might not wish to celebrate the military parade. The film combines home movie footage from the 1992 'Dave Day' event with a more recent example filmed by Deller and Abrahams (likely 2005), setting out a persistent history of resistance, that is reflected stylistically with cross-cutting between images of military marches and Depeche Mode fans processing (Figure 4.5).

For German fans, the band are symbolic of both the moment of freedom and of a revolutionary potential apparent in East Germany immediately prior to the fall of the Berlin Wall. Berlin residents Igor, Helko and Thomas recall the band being a symbol of the cultural and political tensions between East and West Berlin. West German television and radio signals could be received in the East, and so the band's music was available and familiar, but could not be bought. Therefore, the band acted as a sort of Western soft-power, the TV and radio signals breaching the Berlin Wall in a way not possible for ordinary, corporeal Berliners, and tapes were made from radio broadcasts and circulated (Burmeister and Lange 2017: 378–80). This weakening of the barriers between East and West was made even more concrete by the band's 1988 concert in East Berlin, which is the focal point of the Berlin fan's discussion. Igor, Helko and Thomas are interviewed on the former site of the concert venue and Helko recalls there being a sense of insecurity about the number of people who turned up without tickets, suggesting that the authorities were concerned about the revolutionary potential of the gathered masses. Reflecting the subversive nature of 'Dave Day', Thomas, who was working as security, recalls prioritizing his view of the concert over his duties, noting that 'I wasn't the only one to lose my security shirt when [it] started.' Igor explains the power of being able to see the band in the flesh, recalling a newspaper headline that stated 'The Posters Came From the Walls' (Deller and Abraham's alternative title for the film), making it clear that 'You never were able to see your posters alive. And suddenly they were there on the stage singing for you and it was so special. For me it was the first time that really a massive star group came to the DDR. It was the whole wide world coming to your little Socialist country.'

The documentary explores other spaces of oppression, including Iranian fan Peyman's observations that buying commercial copies of Western music remains illegal and that the prospect of a Depeche Mode concert is 'something that I don't believe could happen'. In an interview, Peyman's uncle Andy tells the camera that he moved to Canada to escape the Iranian regime, and he highlights both the struggle 'to find a single poster of Depeche Mode or a single [piece of] music' when he was growing up, but also the dangers involved in self-expression since the 1979 revolution. Andy talks particularly about Martin Gore's tendency towards cross-dressing as being something that was 'really forbidden' in Iran, and photographs of him and his friends with shaved heads, wearing leather jackets and playing guitars accompany his testimony that 'people like us who were following the band, and having the same haircut, and wearing the leather jacket and stuff like this, we were in the spotlight. We used to get caught and beaten by police.' He intimates that there are still dangers for those caught listening to Western music and that 'you can end up in jail or ... they raid your house and destroy everything that you have'. This makes Peyman's contribution to the film – small and seemingly uncontroversial though it is – a political act given that he is still living in Iran. For Andy, there are key implications for self-identity and self-expression. 'What you look like and what you listen to is setting up your culture and who you are', he suggests, 'and when you don't fit in a society because you don't listen to the music they do and you don't look like what they look like, eventually you feel depressed and you feel separated from them.' This sense of separation is not something that is a condition of fandom, but something imposed upon fans by external forces. 'I am nothing without listening to music. I am nothing without playing it and performing it', Andy states, 'and that was one the main reasons that I left Iran'.

Like Igor, Helko and Thomas, Andy understands his attendance at his first Depeche Mode concert in Canada as having a political underpinning. This is also true for Mark, the final subject of *Our Hobby Is Depeche Mode*, a former homeless man from London who describes his three years spent living alone under Hammersmith Bridge, with a small stereo and a copy of Depeche Mode's *101* album as his 'best friend and company'. Mark describes his greatest fear during this time as 'running out of batteries', and his ultimate salvation being his acquisition of a bootleg copy of the band's 1993 album *Songs of Faith and Devotion* and a ticket to the band's Crystal Palace gig of the same year, an event that 'put the fire in my belly' and encouraged him to reeducate himself and find somewhere to live. As with many of the other interviewees in the film, Mark is interviewed in a location significant to his past fan engagement (the banks of the Thames near Hammersmith Bridge), and he declares the gig as 'a huge turning point' because of the way it reconnected him to a wider community: 'Never up to that point had I felt such a part of something. Such an awesome sense of togetherness, of hope, of energy. It made me realise that … surviving isn't enough. For a life to be worth anything you've got to live. And it takes a moment where you actually feel alive to realise that.' Music, and the connections that it fosters both emotionally and socially, is positioned as a fundamental aspect of 'living'.

Music is, therefore, positioned as an important point of connection with society, not as a vehicle of isolation as the pathological view of fandom suggests, and Depeche Mode's fans are not positioned as outsiders *because* of their fandom. For some, their position on the margins is due to personal circumstances, medical contexts or inherent personality traits that position an individual apart from the mainstream. In other cases, a sense of disconnection or isolation from like-minded people is enforced by state apparatus. The combination of the former and the latter draws out the notion that rather than being the cause of 'outsiderness', music is used as a tool to sustain a sense of self-identity in challenging contexts, and fandom can be a means of connecting with wider society, in order to find a sense of place and acceptance. Even those fans who could be positioned at the extreme end of the spectrum of fan behaviours are understood within a wider structure of meaning. Claudia, the German mother and director of her family's music video reenactment, unwittingly mirrors Shane from *Sound It Out* when she argues that 'Other people go to the gym or do sports. Our hobby is Depeche Mode.' Likewise, a group of Russian friends who *also* make their own music videos, explain the importance of the band to their connection *as* individuals operating on the edges of the social acceptance in Russia: 'They help us to live. They help us to survive and to stay ourselves.'

Our Hobby Is Depeche Mode ends in a way that underlines the overriding argument of this chapter: that the 'hysterical mass' of music fans is, in fact, a complex construction of individual music lovers who each have a unique relationship with the object of their fandom, and that *how* that enthusiasm is enacted can inflect our understanding of the fan object. Near the start of the film, teenage fans from California, Orlando and Elana, establish the importance of the live concert as a space for communality, and specifically highlight Gahan's arm-waving during performances of the song 'Never Let Me Down Again' as a shared moment of audience participation. This gesture became ritualized during the 'Music for the Masses' tour and because of its appearance in the *101* tour film, a moment edited into *Our Hobby* at this point.[22] At the conclusion of *Our Hobby*, Mark talks in voice-over about the relative anonymity of the concert crowd as we see him in the audience: 'looking around the crowd you can't tell who's homeless, who's rich, who's first gig, who's been to many. You're almost moving as one.' As 'Never Let Me Down Again' comes to its conclusion, Mark raises his arms in the air and joins those around him in the ritualized performance. He is then joined by the other fans seen in the film as Deller and Abrahams cut between the various groups, replicating the same dance and united in both movement and sound with continuity constructed through the soundtrack. This is not the anonymous mass of Beatles stock footage, but a complex network of inter-connected individuals, united in their differences and each physically and verbally expressing the meaning that they find within the music, within live performance and within the iconography that is produced by, and underpins, the object of their fandom.

Conclusion

Although the representation of fans as a mass entity conveys a clear sense of broad cultural impact/disturbance, and of commercial success, it is the drilling down to individual stories where the music finds its meaning. The first three chapters in this book convey the various ways in which a star image is constructed within the music documentary as part of a wider cultural and commercial media economy. In some circumstances the same is true of fan representations, where documentaries become pedagogic tools to police fan behaviour. However, it is also at the point of reception (of a piece of music, of a live performance, of an in-person encounter) where much of the meaning is made. The impact of the music on the world might be most clearly explored in documentaries that break apart the 'mass' object, and take a sensitive eye to explore what happens to the commercial product (the LP, the CD, the concert film, the poster, the star image itself) once it leaves the control of the producer and begins to enact its meanings in the public realm. It is in the space of reception where music 'means' most, and documentaries that consider the place of music within individual lives seem particularly successful at capturing this meaning in insightful and nuanced ways.

Conclusion

This book has drawn together a range of strands that underpin the pop music documentary in its contemporary form. The overriding concern has been to consider the documentary within an industrial context where it plays an important role as part of the commercial mechanism of pop stardom. However, rather than dismiss such texts from consideration because of a belief that this entanglement with industry means that they are inherently corrupted, I hope that I have shown that this can instead provide an interesting focus for analysis. This also opens avenues of analysis where the project's wider interventions speak to the documentary project more generally. The mosaic nature of the concert film (Chapter 1) constructs the 'ideal' live performance, a manoeuvre that has clear commercial and artistic implications for the recording artist, and has particular relevance for the analysis of other forms of live performance on screen (stand-up comedy, for instance), but also speaks to the ways in which documentaries always work to transform their subject matter into representations. The concept of the documentary backstage (Chapter 2) provides a range of aesthetic spaces in which pop stars are presented to the public by the documentary maker in ways that feeds into the public's understanding of their personality, but it also has wider implications for how documentary makers are able to underwrite documentary's transformative potential by asserting the veracity, intimacy and authenticity of their representations. The obscuring (even erasure) of labour discussed in Chapter 3 has particular implications for how the craft of songwriting is balanced within the popular understanding of pop artists, especially in terms of claims of artistry, ownership and authorship, but it also poses wider questions for how creative acts more generally can be represented in factual media in ways that are both insightful *and* interesting. Chapter 4's arguments about fan representation tell particular stories about how the history of popular music is told and how fan behaviours are regulated, but also make broader claims about the ethics of representation within unequal power dynamics and the recirculation of the resulting images to uphold problematic cultural hierarchies. By taking such an approach, we can also explore the work that music documentaries do in the mediation of pop stardom in a way that encourages scholarly consideration of a wider and more inclusive range of texts that break down cultural hierarchies of taste and value. I hope that it inspires others to conduct their own analysis of the many worthy documentaries that have not made it into this particular monograph.

As I set out in the introduction, a reliance on traditional evaluative hierarchies is reflected in the scholarship around the genre, which has tended to place male subjects (Bob Dylan, The Beatles, David Bowie, The Rolling Stones), conventionally masculine genres (rock) and male traditions of filmmaking (direct cinema) as more worthy of attention, often by contrasting them with more commercialized, emotional, interactive – and feminine – forms and values. This book takes seriously the work that documentaries about popular music do in relation to these evaluative hierarchies. I have attempted to find spaces in which recent music documentaries have challenged such evaluative shackles; the focus on the complex personal stories offered by multi-aged, individualized female fans of boybands that resist stereotypical pathologization, for instance, or the ways in which themes of vulnerability and resilience in portraits of (particularly female) pop stars are elevated as a means of critiquing the industrial and cultural pressures of celebrity commodification. Even when they are not directly addressing these practices, these documentaries reveal the gendered cultural prejudices at work within the music industry, within the culture at large and surrounding the music documentary in particular.

This is not to say that I am making a straightforward argument that the documentaries examined here are primarily interesting for their utility value rather than their aesthetic qualities. The documentary maker's liminal position as undertaking *both* 'a job from behind the lines' and an 'inside job' (Romney 1995: 87) has a tendency to produce texts that exhibit the tension of this dual engagement in interesting ways. One key aspect of this concerns how questions of cultural value when it comes to music documentaries, pop stardom and – often – gender are intertwined, with all three categories devalued by their cross-association. The analysis within has shown that the tensions that might be assumed to destroy artistry (both *within* the music industry *and* in its documentary representation) can actually produce aesthetic and narrative experimentation and enjoyment for audiences. We can see this, for instance in the aesthetics of *20,000 Days on Earth* (2014), where an oneiric aesthetic and tone offers, somewhat counter-intuitively, a genuinely insightful meditation on the nature of pop stardom, or where Beyoncé's manipulation of space and time in *Homecoming* (2019) acts in both an explicitly commercial dimension (it produces the best possible performance) while also pointing towards the political and historical significance of the event and its filmic representation as works of Black artistry.

The tension between documentary enquiry and commercial function has an aesthetic dimension. Meaning emerges not just from the forwarding of commercial interests, but also from the ways in which the stars express their humanity in the face of highly commercial industries which position them (and not just the work they produce) as products for consumption. On the other side of this relationship, the fans who are doing the consuming express the importance of the products of the commercial system (including the documentary texts) to their own identities and their social relationships in meaningful ways. This removes them from the purely commercial dimension and recalibrates them as personal sites of meaning. Across each of these spaces, the documentaries act in transformative ways, and thus the form of the material transcends straightforward observation, producing cinematic (and televisual) artefacts that in their transformativity and interactivity have meaningfully changed the documentary subject *within* the documentary, and worked to produce aesthetic objects that have value beyond their simple utilitarian role as part of the star-making machinery.

The structure of the book reflects the interplay between the music documentary, the pop star, the industry of which they are a part, and their audience. As such, it has a shape that is partly determined by factors external to the documentary. This is a useful approach, but it has the effect of opening several natural avenues of investigation while closing down others, or at least making them less intuitive. For instance, the centring of the star (and latterly the fan) means that documentaries that are less interested in that aspect of popular music are paid less attention than they often deserve. There are documentaries about – to give just a handful of examples – album artwork, specific genres and music scenes, backing singers and supporting musicians that make up a significant portion of the music documentary landscape and offer important alternative perspectives, for which I have not found space within these pages. Other approaches to the same subject could excavate an entirely different set of issues, concerns, aesthetics and topologies, and this book merely scratches the surface of the pop music documentary since 1980.

To conclude I want to set out just a few examples of where this work could continue in the future. This book combines an analysis of film and television texts, and while I have made efforts to consider how their medium-specific qualities inflect the documentary material we see (as, for instance, in the discussion of television aesthetics and series form in Chapter 3), there is a much more complex history of the television music documentary still to be told that places television institutions and production practices at the centre. Notable work exists in this area (Andrews 2021: 151–84; Bennett and Baker 2016; Long and Wall 2010, 2013; Pillai 2017: 83–116; Weston 2021a, b; Williams 2010), but there is still a great deal more that could be done, here, especially in terms of analysis and history.

This also applies to global considerations of the music documentary, and in writing this book, it became increasingly clear that many of the approaches and frameworks to stardom and industry that underpin the discussions of this book are particularly Western in outlook and, as a result, are challenged by films and programmes that do not embody similar sensibilities. A full exploration of the global picture of music documentary is long overdue, and this breadth is largely – and regrettably – absent here, in part because the scope and structure of the book did not allow adequate space to do justice to the nuance and detail required to fully engage with this material.

The question of the future direction of the music documentary also presents a space of mutability and uncertainty. The global circulation of audio-visual products via streaming services has the potential to open up new markets and audiences for regionally produced content, but this rubs against the increasingly proprietorial tendencies with which streaming platforms are containing access to their content. This has also led to a certain homogeneity of programming aimed at a potential global audience, rather than understanding national or regional specificity as advantageous (Piper 2016). On the other hand, social media sites provide fans with ever-more direct access to their idols which, while not explicitly a space for documentary in the traditional sense, extends the concerns with intimacy and access that has been central to this book into a liminal space somewhere between the tightly-controlled image-management of a publicity campaign and talking to a close friend (this is not unlike how I suggest the 'documentary backstage' operates in Chapter 2). These boundaries have been blurred even further during the Covid-19 pandemic, where Instagram feeds, TikTok accounts and other livestreaming platforms were used to host 'lockdown' gigs, often in domestic spaces like living rooms, kitchens and garages, and even – such as in the case of Laura Marling's Instagram account (lauramarling [@lauramarling] 2020) – providing guitar lessons and tutorials. Such examples reformulate the possibilities of the music documentary in a short-form digital space and combine with other industry-disrupting (though more mainstream) activities, such as Taylor Swift's success producing and distributing *The Eras Tour* (2023) outside of the Hollywood system, to open up alternative avenues for 'documenting' music, music making and the lives of those making and consuming music.

This is, therefore, not an exhaustive overview of a multi-media genre that is playing an ever-more important role in both the music industry and the film and television landscape. Rather, I hope I have indicated a number of critical perspectives from which recent music documentaries can be viewed afresh, and a range of methodological approaches which can be used to extend the discussion further, and especially outside of existing frameworks of cultural value. It also demonstrates the depth and richness of the music documentary in its current form and the opportunity for a much more wide-ranging discussion to emerge. I hope that this book proves suitably inspiring to other scholars to take this work further.

Notes

Introduction

1 The $26 million of pre-sales was over 50 per cent higher than the previous record of $16.9 million set by *Spider-Man: No Way Home* in 2021 (Rubin 2023).
2 These figures are derived by combining the reports for the 'Documentary' and 'Concert or Performance' categories on the film statistics website the-numbers.com.
3 This can be understood as part of a broader agenda by Swift to ensure ownership of her creative endeavours. This is most apparent in her re-recording albums originally made when signed to Big Machine Records, for which Swift does not own the master tapes (Bruner 2021).
4 Swift's film was produced as part of an interim agreement with SAG-AFTRA to allow the continuation of projects that met the minimum standards that the unions were negotiating towards as part of the strike action (Kaufman 2023).
5 These include *All of Those Voices* (2023), *Angelheaded Hipster: The Songs of Marc Bolan & T. Rex* (2022), *Bobi Wine: The People's President* (2022), *Carlos* (2023), *Ed Sheeran: The Sum of It All* (2023), *Ghosts of the Chelsea Hotel (and Other Rock & Roll Stories)* (2023), *Have You Got It Yet? The Story of Syd Barett and Pink Floyd* (2023), *Kick Out!: The Newtown Neurotics Story* (2023), *Lewis Capaldi: How I'm Feeling Now* (2023), *Little Richard: I Am Everything* (2023), *Meet Me in the Bathroom* (2022), *Reinventing Elvis: The '68 Comeback* (2023), *Squaring the Circle* (2022), *Robbie Williams* (2023), *Wham!* (2023) and high-profile re-issues of *Dance Craze* (1981), *Stop Making Sense* (1984) and *Ziggy Stardust and the Spiders from Mars* (1979).
6 *Geri* is a particularly rich documentary text, but has been well-discussed elsewhere and so is otherwise absent here (Bruzzi 2006: 203–4; Goode 2015).
7 This is the now-customary footnote to clarify that the correct spelling of the film's title excludes the apostrophe (Wallace 2019: 30–1 fn. 5).
8 For the debates around the identity of MTV, see the work of E. Ann Kaplan (1991) and Andrew Goodwin (1992).
9 Though the focus on live performance in programmes like *MTV Unplugged* (1989–) offered a concurrent space for the continuity of authenticity as a key site of pop-rock credibility.
10 *What Happened, Miss Simone?* (2015) was also nominated.
11 The body of scholarship on observational documentary and direct cinema more generally is vast, but key works include Bruzzi (2006: 73–80), Issari and Paul (1979),

Kuhn (1978), Mamber (1972a; b), Nichols (1991), Saunders (2007) and Winston (1993) as well as numerous interviews with the practitioner.
12 See Bruzzi (2006) for the most comprehensive overview of this debate.
13 Figures derived by combining the reports for the 'Documentary' and 'Concert or Performance' categories on the film statistics website the-numbers.com.
14 See work by Kim Gabbard (1996), Nic Pillai (2017) and Tim Wall and Paul Long (2010) that addresses this.

1 The Concert Film

1 These are *Hannah Montana and Miley Cyrus: Best of Both Worlds Concert* (2008), *Michael Jackson's This is It* (2009), *Justin Bieber: Never Say Never* (2011), *One Direction: This is Us* (2013) and *Taylor Swift: The Eras Tour* (2023). Figures are derived by combining the reports for the 'Documentary' and 'Concert or Performance' categories on the film statistics website the-numbers.com.
2 Mitchell, in particular, is evoked in the black and white photograph used in the publicity for Swift's 2021 single 'All Too Well (Sad Girl Autumn Version)'.
3 It is rare that the audience is omitted from a concert film, though a handful of films, including *Stop Making Sense*, *American Utopia* and *Lou Reed: Berlin* (2007) deliberately keep audience shots to a minimum.
4 Philip Auslander has argued that live events are already closely aligned to their reproductions because of the 'incursion of mediatization' into the live space itself (1999: 7). At an arena concert, for example, 'the spectator sitting in the back rows is present at a live performance, but hardly participates in it … since his/her main experience of the performance is to read it off a video monitor' (Auslander 1999: 24).
5 This is especially the case given the film's status as a Netflix film, so the distance between audience and screen could be a matter of inches.
6 Even for 2D concert films, specific tour dates will usually be staged for the express purpose of being filmed, with warnings put in place that views might be obstructed and sometimes with reduced ticket prices to mitigate these potential disruptions (Deseret News 2007; KATY PERRY [@katyperry] 2011; McGee 2011: 115).
7 It has also become a naturalized element of live performance footage, which is partly an outcome of many concert films sharing creative personnel; Paul Dugdale, for instance, has directed a number of prominent concert films, including *Reputation Stadium Tour*, *Excuse Me, I Love You* and *Coldplay: Music of the Spheres – Live at Rover Plate*, and so his style could be understood as offering a template for the genre.
8 *The Song Remains the Same* even includes several fantasy sequences.

9 The use of black and white for the backstage sequences of *Madonna: Truth or Dare*, *Rattle and Hum* and *Homecoming* is a stylistic tic that attempts to mobilize the aesthetic associations of direct cinema. See Chapter 2 for a more detailed discussion on both the backstage and its associations with black and white cinematography.

10 Versions of the 'stage being readied for a show' montage (usually using time-lapse) can be found in many concert films including, *The Bruce McMouse Show* (2018), *Awesome; I Fuckin' Shot That!* (2006), *Never Say Never* and *Lewis Capaldi: How I'm Feeling Now* (2023).

11 An alternative convention of the concert film is to focus on a single important concert as can be seen in *The Last Waltz* and *Shut up and Play the Hits* which are framed as farewell performances by their respective bands The Band and LCD Soundsystem, and in *Homecoming* and *Gimme Shelter* where the specificities of Coachella and Altamont are centralised.

12 'Baby Don't You Do It' was made famous under that name by Marvin Gaye, but is retitled, here, as simply 'Don't Do It'.

13 Elsewhere, I have discussed D. A. Pennebaker's decision to order songs in *101* for thematic and affective effect (Wallace 2021a), and Laurel Westrup notes similarly non-chronological sequencing in *Monterey Pop* (2021: 45–46).

14 The yellow outfits were worn on the 14 April 2018, the pink versions a week later (Mitchell 2019).

15 It is not necessarily the case that every song will come from the same performance, and there might be a mix-and-match approach to the soundtrack.

16 This doesn't take into account any mixing, over-dubbing and balancing of the soundtrack that might take place in post-production that alter the soundtrack even further from the live sound originally recorded during the performance. Examples of this can be seen in Brett Morgen's *Moonage Daydream* (2022), where the archival audio from live concert performances by David Bowie was played through the PA of a football stadium and re-recorded to produce reverb effects for the Dolby Atmos surround sound mix that were not present on the original recordings. New crowd noise was also recorded in order to create an 'immersive experience' for the cinemagoer. (Brett Morgen [@brettmorgen] 2023a, b).

17 At the start of the third number in *Stop Making Sense*, 'Thank You For Sending Me an Angel', drummer Chris Frantz can be seen picking up a set of headphones playing the previous evening's performance of the song to ensure a consistent tempo across the four performances for ease of editing.

18 Matt Hills, for example, has described slow motion as 'a technique borrowed from fiction film' (2007: 471), though it also has a long heritage in sports broadcasting.

19 An interesting alternative to this can be seen in a sequence in *Dance Craze* where a Steadicam operator almost collides with Pauline Black, lead singer of The

Selecter, who responds by shooting the camera what the singer referred to as a 'dirty look' in a Q&A accompanying a screening of a reissue of the film. Q&A with Pauline Black and Roger Lomas, conducted by Pete Chambers, Coventry Odeon, 23 March 2023.

20 Matt McGee's account of the filming of *Rattle and Hum* suggests that the first night of recording in Denver was undermined because 'cameras follow Bono everywhere, and frustrate his ability to play to the crowd' (2011: 112).

21 See *Gimme Shelter*, *Bring on the Night* (1985), *Ratte and Hum*, *No Distance Left to Run* (2010) and numerous others examples of where factual modes of documentary exploration give way to affective registers as musical performances begin.

22 The visibility of the feet of the performers is another way in which the film viewer is prioritized over the concert audience, given that the feet of the performers on stage are often obscured by the presence of monitors and guitar pedals. The focus on the feet of the performers at key moments in *Monterey Pop*, *Dance Crazy*, *Stop Making Sense* and *American Utopia* is striking because it offers yet another unfamiliar view of the performer that is both physical/sensual and informative.

2 The 'Documentary Backstage'

1 This is the kind of performance of self in everyday life that we all enact in our social interactions, as set out by Erving Goffman (1971) and Judith Butler (1990, 1993).

2 There is another strand of archival documentary film, not examined in detail here, where the archive is combined in ways that purposefully sacrifices its contextual integrity to produce meaning through manipulation and experimental combinations. This includes Brett Morgen's films *Montage of Heck* and *Moonage Daydream* as well as *The Filth and the Fury* (2000), *The Velvet Underground* and *Sisters with Transistors* (2020).

3 I have previously discussed this aspect of found footage as it pertains to mockumentary horror (see Wallace 2021b).

4 Although there are some monochrome shots in the performance sequences of *Homecoming*, monochrome images are much more readily apparent in the behind-the-scenes sequences, aligning the 'informative' strand of the film with black-and-white, as they do in the backstage sequences of *Truth or Dare*, *Rattle and Hum* (1988) and *Shine a Light* (2008).

5 The recordings were used as the basis of a number of biographies of Holiday, including those by Robert O'Meally (2000) and Julia Blackburn (2006), however this is the first time that they have been *heard* by the public.

6 I say 'potential' here, as ineffectual colourization processes can produce their own uncanny effects. See, for example, Grainge's (1999) work on Ted Turner's endeavours to colourize Hollywood classics in the 1980s.
7 For an overview of the introduction of colour television in the UK, see Helen Wheatley (2016: 56–75).
8 Most other surviving television of this era remains because it was telerecorded on 16mm film for preservation or for the purpose of overseas sales (see Bryant 1989; Molesworth 2013).
9 Possibly this is an aesthetic decision enforced *by* the technical limitations of the original moving images.
10 Diaries and notebooks are important means through which insight into Eilish's, Gomez's, Halliwell's and Swift's mental health and relationship with fame are accessed and managed by these documentaries.
11 The 'pet' theme is also evident in *My Mind and Me* where Selena Gomez's dog plays a prominent part.
12 This is also the case with Swift, where close family members – and especially her mother – are a key part of her touring entourage and management team.
13 Eilish's fandom of *The Office* is most apparent in her song 'My Strange Addiction' which samples dialogue from the seventh season episode 'Threat Level Midnight'. See Mills (2004) and Wallace (2019: 119) for more on the style of mockumentary sitcoms.
14 The notion that a subject might 'forget' the presence of the camera crew is another rhetorical trope of direct cinema. Most famous is Richard Leacock's claim about Kennedy forgetting his presence when filming *Primary* (1960), a notion that Bruzzi describes as naïve (2006: 74).
15 Examples of this are numerous and include sequences in *Amy*, *Ed Sheeran: The Sum of It All*, *How I'm Feeling Now*, *Miss Americana*, *My Mind and Me*, *Never Say Never* (2011) and *Part of Me*.
16 For instance, the famous 'Subterranean Homesick Blues' sequence which opens *Dont Look Back* was the last thing shot by Pennebaker for the film. *Gimme Shelter* is a complicated case as it actually concludes in the editing suite with Mick Jagger and Charlie Watts reviewing the Altamont footage, faced with the fatal repercussions of the decision-making that has been the focus of much of the rest of the film. However, the theme of departure remains present in the final freeze-frame of Jagger leaving the editing suite and the final montage of footage of the Altamont crowd dispersing that is shown as the credits roll.
17 The television special eventually became a cinematically released documentary in order to fulfil the band's three-picture contract with United Artists (Doggett 2010: 93).
18 Of course, we do not know for sure that these moments weren't staged.

3 Songwriting

1. Different cuts of *The Beatles Anthology* were broadcast in different international territories. For the purposes of this book, I am referring to the eight-part DVD version which is the most accessible. However, McCartney's comments appear in the third episode of the six-part UK television version, broadcast 10 December 1995.
2. Long and Barber give other examples of songs that have arrived in a similarly serendipitous manner. Dan Wilson recalls dreaming Semisonic's hit 'Secret Smile' and Jimmy Webb suggests that writing occasionally happens so directly that it's like 'a wind blew through the room and left a song on the piano' (2017: 562). A particularly detailed account of the writing of 'Yesterday', which challenges the 'magical' framing of the composition, can be found in Phillip McIntrye and Paul Thompson's work (2021: 73–105).
3. I will use the word 'magical' throughout this chapter to refer to a paradigm of songwriting storytelling that implies that a song was not the product of labour.
4. The *Miss Americana* and *Charlie Is My Darling* sequences also benefit from the songs being collaborations and both involve one partner (Swift and Jagger, respectively) explaining the logic and meaning of their work to the other. Similar sequences can be seen in *Billie Eilish: The World's a Little Blurry* (2021), where Billie and her brother Finneas talk through decisions being made about specific lyrics. This creates an articulation of meaning that can be filmed that is less likely to occur if an artist is working alone.
5. Thompson places such occurrences within a 'systems approach to creativity' that stresses the broad range of fields that influence and inflect the creation of songs (Thompson 2019: 117–47).
6. McCartney's improvisations took place on 7 January 1969 (Sulpy and Schweighardt 2003: 94) was developed further on 9 and 13 January (2003: 168–9) and was not ready to record until 23 January (2003: 246–52). The final version was not recorded until 27 January (2003: 305–6).
7. Both *Let It Be* and *Get Back* feature moments where the arrangement of songs *does* precipitate crises, such as the infamous argument between Harrison and McCartney about how the guitar parts on 'Two of Us' should be arranged, and Harrison subsequently walking out of the band.
8. Prior to Busbee's untimely death in 2019, he and his partner Ben West wrote under the name GoNorthToGoSouth.
9. The original film can be found on the website of the production company, BX Films (2010).
10. Ironically, one of the most in-depth examinations of the process of song production, Jean-Luc Godard's *Sympathy for the Devil* (1968), doesn't even provide a focus on

progress. The musical sections of the film are composed of a handful of long takes of the Rolling Stones recording their well-known song at Olympic Studios in London. However, in-keeping with the wider political and aesthetic approach of Godard's film, the order of the sequences is not explicitly chronological and, as Shaun Inouye notes, 'the film's titular song, at least in Godard's original cut, remains frustratingly incomplete' (2013: 148).

11 A mumble track is where a songwriter sings a nonsense lyric – or sometimes just sounds – that fit an existing melody, 'carving towards words, and then words with meaning' (Tweedy 2020: 136, 140–2).

12 As well as his composition of choral works and musical theatre, Goodall is well known for composing the theme tunes to television series such as *Blackadder* (1983-1989), *Red Dwarf* (1988–9, 2009–20) and *The Vicar of Dibley* (1994–2007) and presenting factual programmes on music history and theory including *Howard Goodall's Choir Works* (1998), *How Music Works* (2006) and *Howard Goodall's Story of Music* (2013).

13 The first episode of *The Life of Rock with Brian Pern* (2014), for instance, features Matt Lucas as now-deaf record producer Ray Thomas, who fails to show off his work with the band Thotch because he is unable to hear that he is playing the wrong sounds from the mixing desk.

14 'Strawberry Fields Forever' is not on the *Sgt. Pepper* album but was one of the first songs recorded during the recording sessions for the album. For an extended discussion of the creation of the song, see Thompson (2019: 117–47).

15 The poster for 'Being for the Benefit of Mr. Kite' is the subject of a documentary short of its own called *Lennon's Poster* (2012).

16 A similar structure, though with more problematic outcomes, is evident in the PJ Harvey documentary *A Dog Called Money* (2019), where we see Harvey travelling to Afghanistan, Kosovo and deprived areas of Washington, DC, to gather inspiration for her *The Hope Six Demolition Project* album. We are given no insight into how Harvey translated this inspiration into song form, and instead move directly to the recording and production process which took the form of an art installation at Somerset House, with Harvey and her band recording inside a glass box as a paying audience filed past. This approach is troubling in this instance, because the lack of meditation on the creative process of writing leaves Harvey's travelogue open to accusations of poverty/trauma tourism and cultural appropriation.

17 A demo version of the song recorded by Lennon at home is included on the *Beatles Anthology 2* album and shows that large portions of the song were, indeed, in place by the time Lennon presented it to Martin.

18 For a broader discussion of television's spectacular qualities, see Wheatley (2016: 1–20).

19 We can see similar instances in McCartney having written the whole of the *Band on the Run* album prior to the start of recording (Kozinn and Sinclair 2022: 602). Similarly, his drive to match the sound in his imagination in the recording studio caused significant friction with fellow band members George Harrison (The Beatles) and Henry McCullough (Wings) who both felt their creativity being stifled by playing pre-determined guitar parts (Kozinn and Sinclair 2022: 671). A counter example is evident, however, in Alan Parsons's and Glynn Johns's accounts of the making of the *Red Rose Speedway* album, which Johns felt was undisciplined and which led to Parsons suggesting that McCartney was 'not very good at describing what it is he's after' (Kozinn and Sinclair 2022: 386–7, 468).

20 This version was issued on the *Beatles Anthology 2* compilation.

21 According to Ian MacDonald, the players were Tony Fisher, Greg Bowen, Derek Watkins and Stanley Roderick (trumpets), and John Hall, Derek Simpson and Normal Jones (cellos) (2005: 212).

22 This is a different approach to that taken in the sequences dedicated to 'Penny Lane' and 'A Day in the Life' where the contributions of instrumentalists *are* highlighted because of the novelties – and thus the availability of stories – apparent within their respective scores. For 'Penny Lane' this concerned McCartney seeing David Mason paying a piccolo trumpet on an episode of BBC2's *Masterworks* (1966–7) series and then asking him to play a part that was in a difficult register (Lewisohn 1989: 240–1). For 'A Day in the Life' this concerned the 'orgasmic' orchestral crescendo that appears twice in the song. This was recorded in a five hour session with a forty-piece orchestra and is – not coincidentally – the source of the only moving image footage of the *Sgt. Pepper* recording sessions (Lewisohn 1989: 244–5).

23 The idea that the methods of production of recorded music are not determined by the technologies used, but also shapes the subsequent development of those technologies can be found in Julien (1999). There is something of an over-simplification in *Musical Revolution*'s account because although the idea of changing the speeds of two separate recordings and joining them together *was* novel, Townsend's vari-speed function (also sometimes referred to as a 'frequency oscillator' or 'frequency changer') was *not* invented specifically to complete this task, but had been created earlier in 1966 as a component in Townsend's Artificial Double Tracking (ADT) system. This had been used on a number of Beatles songs earlier in 1966 including 'Tomorrow Never Knows', 'Doctor Robert', 'Taxman' and 'I'm Only Sleeping' (Everett 1999: 34, 45, 48, 50; Julien 1999: 361; Lewisohn 1989: 70, 74).

24 An example of this is an interview that Damon Albarn gave to the *Los Angeles Times* (Wood 2022) in which he claimed that Taylor Swift did not write her own songs, largely because most of them are co-written. The incident was unusual because despite largely ignoring such criticism, Swift responded quickly to the 'damaging'

(Horton and Snapes 2022) claims, perhaps because they make the commercial labour of songwriting visible and challenge Swift's status as aligning with the 'mythical' conceptualization of the songwriter. The incident also raises a number of facets, including Albarn's presumption that Swift is not inherently the author of her work (presumably because she is a woman working in pop). This relates to the earlier discussion of the separation of song and recording in that it foregrounds the question of *where* and *when* the writing takes place within the chain of song creation; the attack on 'co-written' songs implying that the writing and production are synonymous. Swift has made previous attempts to address such accusations, such as by foregrounding her *Speak Now* album as being entirely self-written, and the inclusion of 'voice memos' on the extended version of her *1989* album, which demonstrate that a number of the songs were well developed *prior* to their recording. Myles McNutt argues that their release was part of a larger discursive project to emphasize Swift's authorship of the *1989* material (2020).

25 The writers of TLC's hit 'No Scrubs' – Kandi Burruss, Tameka Cottle and Kevin Briggs – were given co-writing credits on 'Shape of You' after similarities were identified between the chorus of 'No Scrubs' and the bridge of Sheeran's song. In a *New York Times* video, Sheeran claims that the borrowing was a deliberate decision in order to play up the R'n'B 'feel' of the track, though the co-writing credit was not agreed until after the song's release. (BBC Newsbeat 2017; Beldy et al. 2017).

26 One could argue that Sheeran lacks an appreciation of metaphor, which is more prominent in the 'love yourself' version of the lyric, though this would be to read against the grain of the film.

27 Sheeran has claimed that 'Shape of You' was initially intended as a duet between Rhianna and Rudimental and the session also produced songs recorded by Tim McGraw and Faith Hill ('The Rest of Our Life') and Liam Payne ('Strip that Down') (Beldy et al. 2017).

28 For example, the signature keyboard melody was Steve Mac's creation (Beldy et al. 2017).

4 Fans

1 This foundational work includes, but is not limited to Amesley (1989), Bacon-Smith (1992), Fiske (1992), Jenkins (1992) and Tulloch and Jenkins (1995).

2 Jensen's name is mis-spelled as 'Jenson' in the original publication. I have used the correct spelling here.

3 *Our Hobby Is Depeche Mode* was originally produced with the title *The Posters Came from the Walls*. For consistency I will refer to the film under its current name.

4 The notion that fandom is performative can be found in Matt Hills's argument that fandom 'is an identity which is (dis-)claimed, and which performs cultural work' (2010: x) and in Jones's argument that intra-fandom antagonism can be understood as competing paradigms of fan performance vying for dominance (2016: 61).

5 The narrative of *Mission to Lars*, which Duffett is writing about, revolves entirely around a quest by Kate and Will Spicer to secure a meeting between Metallica drummer Lars Ulrich and their brother Tom, who suffers from Fragile X Syndrome.

6 In general, this remains an example of intimacy at a distance, and this is as much a performance for the camera as it is for the fans. This is addressed in some of the interviews with Swift, but is even more evident in *Katy Perry: Part of Me* (2012), where the fan meet-and-greets become laborious and start to conflict with Perry's exhaustion and emotional fragility.

7 I use the term 'negotiated reading' here in line with ideas proposed by Stuart Hall (2018) and integrated into discussions of fan behaviour by Henry Jenkins (2018: 14–16).

8 It is significant that idol culture values the 'sweetness and purity' of adolescence more than superstar qualities, and that being 'above average in appearance, ability and charm' is valued, but only as long as it is 'just enough to give the illusion that "you can also be a star if you try hard enough"' (Herd 1984: 78).

9 This is the second episode of the series, the first being a programme overview.

10 This is not to suggest that rock music excludes women entirely. This is patently untrue and there has always been a vibrant community of female rock performers who have played the rock 'game' as well as any of their male contemporaries (Debbie Harry, Pat Benatar, Chrissie Hynde, Pauline Black, Rhoda Dakar, Viv Albertine and the Slits, Patti Smith, Poly Styrene and Courtney Love come immediately to mind, as well as journalists like Annie Nightingale). Nevertheless, the discourses around rock *have* tended to prioritize traditionally masculine values and female acceptance within the world of rock has not always been straightforward.

11 There were also genuine concerns for the band's safety.

12 See, for example, Caroline Coon's recognition that Status Quo is often 'written off as lame-brained and limited' (2013).

13 Rebecca Williams highlights other examples of 'stereotypical' fan behaviours in *Pulp: A Film about Life, Death & Supermarkets*, particularly the individual who 'declares "Jarvis Cocker, I love you" while making a heart shape with her fingers' to the camera (2016: 26). Such performances draw on conventions of fan behaviours circulated within media images, and thus can be understood to be shaped *by* and *for* the documentary, but also for the public space in which the performance is enacted.

14 That these are now in a box rather than on her wall is, of course, emblematic of her life-stage. The fan engagement remains – the posters are still in her possession – but is no longer so visible.

15 There is an interesting parallel, here, with Lauren Jade Thompson's (2013) work on post-feminist masculinity in the Hollywood romcom, and especially the relationship between the gendered space of the 'mancave' as a signal of juvenile behaviour.

16 This moment has particular resonance now that Sound It Out has, indeed, closed following Butchart's death in 2023. Shane was present in the shop when Butchart was taken ill and cared for him until the paramedics arrived (Doran and Finlay 2023).

17 One reasons that Jeremy Deller gives for why *Our Hobby Is Depeche Mode* was not released by the band as intended was a perception by the band's record company that prioritizing certain well-known fans – especially a German couple 'who dress their children up as members of the band and … manage to get tickets for the press launches of albums [and] private meet and greets' (Deller n.d.) – might have led to fan resentment and negative feedback.

18 Channel 4's commissioning guidelines have a specific section relating to 'shock-docs' that states 'we've always got an appetite for shock-docs e.g. *Dogging Tales* (2013), *The Paedophile Hunter* (2014) or *Secrets of the Living Dolls* (2014). These films create "water-cooler" moments and generate brilliant headlines, but they need to feel privileged rather than grubby' (Channel 4 n.d.).

19 *I Used to Be Normal* has this potential too, but there is a difference in that the phrase comes directly from one of the participants – Elif – who makes the comment ironically and reflects on it within the film. Furthermore, the film challenges the notion of 'normality' by showing firstly that continued, shifting fan engagement *is* normal: 'How can it be insignificant when everybody does it?' Susan asks at one point.

20 Indications of this approach to sound-making can be seen in the band's mid-1980s television appearances On *Top of the Pops* (1964–2006), Martin Gore can be seen banging an oil can with a mallet for 'People Are People' (1984) and striking parts of a shopping trolley during their performance of 'Shake the Disease' (1985). The performance of 'Blasphemous Rumours' (1984) on the German programme *Thommy's Pop Show* (1982–4) includes Gore hitting a metal pole and a bicycle wheel with a drumstick and Alan Wilder hitting concrete breeze blocks with a sledgehammer.

21 This also goes some way towards explaining the band's relative lack of success in the UK, because the band's music is not so sympathetic to British pop sensibilities.

22 I have written about this moment in *101* in more detail elsewhere (Wallace 2021a: 208–11).

References

Altman, R. (1987), *The American Film Musical*, Bloomington: Indiana University Press.
Amesley, C. (1989), 'How to Watch Star Trek', *Cultural Studies*, 3 (3): 323–39.
Andrews, H. (2017), 'From Unwilling Celebrity to Authored Icon: Reading *Amy* (Kapadia, 2015)', *Celebrity Studies*, 8 (2): 351–4.
Andrews, H. (2021), *Biographical Television Drama*, Cham: Palgrave Macmillan.
Ang, I. (1985), *Watching Dallas: Soap Opera and the Melodramatic Imagination*, London: Methuen.
Aoyagi, H. (2005), *Islands of Eight Million Smiles: Idol Performance and Symbolic Production in Contemporary Japan*, Cambridge: Harvard University Press.
Apple TV+ Press (2020), 'Apple Original Films Releases Trailer and Premiere Date for *Billie Eilish: The World's A Little Blurry*', *Apple TV+ Press (United Kingdom)*. Available online: https://web.archive.org/web/20210421155955/https://www.apple.com/uk/tv-pr/news/2020/12/apple-original-films-releases-trailer-and-premiere-date-for-billie-eilish-the-worlds-a-little-blurry/ (accessed 8 April 2022).
Askwith, I., B. Lundin and A. Romano (2017), 'Industry/Fan Relations: A Conversation', in M. A. Click and S. Scott (eds), *The Routledge Companion to Media Fandom*, 123–31, London: Routledge.
Asquith, D. (2016), 'Crazy about One Direction: Whose Shame Is It Anyway?', in L. Bennett and P. Booth (eds), *Seeing Fans: Representations of Fandom in Media and Popular Culture*, 79–88, New York: Bloomsbury Academic.
Auslander, P. (1999), *Liveness: Performance in a Mediatized Culture*, London: Routledge.
Auslander, P. (2006a), 'Musical Personae', *The Drama Review*, 50 (1): 100–19.
Auslander, P. (2006b), 'Music as Performance: Living in the Immaterial World', *Theatre Survey*, 47 (2): 261–9.
Austin, T. (2016), 'Interiority, Identity and the Limits of Knowledge in Documentary Film', *Screen*, 57 (4): 414–30.
B. X. Films (2010), 'GoNorthToGoSouth', *Vimeo*, 28 May. Available online: https://vimeo.com/12122111 (accessed 18 December 2023).
Bacon-Smith, C. (1992), *Enterprising Women: Television Fandom and the Creation of Popular Myth*, Philadelphia: University of Pennsylvania Press.
Bailey, A. (2019), 'Selena Gomez's "Lose You to Love Me" Lyrics Are Her Goodbye to Justin Bieber', *ELLE*, 23 October. Available online: https://web.archive.org/web/20191023203347/https://www.elle.com/culture/music/a29553902/selena-gomez-lose-you-to-love-me-lyrics-meaning-justin-bieber/ (accessed 18 December 2023).

Baker, M. B. (2011), 'Rockumentary: Style, Performance & Sound in a Documentary Genre', PhD Thesis, Montréal: McGill University.

Baker, M. B. (2014), 'Notes on the Rockumentary Renaissance', *Cinephile: The University of British Columbia's Film Journal*, 10 (1): 4–10.

Baker, M. B. (2015), 'Martin Scorsese and the Music Documentary', in A. Baker (ed.), *A Companion to Martin Scorsese*, 239–58, Chichester: John Wiley.

Baron, J. (2012), 'The Archive Effect: Archival Footage as an Experience of Reception', *Projections*, 6 (2): 102–20.

Bassett, J. (2016), 'Who Is Justin Bieber's "Love Yourself" About?', *NME*, 29 March. Available online:https://web.archive.org/web/20161022170439/https://www.nme.com/blogs/nme-blogs/who-is-justin-biebers-love-yourself-about-an-nme-investigation-769216 (accessed 18 December 2023).

BBC Newsbeat (2017), 'No Scrubs Writers given Credit on Ed Sheeran's Shape of You', *BBC News*, 21 March. Available online: https://web.archive.org/web/20210414152456/https://www.bbc.com/news/newsbeat-39336424 (accessed 18 December 2023).

Beattie, K. (2004), *Documentary Screens: Non-Fiction Film and Television*, Houndmills: Palgrave Macmillan.

Beattie, K. (2005), 'It's Not Only Rock and Roll: "Rockumentary", Direct Cinema, and Performative Display', *Australasian Journal of American Studies*, 24 (2): 21–41.

Beattie, K. (2008), *Documentary Display: Re-Viewing Nonfiction Film and Video*, London: Wallflower.

Beattie, K. (2019), *Dont Look Back*, London: A BFI book published by Palgrave.

Beldy, T., A. DeSantis, A. Eaton, E. Grothjan and G. Roberts (2017), '"Shape of You": Making 2017's Biggest Track', *New York Times*, 9 December. Available online: https://web.archive.org/web/20231218131914/https://www.nytimes.com/video/arts/music/100000005469604/ed-sheeran-shape-of-you.html (accessed 15 December 2023).

Belloni, M. (2023), 'How the Swiftie Cinematic Universe Came to Theaters', *Puck*, 1 September. Available online: https://web.archive.org/web/20230901054631/https://puck.news/how-the-swiftie-cinematic-universe-came-to-theaters/ (accessed 2 October 2023).

Bennett, A. (2006), 'Punk's Not Dead: The Continuing Significance of Punk Rock for an Older Generation of Fans', *Sociology*, 40 (2): 219–35.

Bennett, A. and S. Baker (2016), 'Classic Albums: The Re-Presentation of the Rock Album on British Television', in I. Inglis (ed.), *Popular Music and Television in Britain*, 41–53, Abingdon: Routledge.

Bennett, L. (2020), 'Resisting Technology in Music Fandom: Nostalgia, Authenticity, and Kate Bush's "Before the Dawn"', in J. Gray, C. Sandvoss and C. L. Harrington (eds), *Fandom, Second Edition*, 127–42, New York: New York University Press.

Bennett, L. and P. Booth (eds) (2016a), *Seeing Fans: Representations of Fandom in Media and Popular Culture*, New York: Bloomsbury Academic.

Bennett, L. and P. Booth (2016b), 'Interview with Jeanie Finlay, Director of *Sound It Out* (2011)', in L. Bennett and P. Booth (eds), *Seeing Fans: Representations of Fandom in Media and Popular Culture*, 263–66, New York: Bloomsbury Academic.

Berlant, L. (1998), 'Intimacy: A Special Issue', *Critical Inquiry*, 24 (2): 281–88.

Bingham, D. (2010), *Whose Lives Are They Anyway? The Biopic as Contemporary Film Genre*, New Brunswick: Rutgers University Press.

Blackburn, J. (2006), *With Billie: A New Look at the Unforgettable Lady Day*, New York: Vintage Books.

Booth, P. and L. Bennett (2016), 'Introduction: Seeing Fans', in L. Bennett and P. Booth (eds), *Seeing Fans: Representations of Fandom in Media and Popular Culture*, 1–9, New York: Bloomsbury Academic.

Bordwell, D. (2002), 'Intensified Continuity Visual Style in Contemporary American Film', *Film Quarterly*, 55 (3): 16–28.

Bordwell, D., K. Thompson and J. Smith (2019), *Film Art: An Introduction*, 12th edn, New York: Mc-Graw-Hill.

Brett Morgen [@brettmorgen] (2023a), 'To Create the Concert Scenes in Moonage Daydream, We Had to Separate the Music Stems from the Room and the Crowds. To Create Authentic Reverb, the Sound Team Rented a Football Stadium and Played the Full Mix through the PA, Recording the Ambience on 12 Mics. Here's Jean Genie!', *Twitter*, Tweet, https://web.archive.org/web/20230131181545/https://twitter.com/brettmorgen/status/1612938826741342208 (accessed 18 December 2023).

Brett Morgen [@brettmorgen] (2023b), 'Moonage Daydream Is Designed to Be an Immersive Experience. We Recorded Crowds for Every Performance so We Could Surround the Viewer in Atmos and 12.0 Existing Archival Audio Was Blended w/ New Multitrack Recordings. Here's @NHartstone Directing Group for Station to Station', *Twitter*, Tweet, https://web.archive.org/web/20230130181751/https://twitter.com/brettmorgen/status/1613208589077999616 (accessed 18 December 2023).

Brown, T. and B. Vidal (2014), *The Biopic in Contemporary Film Culture*, New York: Routledge.

Brueggemann, T. (2023), 'Don't Blame Me: Taylor Swift Concert Film and AMC Infuriates Studios, Creates Chaos', *IndieWire*, 31 August. Available online: https://web.archive.org/web/20230901010748/https://www.indiewire.com/news/box-office/taylor-swift-the-eras-tour-amc-infuriates-studios-1234901227/ (accessed 18 December 2023).

Bruner, R. (2021), 'Here's Why Taylor Swift Is Re-Releasing Her Old Albums', *Time*, 25 March. Available online: https://web.archive.org/web/20210325210833/https://time.com/5949979/why-taylor-swift-is-rerecording-old-albums/ (accessed 2 October 2023).

Brunsdon, C. (1981), '"Crossroads" Notes on Soap Opera', *Screen*, 22 (4): 32–7.

Bruzzi, S. (2006), *New Documentary*, 2nd edn, London: Routledge.

Bryant, S. (1989), *The Television Heritage: Television Archiving Now and in an Uncertain Future*, London: BFI Pub.

Burmeister, D. and S. Lange (2017), *Depeche Mode: Monument*, trans. L. R. Jones, New York: Akashic Books.

Burns, L. and J. Watson (2013), 'Spectacle and Intimacy in Live Concert Film: Lyrics, Music, Staging, and Film Mediation in P!Nk's *Funhouse Tour* (2009)', *Music, Sound, and the Moving Image*, 7 (2): 103–40.

Busse, K. (2013), 'Geek Hierarchies, Boundary Policing, and the Gendering of the Good Fan', *Participations: Journal of Audience & Reception Studies*, 10 (1): 73–91.

Butler, J. (1990), *Gender Trouble: Feminism and the Subversion of Identity*, New York: Routledge.

Butler, J. (1993), *Bodies That Matter: On the Discursive Limits of 'Sex'*, New York: Routledge.

Byrne, D. (2013), *How Music Works*, Edinburgh: Canongate Books.

Byrne, D., J. Demme C. Frantz, J. Harrison and T. Weymouth (2009), *Stop Making Sense*, [DVD Commentary], Palm Pictures.

Cain, S. (2024), 'Chappell Roan Blasts "Entitled" Fans for "Creepy Behaviour" amid Her Rapid Rise in Fame', *The Guardian*, 20 August. Available online: Chappell Roan blasts 'entitled' fans for 'creepy behaviour' amid her rapid rise in fame | Chappell Roan | The Guardian (accessed 11 September 2024).

CalHx (2017), 'Justin Bieber's "Love Yourself" May Have Been Inspired By One Of Selena Gomez's Tattoos', *Genius*, 12 February. Available online: https://web.archive.org/web/20170612005833/https://genius.com/a/justin-bieber-s-love-yourself-may-have-been-inspired-by-one-of-selena-gomez-s-tattoos (accessed 21 May 2021).

Capital FM (2015), 'EXCLUSIVE: Justin Bieber Tells Us ALL About His Ed Sheeran Song. We've Got ACTUAL Chills!', *Capital*, 23 October. Available online: https://web.archive.org/web/20151024173701/https://www.capitalfm.com/artists/justin-bieber/news/ed-sheeran-new-song/ (accessed 20 May 2021).

Caves, R. E. (2003), 'Contracts between Art and Commerce', *The Journal of Economic Perspectives*, 17 (2): 73–84.

Cavicchi, D. (1998), *Tramps like Us: Music & Meaning among Springsteen Fans*, New York: Oxford University Press.

Chanan, M. (2013), 'Music, Documentary, Music Documentary', in B. Winston (ed.), *The Documentary Film Book*, 337–44, London: British Film Institute.

Channel 4 (n.d.), 'Documentaries', *Channel 4*. Available online: https://web.archive.org/web/20230609041339/https://www.channel4.com/commissioning/4producers/documentaries (accessed 21 December 2023).

Chapman, W. (2023), 'Taylor Swift's Concert Film Has Changed the Theatrical Release Dates of Five Movies – So Far', *IndieWire*, 8 September. Available online: https://web.archive.org/web/20230912230954/https://www.indiewire.com/gallery/taylor-swift-eras-tour-movie-release-date-changes/ (accessed 18 December 2023).

Choi, J. and R. Maliangkay (2014), 'Introduction: Why Fandom Matters to the International Rise of K-Pop', in J. Choi and R. Maliangkay (eds), *K-Pop: The International Rise of the Korean Music Industry*, 1–18, New York: Routledge.

Clarke, P. (1983), '"A Magic Science": Rock Music as a Recording Art', *Popular Music*, 3: 195–213.

Coates, N. (2003), 'Teenyboppers, Groupies, and Other Grotesques: Girls and Women and Rock Culture in the 1960s and Early 1970s', *Journal of Popular Music Studies*, 15 (1): 65–94.

Cole, P. (2013), 'Searching for Detroit', *Safundi*, 14 (4): 476–81.

Concord (n.d.), 'Concord and Billie Holiday Estate Partner on James Erskine's Documentary Billie', *Concord*. Available online: https://web.archive.org/web/20200813062609/https://concord.com/concord-news/concord-and-billie-holiday-estate-partner-on-james-erskines-documentary-billie/ (accessed 21 June 2022).

Coon, C. (2013), 'Status Quo: "We're Not Musicians – We're Players!"', *The Guardian*, 27 November. Available online: https://web.archive.org/web/20131127154149/https://www.theguardian.com/music/2013/nov/27/status-quo-rocks-backpages-classic-interview (accessed 21 September 2023).

Cooper, S. (2006), *Selfless Cinema? Ethics and French Documentary*, London: Legenda.

Corner, J. (1995), *Television Form and Public Address*, London: Edward Arnold.

Corner, J. (2003), 'Television, Documentary and the Category of the Aesthetic', *Screen*, 44 (1): 92–100.

Corner, J. and A. Rosenthal (2005), 'Introduction', in A. Rosenthal and J. Corner (eds), *New Challenges for Documentary*, 2. ed, 1–13, Manchester: Manchester University Press.

Cousins, M. and K. Macdonald (2005), *Imagining Reality: The Faber Book of Documentary*, Rev. edn, London: Faber.

Davies, S. (2012), 'Searching for Sugar Man', *Sight and Sound*, 22 (8): 70.

Deller, J. (n.d.), 'Jeremy Deller – Our Hobby Is Depeche Mode'. Available online: https://web.archive.org/web/20230529190814/http://www.jeremydeller.org/OurHobbyIsDepechMode/OurHobbyIsDepecheMode_Video.php (accessed 6 August 2021).

Deseret News. (2007), 'Hannah Montana Adds Second Salt Lake Tour Date', *Deseret News*, 19 October. Available online: https://web.archive.org/web/20211021202335/https://www.deseret.com/2007/10/19/20048282/hannah-montana-adds-second-salt-lake-tour-date (accessed 17 November 2022).

Doggett, P. (2010), *You Never Give Me Your Money: The Battle for the Soul of the Beatles*, London: Vintage Books.

Doherty, T. (1985), 'Stop Making Sense', *Film Quarterly*, 38 (4): 12–16.

Donahue, A. (2008), 'Screen Sirens: "Hannah Montana," U2 Use A New Generation of Concert Films to Lure Audiences', *Billboard*, 23 February: 14.

Donnelly, K. J. (2013), 'Visualizing Live Albums: Progressive Rock and the British Concert Film in the 1970s', in R. Edgar, K. Fairclough-Isaacs and B. Halligan (eds),

The Music Documentary: Acid Rock to Electropop, 171–82, London: Taylor & Francis Group.

Donnelly, K. J. (2015), *Magical Musical Tour: Rock and Pop in Film Soundtracks*, New York: Bloomsbury Academic.

Donnelly, M. (2023), 'Beyonce in Final Talks to Release "Renaissance" Concert Film Through AMC Theatres Following Taylor Swift Deal (EXCLUSIVE)', *Variety*, 30 September. Available online: https://web.archive.org/web/20230930191143/https://variety.com/2023/film/news/beyonce-renaissance-concert-film-amc-theatres-1235741062/ (accessed 18 December 2023).

Doran, J. and J. Finlay (2023), 'Remembering Tom Butchart of Sound It Out Records', *The Quietus*, 19 July. Available online: https://thequietus.com/articles/33192-tom-butchart-sound-it-out-records-obituary (accessed 19 September 2023).

Doss, E. (1999), *Elvis Culture: Fans, Faith, & Image*, Lawrence: University Press of Kansas.

Douglas, E. (2021), 'Cinematographer Spotlight: Jenna Rosher Talks about Shooting the Billie Eilish Doc', *Below the Line*, 24 March. Available online: https://web.archive.org/web/20210324165553/https://www.btlnews.com/crafts/camera/jenna-rosher-billie-eilish/ (accessed 7 April 2022).

Duffett, M. (2013), 'Multiple Damnations: Deconstructing the Critical Response to Boy Band Phenomena', *Popular Music History*, 7 (2): 185–97.

Duffett, M. (2016), 'Beyond Exploitation Cinema: Music Fandom, Disability, and Mission to Lars', in L. Bennett and P. Booth (eds), *Seeing Fans: Representations of Fandom in Media and Popular Culture*, 13–22, New York: Bloomsbury Academic.

Duffett, M. (2017), 'I Scream Therefore I Fan? Music Audiences and Affective Citizenship', in J. Gray, C. Sandvoss and C. L. Harrington (eds), *Fandom: Identities and Communities in a Mediated World*, 143–56, New York: New York University Press.

Dyer, R. (1991), 'A Star Is Born and the Construction of Authenticity', in C. Gledhill (ed.), *Stardom: Industry of Desire*, 136–44, London: Routledge.

Dyer, R. (2002), *Only Entertainment*, 2nd edn, New York: Routledge.

Dyer, R. (2004), *Heavenly Bodies: Film Stars and Society*, 2nd edn, London: Routledge.

Edgar, R., K. Fairclough-Isaacs and B. Halligan, eds. (2013a), *The Music Documentary: Acid Rock to Electropop*, New York: Routledge.

Edgar, R., K. Fairclough-Isaacs and B. Halligan (2013b), 'Preface', in R. Edgar, K. Fairclough-Isaacs and B. Halligan (eds), *The Music Documentary: Acid Rock to Electropop*, xi–xvi, London: Taylor & Francis Group.

Edgar, R., K. Fairclough-Isaacs and B. Halligan (2013c), 'Introduction: Music Seen: The Formats and Functions of the Music Documentary', in R. Edgar, K. Fairclough-Isaacs and B. Halligan (eds), *The Music Documentary: Acid Rock to Electropop*, 1–21, London: Taylor & Francis Group.

Edgerton, G. R. (1997), '"Mystic Chords of Memory": The Cultural Voice of Ken Burns', in Gary Richard Edgerton, M. T. Marsden, J. G. Nachbar and Gary R. Edgerton (eds), *In the Eye of the Beholder: Critical Perspectives in Popular Film and Television*, 11–26, Bowling Green: Bowling Green State University Popular Press.

Ehrenreich, B., E. Hess and G. Jacobs (1987), *Re-Making Love. The Feminization of Sex*, London: Fontana.

Ellis, J. (1982), 'Star/Industry/Image', in C. Gledhill (ed.), *Star Signs: Papers from a Weekend Workshop*, 1–12, London: BFI Education.

Ellis, J. (1992), *Visible Fictions: Cinema, Television, Video*, Rev. edn, London: Routledge.

Ellis, J. (2012), *Documentary: Witness and Self-Revelation*, London: Routledge.

Erickson, D. (2021), 'New Lens Series. Revisiting RAM-McCartney's Eccentric Masterpiece (Pt 2). With Duncan Driver', *One Sweet Dream: A Beatles Podcast*, 27 March. Available online: https://web.archive.org/web/20230330140614/https://onesweetdreampodcast.com/episodes/new-lens-series-revisiting-rammccartneys-eccentric-masterpiece-pt-2-with-duncan-driver-107 (accessed 18 December 2023).

Everett, W. (1999), *The Beatles as Musicians: Revolver through the Anthology*, New York: Oxford University Press.

Fast, S. (2013), 'U2 3D: Concert Film and/as Live Performance', in N. Cook and R. Pettengill (eds), *Taking It to the Bridge: Music As Performance*, 20–36, Ann Arbor: University of Michigan Press.

Ferris, K. O. and S. R. Harris (2010), *Stargazing: Celebrity, Fame, and Social Interaction*, London: Routledge.

Feuer, J. (1977), 'The Self-reflective Musical and the Myth of Entertainment', *Quarterly Review of Film Studies*, 2 (3): 313–26.

Fiske, J. (1992), 'The Cultural Economy of Fandom', in L. A. Lewis (ed.), *The Adoring Audience: Fan Culture and Popular Media*, 30–49, London: Routledge.

Fossen, I. (2014), 'Buena Vista Social Club', *Senses of Cinema*, 72. Available online: https://web.archive.org/web/20141008113751/https://www.sensesofcinema.com/2014/cteq/buena-vista-social-club/ (accessed 18 December 2023).

Fraser, N. (2013), 'Foreword: Why Documentaries Matter', in B. Winston (ed.), *The Documentary Film Book*, x–xv, London: British Film Institute.

Freeman, L. (2018), 'Colouring in the Past', *The Spectator*, 4 August. Available online: https://web.archive.org/web/20200516133608/https://www.spectator.co.uk/article/colouring-in-the-past (accessed 11 April 2022).

Frith, S. (1989), 'Why Do Songs Have Words?', *Contemporary Music Review*, 5 (1): 77–96.

Frith, S. (2002), 'Look! Hear! The Uneasy Relationship of Music and Television', *Popular Music*, 21 (3): 277–90.

Gabbard, K. (1996), *Jammin' at the Margins: Jazz and the American Cinema*, Chicago: University of Chicago Press.

Galbraith, P. W. (2021), 'Idol Economics: Television, Affective and Virtual Models in Japan', in A. Hiroshi, P. W. Galbraith and M. Kovacic (eds), *Idology in Transcultural Perspective: Anthropological Investigations of Popular Idolatry*, 65–89, Cham: Palgrave Macmillan.

Gardner, A. and G. Moorey (2016), 'Raiders of the Lost Archives', *Popular Communication*, 14 (3): 169–77.
Garner, R. (2018), 'Not My Lifeblood: Autoethnography, Affective Fluctuations and Popular Music Antifandom', in P. Booth (ed.), *A Companion to Media Fandom and Fan Studies*, 91–106, Hoboken: Wiley Blackwell.
Garratt, S. (2007), 'Teenage Dreams', Reprinted, in S. Frith and A. Goodwin (eds), *On Record: Rock, Pop, and the Written Word*, 399–409, London: Routledge.
Goffman, E. (1971), *The Presentation of Self in Everyday Life*, London: Penguin Press.
Goode, I. (2015), 'Living with Fame: Geri and Livig with Michael Jackson', in S. Redmond (ed.), *The Star and Celebrity Confessional*, 68–81, London: Routledge.
Goodwin, A. (1992), *Dancing in the Distraction Factory: Music Television and Popular Culture*, Minneapolis: University of Minnesota Press.
Gorky, M. (2005), 'The Kingdom of Shadows', in M. Cousins and K. Macdonald (eds), *Imagining Reality: The Faber Book of Documentary*, Rev. edn, 6–10, London: Faber.
Grainge, P. (1999), 'Reclaiming Heritage: Colourization, Culture Wars and The Politics of Nostalgia', *Cultural Studies*, 13 (4): 621–38.
Grainge, P. (2002), *Monochrome Memories: Nostalgia and Style in Retro America*, Westport: Praeger.
Grant, C. (2012), 'The Numbers: Searching for Sugar Man', *Sight and Sound*, 22 (10): 19.
Gregory, G. (2019), *Boy Bands and the Performance of Pop Masculinity*, London: Routledge.
Grochowski, T. (2019), '"The Beginning of the Beginning of the End of the Beginning": *The Last Waltz* and/as Adaptation', *Literature/Film Quarterly*, 47 (3). Available online: https://lfq.salisbury.edu/_issues/47_3/the_beginning_of_the_end_of_the_beginning_the_last_waltz_adaptation.html (accessed 18 December 2023).
Guerrier, S. (2017), *The Evil of the Daleks*, Edinburgh: Obverse Books.
Gunning, T. (2006), 'The Cinema of Attraction[s]: Early Film, Its Spectator and the Avant-Garde', in W. Strauven (ed.), *The Cinema of Attractions Reloaded*, 381–8, Amsterdam: Amsterdam University Press.
Häkkänen-Nyholm, H. (2021), 'Bruce Springsteen Fan Behavior and Identification', *Psychology of Music*, 49 (4): 691–703.
Haleff, M. (1964), 'The Maysles Brothers and "Direct Cinema"', *Film Comment*, 2 (2): 19–23.
Hall, S. (2018), 'Encoding and Decoding in the Television Discourse', in D. Morley (ed.), *Essential Essays, Volume 1: Foundations of Cultural Studies*, 257–76, Durham: Duke University Press.
Hans, S. (2023), 'Stories in Unlikely Places: A Conversation with Jeanie Finlay', *The Criterion Collection*, 14 June. Available online: https://web.archive.org/web/20230614193121/https://www.criterion.com/current/posts/8174-stories-in-unlikely-places-a-conversation-with-jeanie-finlay (accessed 21 September 2023).
Harbert, B. J. (2018), *American Music Documentary: Five Case Studies of Ciné-Ethnomusicology*, Middletown: Wesleyan University Press.

Harrington, C. L. and D. D. Bielby (2010), 'A Life Course Perspective on Fandom', *International Journal of Cultural Studies*, 13 (5): 429–50.

Hassan, N. (2015), 'Hidden Fans? Fandom and Domestic Musical Activity', First issued in paperback, in M. Duffett (ed.), *Popular Music Fandom: Identities, Roles and Practices*, 55–70, New York: Routledge.

Helgesson, S. (2013), '*Sugar Man* and Anglo-Sweden', *Safundi*, 14 (4): 481–4.

Hemingway, T. (2021), 'The Aesthetics of Post-Broadcast Comedy Television', PhD Thesis, Coventry: University of Warwick.

Hepworth, D. (2018), *Nothing Is Real: The Beatles Were Underrated and Other Sweeping Statements about Pop*, London: Bantam Press.

Herd, J. A. (1984), 'Trends and Taste in Japanese Popular Music: A Case-Study of the 1982 Yamaha World Popular Music Festival', *Popular Music*, 4: 75–96.

Hernández, T. K. (2002), 'The Buena Vista Social Club: The Racial Politics of Nostalgia', in M. Habell-Pallán and M. Romero (eds), *Latino/a Popular Culture*, 61–72, New York: New York University Press.

Highmore, B. (2013), 'TV Times: Archive, Mood, Media', *Key Words: A Journal of Cultural Materialism*, (11): 44–57.

Hills, M. (2005), 'Patterns of Surprise: The "Aleatory Object" in Psychoanalytic Ethnography and Cyclical Fandom', *American Behavioral Scientist*, 48 (7): 801–21.

Hills, M. (2007), 'Michael Jackson Fans on Trial? "Documenting" Emotivism and Fandom in *Wacko About Jacko*', *Social Semiotics*, 17 (4): 459–77.

Hills, M. (2010), *Fan Cultures*, London: Routledge.

Hills, M. (2016), '"Twilight" Fans Represented in Commercial Paratexts and Inter-Fandoms: Resisting and Repurposing Negative Fan Stereotypes', in A. Morey (ed.), *Genre, Reception, and Adaptation in the 'Twilight' Series*, 113–29, London: Routledge.

Hodkinson, P. (2013), 'Spectacular Youth Cultures and Ageing: Beyond Refusing to Grow Up', *Sociology Compass*, 7 (1): 13–22.

Hopkins, M. and J. Treadwell (eds) (2014), *Football Hooliganism, Fan Behaviour and Crime*, London: Palgrave Macmillan UK.

Horton, A. (2021), 'I Used to Be Normal: A Boyband Fangirl Story Review – Tears, Squeals and Boundless Devotion', *The Guardian*, 27 May. Available online, https://web.archive.org/web/20210527082805/https://www.theguardian.com/film/2021/may/27/i-used-to-be-normal-a-boyband-fangirl-story-review-one-direction-beatles (accessed 19 December 2023).

Horton, A. and L. Snapes (2022), 'Taylor Swift Criticises Damon Albarn for Saying She Doesn't Write Her Own Songs', *The Guardian*, 25 January. Available online: https://web.archive.org/web/20220124215326/https://www.theguardian.com/music/2022/jan/24/taylor-swift-damon-albarn-write-own-songs (accessed 18 December 2023).

Huber, A. (2011), 'Remembering Popular Music, Documentary Style: Tony Palmer's History in All You Need Is Love', *Television & New Media*, 12 (6): 513–30.

Hyslop, J. (2013), '"Days of Miracle and Wonder"? Conformity and Revolt in *Searching for Sugar Man*', *Safundi*, 14 (4): 490–501.

Inouye, S. (2013), 'Indicting Truth: Jean-Luc Godard's Sympathy for the Devil and 1960s Documentary Cinema', *Studies in Documentary Film*, 7 (2): 147–60.

Irwin, C. (2021), 'Watch Paul McCartney Craft Beatles' "Get Back" in Two Minutes', *Ultimate Classic Rock*, 1 December. Available online: https://web.archive.org/web/20230204034456/https://ultimateclassicrock.com/paul-mccartney-beatles-get-back/ (accessed 26 October 2023).

Issari, M. A. and D. A. Paul (1979), *What Is Cinéma Vérité?*, Metuchen: Scarecrow Press.

Iversen, G. and S. MacKenzie, eds. (2021a), *Mapping the Rockumentary: Images of Sound and Fury*, Edinburgh: Edinburgh University Press.

Iversen, G. and S. MacKenzie (2021b), 'Introduction: Images of Sound and Fury', in G. Iversen and S. MacKenzie (eds), *Mapping the Rockumentary: Images of Sound and Fury*, 1–18, Edinburgh: Edinburgh University Press.

Jacobs, J. (2000), *The Intimate Screen: Early British Television Drama*, Oxford: Oxford University Press.

Jacobs, J. (2011), 'Television, Interrupted: Pollution or Aesthetic?', in J. Bennett and N. Strange (eds), *Television as Digital Media*, 255–80, Durham: Duke University Press.

James, D. E. (2016), *Rock 'n' Film: Cinema's Dance with Popular Music*, New York: Oxford University Press.

Jenkins, H. (1992), *Textual Poachers: Television Fans & Participatory Culture*, New York: Routledge.

Jenkins, H. (2018), 'Fandom, Negotiation, and Participatory Culture', in P. Booth (ed.), *A Companion to Media Fandom and Fan Studies*, 11–26, Hoboken: Wiley Blackwell.

Jenner, M. (2018), *Netflix and the Re-Invention of Television*, Cham: Springer International Publishing: Imprint: Palgrave Macmillan.

Jensen, J. (1992), 'Fandom as Pathology: The Consequences of Characterization', in L. A. Lewis (ed.), *The Adoring Audience: Fan Culture and Popular Media*, 9–29, London: Routledge.

Jones, B. (2016), '"I Will Throw You off Your Ship and You Will Drown and Die": Death Threats, Intra-Fandom Hate, and the Performance of Fangirling', in L. Bennett and P. Booth (eds), *Seeing Fans: Representations of Fandom in Media and Popular Culture*, 53–65, New York: Bloomsbury Academic.

Jones, M. (2002), 'The Music Industry as Workplace: An Approach to Analysis', in Beck, Andrew (ed.), *Cultural Work: Understanding the Cultural Industries*, 147–56, London: Taylor & Francis Group.

Jones, M. (2005), 'Writing for Your Supper – Creative Work and the Contexts of Popular Songwriting', in J. G. William (ed.), *Words and Music*, 219–50, Liverpool: University of Liverpool Press.

Joyrich, L. (1993), 'Elvisophilia: Knowledge, Pleasure, and the Cult of Elvis', *differences*, 5 (1): 73–91.

Julien, O. (1999), 'The Diverting of Musical Technology by Rock Musicians: The Example of Double-Tracking', *Popular Music*, 18 (3): 357–65.

Kael, P. (1970), 'Gimme Shelter', in M. Cousins and K. Macdonald (eds), *Imagining Reality: The Faber Book of Documentary*, 273–78, London: Faber and Faber.

Kael, P. (2016), 'Three Cheers', *DavidByrne.com*. Available online: https://web.archive.org/web/20160304123806/http://www.davidbyrne.com/archive/film/Stop_Making_Sense/s_m_s_press/s_m_s_pauline_kael_nyer.php (accessed 3 October 2023).

Kang, I. (2014), 'The Political Economy of Idols', in J. Choi and R. Maliangkay (eds), *K-Pop: The International Rise of the Korean Music Industry*, 51–65, New York: Routledge.

Kaplan, E. A. (1991), *Rocking around the Clock: Music Television, Postmodernism, and Consumer Culture*, New York: Routledge.

KATY PERRY [@katyperry] (2011), 'Remember, We're Filming Tonight for Our Tour DVD so Make Sure You WILD out for the Teevee! See You Soon.', *Twitter*, Tweet, 23 November. Available online: https://web.archive.org/web/20160304133617/https://twitter.com/katyperry/status/139528631197241344 (accessed 18 December 2023).

Kaufman, G. (2023), 'How Taylor Swift Filmed Her "Eras Tour" Movie in the Midst of the Hollywood Strike', *Billboard*, 31 August 2023. Available online: https://web.archive.org/web/20230901022417/https://www.billboard.com/music/music-news/taylor-swift-eras-tour-movie-hollywood-strike-1235404250/ (accessed 18 December 2023).

Kim, S.-Y. (2018), *K-Pop Live: Fans, Idols, and Multimedia Performance*, Stanford: Stanford University Press.

Kinik, A. (2021), 'Minimum and Maximum Rock "n" Roll: Nick Cave and the Bad Seeds and Rockumentary Form', in G. Iversen and S. MacKenzie (eds), *Mapping the Rockumentary: Images of Sound and Fury*, 198–211, Edinburgh: Edinburgh University Press.

Klein, A. A. (2021), *Millennials Killed the Video Star: MTV's Transition to Reality Programming*, Durham: Duke University Press.

Kolker, R. P. (1971), 'Circumstantial Evidence: An Interview with David and Albert Maysles', *Sight and Sound*, 40 (4): 183–6.

Kossakowski, R. (2021), *Hooligans, Ultras, Activists: Polish Football Fandom in Sociological Perspective*, Cham: Palgrave Macmillan.

Kozinn, A. and A. Sinclair (2022), *The McCartney Legacy. Volume 1, 1969–73*, New York: Dey St.

Krueger, A. B. (2005), 'The Economics of Real Superstars: The Market for Rock Concerts in the Material World', *Journal of Labor Economics*, 23 (1): 1–30.

Kuhn, A. (1978), 'Documentary: The Camera I Observations on Documentary', *Screen*, 19 (2): 71–84.

lauramarling [@lauramarling] (2020), 'Tutorial: Tap At My Window/ Nouel – Standard Tuning', *Instagram*, Reel, 24 March. Available online: https://www.instagram.com/reel/B-HiJ30DQoc/ (accessed 22 December 2023).

Lewisohn, M. (1989), *The Beatles: Recording Sessions*, New York: Harmony Books.

Lewsen, S. (2013), 'On Music, Censorship, and Globalization', *Safundi*, 14 (4): 455–66.

Locker, M. (2014), 'David Byrne and Jonathan Demme on The Making of Stop Making Sense', *Time*, 15 July. Available online: https://web.archive.org/web/20140715162305/https://time.com/2980989/stop-making-sense-anniversary-david-byrne-jonathan-demme/ (accessed 18 November 2022).

Lombardo, A. (2017), 'Fame and Chronic Pain: Lady Gaga's Hip Injury', *Medtruth*, 12 October. Available online: https://web.archive.org/web/20200925132918/https://medtruth.com/articles/health-features/lady-gaga-hip-injury/ (accessed 8 April 2022).

Long, P. and S. Barber (2015), 'Voicing Passion: The Emotional Economy of Songwriting', *European Journal of Cultural Studies*, 18 (2): 142–57.

Long, P. and S. Barber (2017), 'Conceptualizing Creativity and Strategy in the Work of Professional Songwriters', *Popular Music and Society*, 40 (5): 556–72.

Long, P. and T. Wall (2010), 'Constructing The Histories of Popular Music: The *Britannia* Series', in I. Inglis (ed.), *Popular Music And Television In Britain*, 11–26, London: Routledge.

Long, P. and T. Wall (2013), 'Tony Palmer's *All You Need I Love*: Television's First Pop History', in R. Edgar, K. Fairclough-Isaacs and B. Halligan (eds), *The Music Documentary: Acid Rock to Electropop*, Routledge music and screen media series, 25–41, New York: Routledge.

Lury, K. (2003), 'Closeup: Documentary Aesthetics', *Screen*, 44 (1): 101–5.

Lynch, J. (2014), 'Nick Cave Explains the Truth Behind His Staged Documentary "20,000 Days on Earth"', *Billboard*, 23 September. Available online: https://web.archive.org/web/20211218120223/https://www.billboard.com/music/music-news/nick-cave-explains-the-truth-behind-his-staged-documentary-20000-days-on-earth-6259198/ (accessed 20 October 2021).

MacCannell, D. (1973), 'Staged Authenticity: Arrangements of Social Space in Tourist Settings', *American Journal of Sociology*, 79 (3): 589–603.

MacDonald, I. (2005), *Revolution in the Head: The Beatles' Records and the Sixties*, 2nd rev. edn, London: Pimlico.

Mamber, S. (1972a), 'Cinema-Verite in America, Part I', *Screen*, 13 (2): 79–108.

Mamber, S. (1972b), 'Cinema-Verite in America: Part II – Direct Cinema and the Crisis Structure', *Screen*, 13 (3): 114–36.

Manning, E. (2016), 'Revisiting Madonna's 1991 "truth or Dare" Documentary with Its Director', 29 August. Available online: https://web.archive.org/web/20220928163555/https://i-d.vice.com/en/article/mbe84b/revisiting-madonnas-1991-truth-or-dare-documentary-with-its-director (accessed 18 October 2022).

Manovich, L. (2001), *The Language of New Media*, Cambridge: MIT Press.

Marcus, D. and S. Kara (2016), 'Introduction', in D. Marcus and S. Kara (eds), *Contemporary Documentary*, 1–6, London: Routledge.

Marquis, E. (2014), 'Conceptualizing Documentary Performance', *Studies in Documentary Film*, 7 (1): 45–60.

Marshall, C. (2021), 'Watch Paul McCartney Compose The Beatles Classic "Get Back" Out of Thin Air (1969)', *Open Culture*, 30 November. Available online: https://web.archive.org/web/20211201032257/https://www.openculture.com/2021/11/watch-paul-mccartney-compose-the-beatles-classic-get-back-out-of-thin-air-1969.html (accessed 18 December 2023).

Martin, G. and W. Pearson (1995), *Summer of Love*, London: Pan Books.

McElhaney, J. (2009), *Albert Maysles*, Urbana: University of Illinois Press.

McGee, M. (2011), *U2: A Diary*, London: Omnibus Press.

McIntyre, P. and P. Thompson (2021), *Paul McCartney and His Creative Practice: The Beatles and Beyond*, Cham: Palgrave Macmillan.

McNutt, M. (2020), 'From "Mine" to "Ours": Gendered Hierarchies of Authorship and the Limits of Taylor Swift's Paratextual Feminism', *Communication, Culture and Critique*, 13 (1): 72–91.

McVeigh, T. (2016), 'Lily Allen on Being Stalked: "I Was Asleep. He Steamed into the Bedroom and Started Screaming"', *The Observer*, 16 April. Available online: https://www.theguardian.com/music/2016/apr/16/lily-allen-stalked-singer-police (accessed 11 September 2024).

Miles, B. (1998), *Paul McCartney: Many Years from Now*, London: Vintage.

Miles, C. (1998), 'Spatial Politics: A Gendered Sense of Place', in S. Redhear, D. Wynne and J. O'Connor (eds), *The Clubcultures Reader: Readings in Popular Cultural Studies*, 48–59, Oxford: Blackwell.

Miller, J. (2008), *Stripped: Depeche Mode*, Updated edn, London: Omnibus.

Mills, B. (2004), 'Comedy Verite: Contemporary Sitcom Form', *Screen*, 45 (1): 63–78.

Mitchell, M. (2019), 'Beyonce Homecoming Documentary: Why Does Her Jumper Change Colour?', *Express.co.uk*, 23 April. Available online: https://web.archive.org/web/20190423193935/https://www.express.co.uk/entertainment/films/1117897/Beyonce-Homecoming-documentary-Netflix-yellow-pink-jumper-Balmain-BAC-costume (accessed 28 March 2023).

Modleski, T. (1979), 'The Search for Tomorrow in Today's Soap Operas: Notes on a Feminine Narrative Form', *Film Quarterly*, 33 (1): 12–21.

Molderings, H. (1984), 'Life Is No Performance: Performance by Jochen Gerz', in G. Battock and Rovert Nickas (eds), *The Art of Performance: A Critical Anthology*, 166–80, New York: E. P. Dutton.

Molesworth, R. (2013), *Wiped! Doctor Who's Missing Episodes*, Canterbury: Telos Publishing Ltd.

Murphy, P., J. Williams and E. Dunning (1990), *Football on Trial: Spectator Violence and Development in the Football World*, London: Routledge.

Neaverson, B. (1997), *The Beatles Movies*, New York: Cassell.

Negus, K. (1995), 'Where the Mystical Meets the Market: Creativity and Commerce in the Production of Popular Music', *The Sociological Review*, 43 (2): 316–41.

Negus, K. (1999), *Music Genres and Corporate Cultures*, London: Routledge.

Netflix Media Center (2017), 'Gaga: Five Foot Two', *Netflix Media Center*, 22 September. Available online: https://web.archive.org/web/20231218145602/https://media.netflix.com/en/only-on-netflix/80196586 (accessed 8 April 2022).

Netflix Media Center (2020), 'Miss Americana', *Netflix Media Center*, 31 January. Available online: https://web.archive.org/web/20221004233955/https://media.netflix.com/en/only-on-netflix/81028336 (accessed 8 April 2022).

Nichols, B. (1991), *Representing Reality: Issues and Concepts in Documentary*, Bloomington: Indiana University Press.

Nichols, B. (2016), *Speaking Truths with Film: Evidence, Ethics, Politics in Documentary*, Oakland: University of California Press.

Niebling, L. (2018), *Rockumentary: Theorie, Geschichte und Industrie*, Marburg: Schüren.

Niebling, L. (2021), '"I Don't Make Culture, I Sell It!": The Early History of Music Documentation, 1920s–1970s', in G. Iversen and S. MacKenzie (eds), *Mapping the Rockumentary: Images of Sound and Fury*, 24–36, Edinburgh: Edinburgh University Press.

O'Meally, R. G. (2000), *Lady Day: The Many Faces of Billie Holiday*, New York: Da Capo Press.

Palmer, L. (2023), 'Engineering the "Sense of Being There": Electronovision and the Invention of the Stage Performance Documentary', *Historical Journal of Film, Radio and Television*, 43 (4): 1157–82.

Papies, D. and H. J. van Heerde (2017), 'The Dynamic Interplay Between Recorded Music and Live Concerts: The Role of Piracy, Unbundling, and Artist Characteristics', *Journal of Marketing*, 81 (4), pp. 67–87.

Pennington, A. (2021), 'Jenna Rosher / *Billie Eilish: The World's a Little Blurry*', *British Cinematographer*, 19 May. Available online: https://web.archive.org/web/20220407102311/https://britishcinematographer.co.uk/jenna-rosher-billie-eilish-the-worlds-a-little-blurry/ (accessed 7 April 2022).

Perryman, M., ed. (2002), *Hooligan Wars: Causes and Effects of Football Violence*, New edn, Edinburgh: Mainstream.

Pillai, N. (2017), *Jazz as Visual Language: Film, Television and the Dissonant Image*, London: I.B. Tauris.

Piotrowska, A. (2014), *Psychoanalysis and Ethics in Documentary Film*, New York: Routledge.

Piper, H. (2016), 'Broadcast Drama and the Problem of Television Aesthetics: Home, Nation, Universe', *Screen*, 57 (2): 163–83.

Plantinga, C. (1987), 'Defining Documentary: Fiction, Nonfiction, and Projected Worlds', *Persistence of Vision*, (5): 44–54.

Plantinga, C. (2005), 'What a Documentary Is, After All', *The Journal of Aesthetics and Art Criticism*, 63 (2): 105–17.

Plantinga, C. (2013), '"I'll Believe It When I Trust the Source": Documentary Images and Visual Evidence', in B. Winston (ed.), *The Documentary Film Book*, 40–7, London: British Film Institute.

Plasketes, G. M. (1989), 'Rock on Reel: The Rise and Fall of the Rock Culture in America Reflected in a Decade of "Rockumentaries"', *Qualitative Sociology*, 12 (1): 55–71.

Polaschek, B. (2018), 'The Dissonant Personas of a Female Celebrity: *Amy* and the Public Self of Amy Winehouse', *Celebrity Studies*, 9 (1): 17–33.

Proctor, W. (2016), 'A New Breed of Fan?: Regimes of Truth, One Direction Fans, and Representations of Enfreakment', in L. Bennett and P. Booth (eds), *Seeing Fans: Representations of Fandom in Media and Popular Culture*, 67–78, New York: Bloomsbury Academic.

Radway, J. A. (1994), *Reading the Romance: Women, Patriarchy, and Popular Literature*, London: Verso.

Railton, D. (2001), 'The Gendered Carnival of Pop', *Popular Music*, 20 (3): 321–31.

Redmond, S. (2015), 'Introduction', in S. Redmond (ed.), *The Star and Celebrity Confessional*, 1–6, London: Routledge.

Regev, M. (2013), *Pop-Rock Music: Aesthetic Cosmopolitanism in Late Modernity*, Cambridge: Polity.

Reiter, R. (2008), *The Beatles on Film: Analysis of Movies, Documentaries, Spoofs and Cartoons*, Bielefeld: Transcript.

Rommen, T. (2013), 'Some Cold Facts about Circuits and Circuit Breakers', *Safundi*, 14 (4): 471–5.

Romney, J. (1995), 'Access All Areas: The Real Space of Rock Documentary', in J. Romney and A. Wootton (eds), *Celluloid Jukebox: Popular Music and the Movies since the 50s*, 82–93, London: British Film Institute.

Rothman, W. (1997), *Documentary Film Classics*, New York: Cambridge University Press.

Roush, T. (2023), 'Taylor Swift's "The Eras Tour" Movie Earns $26 Million In Presale Tickets—AMC's Single-Day Record', *Forbes*, 1 September. Available online: https://web.archive.org/web/20230901191404/https://www.forbes.com/sites/tylerroush/2023/09/01/taylor-swifts-the-eras-tour-earns-26-million-in-presale-tickets-amcs-single-day-record/ (accessed 2 October 2023).

Rubin, R. (2023), '"Taylor Swift: Eras Tour" Film Earns Record-Breaking $26 Million in Presales at AMC Theatres', *Variety*, 1 September. Available online: https://web.archive.org/web/20230901125748/https://variety.com/2023/film/box-office/taylor-swift-eras-tour-film-record-breaking-presales-1235710568/ (accessed 18 December 2023).

Rüther, T., A. Matthews and T. Rüther (2014), *Heroes: David Bowie and Berlin*, London: Reaktion Books.

Sandbrook, D. (2009), *White Heat: A History of Britain in the Swinging Sixties*, London: Abacus.

Sanderson, C. (2018), 'Author Interviews: Dan Jones and Marina Amaral', *The Bookseller*, 1 June. Available online: https://web.archive.org/web/20231218150455/https://www.thebookseller.com/author-interviews/profile-dan-jones-marina-amaral-802486 (accessed 21 June 2022).

Sarchett, B. W. (1994), '"Rockumentary" As Metadocumentary: Martin Scorsese's *The Last Waltz*', *Literature/Film Quarterly*, 22 (1): 28–35.

Saunders, D. (2007), *Direct Cinema: Observational Documentary and the Politics of the Sixties*, London: Wallflower Press.

Saunders, D. (2010), *Documentary*, London: Routledge.

Scannell, P. (1996), *Radio, Television, and Modern Life: A Phenomenological Approach*, Oxford: Blackwell.

Scott, N. (2019), 'Revelation of a Documentary Triptych: Defining Metal Through *Some Kind of Monster, Anvil! The Story of Anvil* and *Beyond the Lighted Stage*', in G. Bayer (ed.), *Heavy Metal at the Movies*, 112–28, London: Routledge.

Seabrook, J. (2023), 'The Case for and Against Ed Sheeran', *The New Yorker*, 5 June. Available online: https://web.archive.org/web/20230601100445/https://www.newyorker.com/magazine/2023/06/05/ed-sheeran-copyright-infringement-lawsuit-marvin-gaye (accessed 8 November 2023).

Severn, S. E. (2002), 'Robbie Robertson's Big Break: A Reevaluation of Martin Scorsese's The Last Waltz', *Film Quarterly*, 56 (2): 25–31.

Sharma, S. (2016), 'Netflix and the Documentary Boom', in K. McDonald and D. Smith-Rowsey (eds), *The Netflix Effect: Technology and Entertainment in the 21st Century*, New York: Bloomsbury Academic.

Shenk, J. W. (2014), *Powers of Two: Finding the Essence of Innovation in Creative Pairs*, Boston: Eamon Dolan/Houghton Mifflin Harcourt.

ShotDeck (2022), 'BILLIE EILISH | Documentary Director RJ Cutler & DP Jenna Rosher | ShotDeck: Shot Talk', *YouTube*, 26 January. Available online: https://web.archive.org/web/20220307085348/https://www.youtube.com/watch?v=cVoyYKDnwHg (accessed 7 April 2022).

Siegel, T. (2019), 'Music Documentary Market Booms: "It's a Land Grab Right Now"', *The Hollywood Reporter*, 13 December. Available online: https://web.archive.org/web/20210728153222/https://www.hollywoodreporter.com/news/general-news/music-documentary-market-booms-a-land-grab-right-now-1262346/ (accessed 18 December 2023).

Sontag, S. (1966), 'Film and Theatre', *The Tulane Drama Review*, 11 (1): 24–37.

Soteriou, S. (2024), 'Chappell Roan Just Detailed The Terrifying Fan Encounters That Prompted Those Divisive TikTok Videos', *BuzzFeed News*. Available online: https://www.buzzfeednews.com/article/stephaniesoteriou/chappell-roan-terrifying-fan-encounters-elton-john-support (accessed 11 September 2024).

Sounes, H. (2010), *An Intimate Life of Paul McCartney*, London: HarperCollins Publishers Ltd.

Spangler, T. (2024a), 'Taylor Swift: The Eras Tour Disney+ Premiere Date, 5 Bonus Songs'. Available online: https://variety.com/2024/digital/news/taylor-swift-eras-tour-disney-plus-premiere-date-bonus-songs-1235901364/ (accessed 30 July 2024).

Spangler, T. (2024b), 'Taylor Swift Sells "Eras Tour" Concert Film to Disney+ for $75 Million'. Available online: https://variety.com/2024/digital/news/taylor-swift-disney-deal-eras-tour-concert-film-1235905787/ (accessed 30 July 2024).

Stahl, M. (2013), *Unfree Masters: Recording Artists and the Politics of Work*, Durham: Duke University Press.

Strachan, R. and M. Leonard (2009), 'Rockumentary: Reel to Real: Cinema Verité, Rock Authenticity and the Rock Documentary', in G. Harper (ed.), *Sound and Music in Film and Visual Media: A Critical Overview*, 284–300, London: Bloomsbury Academic.

Stutz, C. (2018), 'Apple Buys Ed Sheeran "Songwriter" Documentary', *Billboard*. Available online: https://web.archive.org/web/20210227015423/https://www.billboard.com/articles/columns/pop/8372679/ed-sheeran-songwriter-documentary-apple-buys (accessed 2 August 2021).

Sulpy, D. and R. Schweighardt (2003), *Get Back: The Beatles' Let It Be Disaster*, London: Helter Skelter Publishing.

Taylor Swift (@taylorswift) (2023), 'The Eras Tour Has Been the Most Meaningful, Electric Experience of My Life so Far and I'm Overjoyed to Tell You That It'll Be Coming to the Big Screen Soon 😊 Starting Oct 13th You'll Be Able to Experience the Concert Film in Theaters in North America! Tickets Are on Sale Now. Eras Attire, Friendship Bracelets, Singing and Dancing Encouraged 🫶 1, 2, 3 LGB!!!! (Iykyk)', *Instagram*, 31 August. Available online: https://www.instagram.com/reel/Cwm810ahz3u/ (accessed 1 December 2023).

Terry, J. (2021), 'Why Are There Suddenly So Many Music Documentaries?', *Vice*, 28 July. Available online: https://web.archive.org/web/20210728143312/https://www.vice.com/en/article/epnqyk/our-favorite-music-documentaries-framing-britney-spears-mccartney-3-2-1-woodstock-99-2021 (accessed 4 August 2021).

Thompson, L. J. (2013), 'Mancaves and Cushions: Marking Masculine and Feminine Domestic Space in Postfeminist Romantic Comedy', in J. Gwynne and N. Muller (eds), *Postfeminism and Contemporary Hollywood Cinema*, 149–65, London: Palgrave Macmillan UK.

Thompson, P. (2019), *Creativity in the Recording Studio: Alternative Takes*, Cham: Palgrave Macmillan.

Tibbetts, J. C. (2005), 'Ken Russell's *The Debussy Film* (1965)', *Historical Journal of Film, Radio and Television*, 25 (1): 81–99.

Titlestad, M. (2013), 'Searching for the Sugar-Coated Man', *Safundi*, 14 (4): 466–70.

Toynbee, J. (2000), *Making Popular Music: Musicians, Creativity and Institutions*, London: Oxford University Press.

Tulloch, J. and H. Jenkins (1995), *Science Fiction Audiences: Watching Doctor Who and Star Trek*, Popular fiction series, London: Routledge.

Turner, G. (2015), 'Genre, Hybridity and Mutation', in G. Creeber (ed.), *The Television Genre Book*, 3rd edn, London: Palgrave Macmillan.

Tweedy, J. (2020), *How to Write One Song*, London: Faber & Faber.

Vannini, P. (2004), 'The Meaning of a Star: Interpreting Pop Music Fans' Reviews', *Symbolic Interaction*, 27(1): 47–69.

Vaughan, D. (1999), *For Documentary: Twelve Essays*, Berkeley: University of California Press.

Verhoeven, B. (2021), 'Questlove's "Summer of Soul" Doc Sells to Searchlight, Hulu', *TheWrap*, 4 February. Available online: https://web.archive.org/web/20210205041402/https://www.thewrap.com/questloves-summer-of-soul-doc-sells-to-hulu-searchlight/ (accessed 19 December 2023).

Vermorel, F. and J. Vermorel (2007), 'Starlust', in S. Frith and A. Goodwin (eds), *On Record: Rock, Pop, and the Written Word*, 481–90, London: Routledge.

Vincent, M. (2021), 'Interview: Cinematographer Jenna Rosher on Working with Billie Eilish in "The World's A Little Blurry"', *Awards Radar*, 26 May. Available online: https://web.archive.org/web/20210526125427/https://awardsradar.com/2021/05/26/interview-cinematographer-jenna-rosher-on-working-with-billie-eilish-in-the-worlds-a-little-blurry/ (accessed 18 December 2023).

Vogels, J. B. (2005), *The Direct Cinema of David and Albert Maysles*, Carbondale: Southern Illinois University Press.

Vroomen, L. (2004), 'Kate Bush: Teen Pop and Older Female Fans', in A. Bennett and R. A. Peterson (eds), *Music Scenes: Local, Translocal, and Virtual*, 238–54, Nashville: Vanderbilt University Press.

Wall, T. and P. Long (2010), 'Jazz Britannia: Mediating the Story of British Jazz on Televisions', *Jazz Research Journal*, 3 (2): 145–70.

Wall, T. and N. Pillai (2018), 'Screening Popular Music's Past: Music Documentary and Biopics', *The Routledge Companion to Popular Music History and Heritage*, 97–107, Abingdon: Routledge.

Wallace, R. (2019), *Mockumentary Comedy: Performing Authenticity*, Cham: Palgrave Macmillan.

Wallace, R. (2021a), '"Good Evening Pasadena!": Fantastical Performance Spaces in the Rock Documentary', in J. L. Wright and M. Shearer (eds), *Musicals at the Margins: Genre, Boundaries, Canons*, 199–213, London: Bloomsbury Academic.

Wallace, R. (2021b), 'Documentary Style as Post-Truth Monstrosity in the Mockumentary Horror Film', *Quarterly Review of Film and Video*, 38 (6): 519–40.

Watson, D. (2013), 'Letting Go of the Cold Facts', *Safundi*, 14 (4): 485–90.

Waugh, T. (2011), *The Right to Play Oneself: Looking Back on Documentary Film*, Minneapolis: University of Minnesota Press.

Weetch, O. (2016), *Expressive Spaces in Digital 3D Cinema*, London: Palgrave Macmillan.

Weston, L. (2021a), 'Fascinating Rhythms: Music Programming, Memory and Materiality in Visual Culture', PhD Thesis, Coventry: University of Warwick.

Weston, L. (2021b), '(Re)Writing Music History: Television, Memory, and Nostalgia in The People's History of Pop', *The Velvet Light Trap*, 88 (1): 59–70.

Weston, L. and M. Samuel (2022), 'The Last Broadcast: Reflections on the Life and Legacy of BBC Four', *Critical Studies in Television*, 17 (2): 178–86.

Westrup, L. (2021), 'Monterey Pop and the Maturation of the Concert Film', in G. Iversen and S. MacKenzie (eds), *Mapping the Rockumentary: Images of Sound and Fury*, 37–49, Edinburgh: Edinburgh University Press.

Wheatley, H. (2016), *Spectacular Television: Exploring Televisual Pleasure*, London: I. B. Tauris.

Whitten, S. (2023), 'Taylor Swift Could Change the Movie Theater Industry with Her Eras Tour Concert Film – Here's How', *CNBC*, 10 September. Available online: https://web.archive.org/web/20230911030638/https://www.cnbc.com/2023/09/10/taylor-swift-eras-tour-movie-theaters.html (accessed 2 October 2023).

Wilkinson, M. (2019), '"Taylor Swift: The Hardest Working, Zaniest Girl in Show Business…"', *Celebrity Studies*, 10 (3): 441–4.

Williams, A. (2010), '"Pay Some Attention to the Man Behind the Curtain": Unsung Heroes and the Canonization of Process in the Classic Albums Documentary Series, *Journal of Popular Music Studies*, 22 (2): 166–79.

Williams, C. (2001), 'Does It Really Matter? Young People and Popular Music', *Popular Music*, 20 (2): 223–42.

Williams, R. (1974), *Television: Technology and Cultural Form*, London: Fontana.

Williams, R. (1977), *Marxism and Literature*, Marxist introductions, Oxford: Oxford university press.

Williams, R. (2014), 'Culture Is Ordinary', in J. McGuigan (ed.), *Raymond Williams on Culture & Society: Essential Writings*, 1–18, London: SAGE Publications Ltd.

Williams, R. (2016), '"We Live Round Here Too": Representing Fandom and Local Celebrity in *Pulp: A Film About Life, Death & Supermarkets*', in L. K. Bennett and P. Booth (eds), *Seeing Fans: Representations of Fandom in Media and Popular Culture*, 23–32, New York: Bloomsbury Academic.

Winston, B. (1993), 'The Documentary as Scientific Inscription', in M. Renov (ed.), *Theorizing Documentary*, 37–57, New York: Routledge.

Winston, B. (2000), *Lies, Damn Lies and Documentaries*, London: BFI Publishing.

Wlömert, N., and Dominik P. (2016), 'On-Demand Streaming Services and Music Industry Revenues — Insights from Spotify's Market Entry', *International Journal of Research in Marketing*, 33 (2), pp. 314–27.

Wolff, J. (1995), *Resident Alien: Feminist Cultural Criticism*, Cambridge: Polity Press.

Womack, K. (2019), *Solid State: The Story of Abbey Road and the End of the Beatles*, Ithaca: Cornell University Press.

Wood, J., ed. (2018), *Nick Broomfield: Documenting Icons*, London: Faber and Faber Limited.

Wood, M. (2022), 'For Damon Albarn, Modern Life Is Still Pretty Much Rubbish', *Los Angeles Times*. Available online: https://www.latimes.com/entertainment-arts/music/story/2022-01-23/damon-albarn-blur-gorillaz (accessed 18 December 2023).

Wootton, A. (1995), 'The Do's and Don'ts of Rock Documentaries', in J. Romney and A. Wootton (eds), *Celluloid Jukebox: Popular Music and the Movies since the 50s*, 94–105, London: British Film Institute.

Wright, J. L. (2013), 'The Good, The Bad and The Ugly '60s: The Opposing Gazes of Woodstock and Gimme Shelter', in R. Edgar, K. Fairclough-Isaacs and B. Halligan (eds), *The Music Documentary: Acid Rock to Electropop*, 71–86, London: Taylor & Francis Group.

Zryd, M. (2003), 'Found Footage Film as Discursive Metahistory: Craig Baldwin's *Tribulation 99*', *The Moving Image*, 3 (2): 40–61.

Filmography

20 Feet from Stardom (2013), [Film] Dir. Morgan Neville, USA: Gil Friesen Productions, Tremolo Productions.
20,000 Days on Earth (2014), [Film] Dir. Iain Forsyth, Jane Pollard, UK: Corniche Media, British Film Institute, Film4, JW Films, Pulse Films.
All of Those Voices (2023), [Film] Dir. Charlie Lightening, USA: 78 Productions, Trafalgar Releasing.
Amy (2015), [Film] Dir. Asif Kapadia, UK: Film4, On the Corner Films.
An Inconvenient Truth (2006), [Film] Dir. Davis Guggenheim, USA: Lawrence Bender Productions, Participant Productions.
André Rieu's 2023 Maastricht Concert: Love Is All Around (2023), [Film] Dir. Michael Wiseman, Portugal: André Rieu Productions, Piece of Magic Entertainment.
Angelheaded Hipster: The Songs of Marc Bolan & T.Rex (2022), [Film] Dir. Ethan Silverman, USA: bmg Rights Management.
Anvil! The Story of Anvil (2008), [Film] Dir. Sacha Gervasi, Canada: Ahimsa Films.
Ariana Grande: Excuse Me, I Love You (2020), [Film] Dir. Paul Dugdale, USA: Den of Theives, Federal Films, SB Projects, SiFi Films.
Awesome; I Fuckin' Shot That! (2006), [Film] Dir. Adam Yauch, USA: Oscilloscope.
Barbra: The Music… The Mem'ries…The Magic! (2017), [Film] Dir. Jim Gable, Barbra Streisand, USA: Barwood Films.
The Beastie Boys Story (2020), [Film] Dir. Spike Jonze, USA: Fresh Bread, Oscilloscope, Polygram, Pulse Films.
The Beatles: Eight Days a Week – The Touring Years (2016), [Film] Dir. Ron Howard, UK/USA: Apple Corps., Aimimage Productions, Diamond Docs, Image Entertainment, OVOW Productions, Universal Music Group International, White Horse Pictures.
Billie (2019), [Film] Dir. James Erskine, UK: Altitude Film Entertainment, Moving Picture Company (MPC), New Black Films, REP Documentary, Concord, BBC Music, Belga Productions, Polygram Entertainment, Reliance Entertainment.
Billie Eilish: The World's a Little Blurry (2021), [Film] Dir. R. J. Cultler, USA: Apple Original Films, Interscope Films, Lighthouse Management & Media, Matador Content, The Darkroom, This Machine.
Bobi Wine: The People's President (2022), [Film] Dir. Moses Bwayo, Christopher Sharp, UK/Uganda/USA: Southern Films, Ventureland.
Bowling for Columbine's (2022), [Film] Dir. Michael Moore Canada/Germany/USA: United Artists, Alliance Atlantis Communications, Salter Street Films

International, Vif Babelsberger Filmproduktion GmbH & Co. Zweite KG, God Eat Dog Films, Iconolatry Productions Inc., TiMe Film- und TV-Produktions GmbH, United Broadcasting Inc.

Bring on the Night (1985), [Film] Dir. Mihael Apted, USA: A&M Films.

Burden of Dreams (1982), [Film] Dir. Les Blank, Germany/USA: Flower Films, Independent Documentary Fund, The National Endowment for the Arts, Ford Foundation, Corporation for Public Broadcasting, Public Television Stations, SDR Fernsehen.

The Bruce McMouse Show (2018), [Film] Dir. Barry Chattington, UK: MPL Communications Ltd.

Cameraperson (2016), [Film] Dir. Kirsten Johnson, USA: Big Mouth Productions, Fork Films.

Carlos (2023), [Film] Dir. Rudy Valdez, USA: Imagine Documentaries, Sony Music Entertainment.

Charlie Is My Darling (1966), [Film] Dir. Peter Whitehead, UK: Because Entertainment.

Cobain: Montage of Heck (2015), [Film] Dir. Brett Morgen, USA: HBO Documentary Films, Polder Animation, Primary Wave Entertainment.

Coldplay: Music of the Spheres – Live at River Plate (2023), [Film] Dir. Paul Dugdale, UK: Infinity Station Films, SiFi Films.

Dance Craze (1981), [Film] Dir. Joe Massot, UK: Chrysalis Records, Osiris Films.

David Byrne's American Utopia (2020), [Film] Dir. Spike Lee, USA: 40 Acres & A Mule Filmworks, HBO Documentary Films, Participant, RadicalMedia, River Road Entertainment, Spike Lee Joint, Todo Mundo, Warner Music Group.

Demi Lovato: Stay Strong (2012), [Film] Dir. Davi Russo, USA: RadicalMEdia.

Depeche Mode: 101 (1989), [Film] Dir. David Dawkins, Chris Hegedus, D. A. Pennebaker, UK/USA: Mute Film, Pennebaker Associates.

The Devil and Daniel Johnston (2005), [Film] Dir. Jeff Feuerzeig, USA: Complex Corporation, This Is That Productions.

Dig! (2004), [Film] Dir. Ondi Timoner, USA: Interloper Films.

A Dog Called Money (2019), [Film] Dir. Seamus Murphy, Ireland/UK/USA: Pulse Films, Blinder Films, JW Films, ATC Management, Artangel, Fís Éireann, Great Point Media, Somerset House.

Dont Look Back (1967), [Film] Dir. D. A. Pennebaker, USA: Leacock-Pennebaker.

Dumb Money (2023), [Film] Dir. Craig Gillespie, USA: Black Bear, Columbia Pictures, Ryder Picture Company, Sony Pictures Entertainment, Stage 6 Films.

The Exorcist: Believer (2023), [Film] Dir. David Gordon Green, USA: Universal Pictures, Blumhouse Productions, Morgan Creek Entertainment, Rough House Picture.

Fahrenheit 9/11 (2004), [Film] Dir. Michael Moore, USA: Fellowship Adventure Group, Dog Eat Dog Films, Miramax.

The Filth and the Fury (2000), [Film] Dir. Julien Temple, UK/USA: FilmFour, Jersey Shore, Nitrate Films, Panacea Entertainment, The Sex Pistols Residuals.

Finding Fela (2014), [Film] Dir. Alex Gibney, USA: Jigsaw Productions.
The First Wives Club (1996), [Film] Dir. Hugh Wilson, USA: Paramount Pictures.
Folklore: The Long Pond Studio Sessions (2020), [Film] Dir. Taylor Swift, USA: Big Brance, Taylor Swift Productions.
Gaga: Five Foot Two (2017), [Film] Dir. Chris Moukarbel, USA: Live Nation Productions, Mermaid Films II, Permanent Wave.
Ghosts of the Chelsea Hotel (and Other Rock & Roll Stories) (2023), [Film] Dir. Danny Garcia, Spain: Chip Baker Films.
Gimme Shelter (1970), [Film] Dir. Albert Maysles, David Maysles, Charlotte Zwerin, USA: Maysles Films, Penforta.
Hannah Montana and Miley Cyrus: Best of Both Worlds Concert (2008), [Film] Dir. Bruce Hendricks, USA: PACE, Walt Disney Pictures.
Happier Than Every: A Love Letter to Los Angeles (2021), [Film] Dir.
Have You Got It Yet? The Story of Syd Barett and Pink Floyd (2023), [Film] Dir. Roddy Bogawa, Storm Thorgerson, UK: A Cat Called Rover, Believe Media, Mercury Studios.
Homecoming: A Film By Beyoncé (2019), [Film] Dir. Beyoncé, Ed Burke, USA: PRG, Southpaw Productions.
I Used to Be Normal: A Boyband Fangirl Story (2018), [Film] Dir. Jessica Leski, Australia/USA: Over Here Productions.
I'll Sleep When I'm Dead (2016), [Film] Dir. Justin Krook, USA: City Room Creative, Hyperion Media Group, MediaWeaver Entertainment, MediaWeaver Productions, Veracity Productions.
It All Begins with A Song (2018), [Film] Dir. Chusy, USA: Plan A Films.
Janis: Little Girl Blue (2015), [Film] Dir. Amy Berg, USA: Disarming Films, Jigsaw Productions.
Jazz on a Summer's Day, (1959) [Film] Dir. Bert Stern, Aram Avakian, USA: Galaxy Productions, Raven Films.
j-hope IN THE BOX (2023), [Film] Dir. Jun-Soo Park, South Korea: Disney Media Distribution.
Justin Bieber: Never Say Never (2011), [Film] Dir. Jon M. Chu, USA: Paramount Pictures, Scooter Braun Films, L.A. Reid Media, AEG Live, Insurge Pictures, Island Def Jam Music Group, MTV Films, Magic Elves Productions.
Katy Perry: Part of Me (2012), [Film] Dir. Dan Cutforth, Jane Lipsitz, USA: Insurge Pictures, MTV Films, Imagine Entertainment, Perry Productions, Direct Management Group, AEG Live, EMI Music, Pulse Films, Magic Elves Productions, Splinter Films.
Kick Out!: The Newtown Neurotics Story (2023), [Film] Dir. Luke J. Baker, UK: Cruel Binary.
Killers of the Flower Moon (2023), [Film] Dir. Martin Scorsese, USA: Apple Studios, Imperative Entertainment, Sikelia Productions, Appian Way.

Ladies and Gentlemen: The Rolling Stones (1974), [Film] Dir. Rollin Binzer, USA: Butterfly, Chesscol Bingo, Musicfilm.

The Last Waltz (1978), [Film] Dir. Martin Scorsese, USA: FM Productions, Last Waltz Inc..

Lennon's Poster (2012), [Film], Dir. Nick Esdaile, Joe Fellows, UK: Make Productions.

Let It Be (1970), [Film] Dir. Michael Lindsay-Hogg, UK: Apple Corps..

Lewis Capaldi: How I'm Feeling Now (2023), [Film] Dir. Joe Pearlman, UK: BMG, Netflix, Pulse Films.

Little Richard: I Am Everything (2023), [Film] Dir. Lisa Cortes, USA: Bungalow Media + Entertainment, CNN Films, Rolling Stone.

Lonely Boy (1962), [Film] Dir. Wolf Koenig, Roman Kroitor, Canada: National Film Board of Canada.

Lou Reed: Berlin (2007), [Film] Dir. Julian Schnabel, UK/USA: Waterboy Productions.

Madonna: Truth or Dare (1991), [Film] Dir. Alek Keshishian, USA: Boy Toy, Miramax, Propaganda Films.

March of the Penguins (2005), [Film] Dir. Luc Jacquet, France: National Geographic Films, Bonne Pioche, Wild Bunch, Alliance de Production Cinematographique, Buena Vista International Film Production France, Canal+, L'Institut Polare Français Paul-Émile Victor.

Meet Me in the Bathroom (2022), [Film] Dir. Will Lovelace, Dylan Southern, Andrew Cross, UK: Pulse Films, XTR.

Metallica: M72 World Tour Live from Texas – Night 1 (2023), [Film] Dir. Gene McAuliffe, USA: Trafalgar Releasing.

Metallica: Some Kind of Monster (2004), [Film] Dir. Joe Berlinger, Bruce Sinofsky, USA: Radical Media, Third Eye Motion Picture Company.

Michael Jackson's This is It (2009), [Film] Dir. Kenny Ortega, USA: Columbia Pictures, The Michael Jackson Company, AEG Live.

Miss Americana (2020), [Film] Dir. Lana Wilson, USA: Tremolo Productions.

Mission to Lars (2012), [Film] Dir. James Moore, Milliam Spicer, UK/USA: Spicer and Moore.

Mistaken for Strangers (2013), [Film] Dir. Tom Berninger, USA: Starz Digital Media, Abramorama.

Momma Don't Allow (1956), [Film] Dir. Karel Reisz, Tony Richardson, UK: British Film institute.

Monterey Pop (1968), [Film] Dir. D. A. Pennebaker, USA: John Phillips-Lou Adler, Leacock-Pennebaker.

Moonage Daydream (2022), [Film] Dir. Brett Morgen, Germany/USA: BGM, Live Nation Productions, Public Road Productions.

Neil Young: Heart of Gold (2006), [Film] Dir. Jonathan Demme, USA: Clinica Estetico, Playtone, Shakey Pictures, Shangri-La Entertainment.

No Distance Left to Run (2010), [Film] Dir. Will Lovelance, Dylan Southern, UK: Pulse Films.

One Direction: This Is Us (2013), [Film] Dir. Morgan Spurlock, UK/USA: Fulwell 73, Syco Entertainment, TriStar Pictures, Warrior Poets.

Ordinary Angels (2024), [Film] Dir. Jon Gunn, USA: Kingdom Story Company, Green Hummingbird Entertainment, Stampede Ventures, Stolen Sky Productions, Vertigo Entertainment.

Orion: The Man Who Would Be King (2015), [Film] Dir. Jeanie Finlay, uk/usa: Glimmer Films, BBC Storyville, Broadway, Nottingham, Creative England, Ffilm Cymru Wales, MetFilm Production, Truth Department.

Our Hobby is Depeche Mode / The Posters Came from the Walls (2007), [Film] Dir. Jeremy Deller, Nicholas Abrahams, UK: Hudson, Mute Records.

The Persian Version (2023), [Film] Dir. Maryam Keshavarz, USA: A Bigger Boat, AgX, Archer Gray, Karma Film Prod, Marakesh Films.

Primary (1960), [Film] Dir. Robert Drew, USA: Drew Associates, Time.

The Proposition (2005), [Film] Dir. John Hillcoat, Australia/UK: UK Film Council, Surefire Film Productions, Autonomous, Jackie O Productions, Pictures in Paradise, Pacific Film and Television Commission, Film Consortium, National Lottery.

Pulp: A Film About Life, Death & Supermarkets (2014), [Film] Dir. Florian Habicht, UK: Pistachio Pictures, British Film Company.

Reinventing Elvis: The '68 Comeback (2023) Dir. John Scheinfeld, USA: MTV Studios, Meteor 17, Paramount+.

Renaissance: A Film By Beyoncé (2023), [Film] Dir. Dir. Beyoncé, Ed Burke, USA: Parkwood Entertainment, Southpaw Productions.

Roadmovie (1996), [Film] Dir. Peter Care, USA: Satellite Films.

Rolling Thunder Revue: A Bob Dylan Story by Martin Scorsese (2019), [Film] Dir. Martin Scorsese, USA: Grey Water Park Productions, Sikelia Productions.

Salesman (1969), [Film] Dir. Albert Maysles, David Maysles, Charlotte Zwerin, USA: Maysles Films.

Searching for Sugar Man (2012), [Film] Dir. Malik Bendjelloul, Finland/Sweden/UK: Red Box Films, Passion Pictures, Canfield Pictures, The Documentary Company, Hysteria Film, Saperi Film, Sveriges Television, YLE Co-Productions.

Selena Gomez: My Mind and Me (2022), [Film] Dir. Alek Keshishian, USA: Lighthouse Management & Media.

Shine a Light (2008), [Film] Dir. Martin Scorsese, USA: Paramount Vantage, Concert Productions International, Shangri-La Entertainment, Grand Entertainment, Shine A Light.

Shut up and Play the Hits (2012), [Film] Dir. Will Lovelace, Dylan Southern, UK/US: Pulse Films, Killer Films.

Sisters with Transistors (2020), [Film] Dir. Lisa Rovner, France/UK/USA: Willow Glen Films, Anna Lena Films.

The Song Remains the Same (1976), [Film] Dir. Peter Clifton, Joe Massot, UK/USA: Swan Song.

Songwriter (2018), [Film] Dir. Murray Cummings, UK: Murray Pictures.

Sound It Out (2011), [Film] Dir. Jeanie Finlay, UK: Glimmer Films.

Spider-Man: No Way Home (2021), [Film] Dir. Jon Watts, USA: Columbia Pictures, Pascal Pictures, Marvel Studios.

Squaring the Circle (2022), [Film] Dir. Anton Corbijn, UK: Raindog Films.

Stop Making Sense (1984), [Film] Dir. Jonahan Demme, USA: Talking Heads, Arnold Stiefel Company.

Stories We Tell (2012), [Film] Dir. Sarah Polley, Canada: National Film Board of Canada.

SUGA: Road to D-Day (2023), [Film] Dir. Jun-Soo Park, South Korea: Disney Media Distribution.

Summer of Soul (…Or, When the Revolution Could Not Be Televised) (2021), [Film] Dir. Questlove, USA: Mass Distraction Media, RadicalMedia, Vulcan Productions, Concordia Studio, Play/Action Pictures, LarryBilly Productions.

Super Size Me (2004), [Film] Dir. Morgan Spurlock, USA: The Con, Kathbur Pictures, Studio On Hudson.

Sympathy for the Devil (1967), [Film] Dir. Jean-Luc Godard, UK, Cupid Productions.

Taylor Swift: The Eras Tour (2023), [Film] Dir. Sam Wrench, USA: Taylor Swift Productions.

Taylor Swift: Reputation Stadium Tour (2018), [Film] Dir. Paul Dugdale, USA: Den of Thieves, SR Films, Taylor Swift Productions.

The Thin Blue Line (1988), [Film] Dir. Errol Morris, USA: American Playhouse, Corporation for Public Broadcasting, Program Development Company Productions Inc., Public Television Stations, The Chubb Group of Insurance Companies.

This Is Spinal Tap (1984), [Film] Dir. Rob Reiner, USA: Spinal Tap Prod., Goldcrest Films International.

Tokyo Idols (2017), [Film] Dir. Kyoko Miyake, Canada/Japan/UK: Brakeless Ltd, EyeSteelFilm Classics Inc.

Touching the Void (2003), [Film] Dir. Kevin Macdonald, UK/USA: FilmFour, UK Film Council, Darlow Smithson Productions, Channel 4 Television Corporation, Public Broadcasting Service, UK Film Council's New Cinema Fund.

U2 3D (2008), [Film] Dir. Catherine Owens, Mark Pellington, USA: 3ality Digital Entertainment.

U2: Rattle and Hum (1988), [Film] Dir. Phil Joanou, USA: Paramount Pictures, Midnight Films.

The Velvet Underground (2021), [Film] Dir. Todd Haynes, USA: Motto Pictures, Killer Content, Digital One, Killer Films, Polygram Entertainment.

What Happens Later? (2023), [Film] Dir. Meg Ryan, USA: Prowess Pictures, Ten Acre Films, Rockhill Studios, Das Films.

What Happened, Miss Simone? (2015), [Film] Dir. Liz Garbus, USA: Moxie Firecracker Films, Netflix, RadicalMedia.
Whitney: Can I Be Me (2017), [Film] Dir. Nick Broomfield, Rudi Dolezal, UK/USA: Lafayette Films, Passion Pictures, Showtime Networks.
The Who: The Kids Are Alright (1979), [Film] Dir. Jeff Stein, UK: The Who Films.
The Wizard of Oz (1939), [Film] Dir. Victor Fleming, USA: MGM.
Woodstock (1970), [Film] Dir. Michael Wadleigh, USA: Wadleigh-Maurice.
Ziggy Stardust and the Spiders from Mars (1979), [Film] Dir. D.A. Pennebaker, UK: Mainman, Bewlay Bros. Miramax.

Teleography

15 Kids and Counting (2012), [TV programme], Channel 4.
All You Need Is Love: The Story of Popular Music, 'God's Children: The Beginnings' (1977), [TV programme], ITV, 19 February.
American Bandstand (1952–2002), [TV programme], WFIL-TV, ABC, USA Network.
Around the World in 80 Days with Michael Palin (1989), BBC1.
The Beatles Anthology, 'Part 3' (1995), [TV programme], ITV, 10 December.
The Beatles: Get Back (2021), [TV programme], Disney+.
Benefits Street (2015–15), [TV programme], Channel 4.
Big Fat Gypsy Weddings (2010–14), [TV programme], Channel 4.
Blackadder (1983–9), [TV programme], BBC1.
Boy Whose Skin Fell Off (2004), [TV programme], Channel 4, 25 March.
Chelsea at Nine (1957–60), [TV programme], ITV.
Classic Albums (1992–2001), [TV programme], BBC, ITV, Sky Arts, VH1/VH1 Classic.
Crazy about One Direction (2013), [TV programme], Channel 4, 15 August.
The Defiant Ones (2017), [TV programme], HBO.
Dogging Tales (2013), [TV programme], Channel 4, 4 April.
Ed Sheeran: The Sum of It All (2023), [TV programme], Disney+.
Geri (1999), [TV programme], Channel 4.
Howard Goodall's Choir Works (1998), [TV programme], Channel 4.
Howard Goodall's Story of Music (2013), BBC2.
How Music Works (2006), [TV programme], Channel 4.
Keeping Up with the Kardashians (2007–21), [TV programme], E!.
The Life of Rock with Brian Pern, 'Birth of Rock' (2014), [TV programme], BBC4, 10 February.
Masterworks, Bach: Part 2: Brandenburg Concertos No.2 and No.3' (1967), [TV programme], BBC1, 11 January.
McCartney 3,2,1 (2021), [TV programme], Hulu.
Nashville (2012–18), [TV programme], ABC, CMT.
The Office: An American Workplace, 'Threat Level Midnight' (2011), [TV programme], NBC, 17 February.
The Osbournes (2002–5), [TV programme], MTV.
The Paedophile Hunter (2014), [TV programme], Channel 4, 1 October.
People's History of Pop (2016), [TV programme], BBC4.
Red Dwarf (1988–99, 2009–20), [TV programme], BBC2, Dave.

ReMastered, 'Who Killed Jam Master Jay?' (2018), [TV programme], Netflix, 7 December.
ReMastered, 'Who Shot the Sherrif?' (2018), [TV programme], Netflix, 12 October.
Robbie Williams (2023), [TV programme], Netflix.
Secrets of the Living Dolls (2014), [TV programme], Channel 4, 6 January.
Sgt. Pepper's Musical Revolution with Howard Goodall, [TV programme], BBC2, 3 June.
Song Exploder (2020), [TV programme], Netflix.
The South Bank Show, 'The Making of Sgt. Pepper' (1992), [TV programme], ITV, 14 June.
Storyville (1997–), [TV programme], BBC.
Taylor Swift: Journey to Fearless, 'Becoming Fearless' (2010), [TV programme], The Hub, 23 October.
Teenland (2007), [TV programme], BBC4.
Thommy's Pop Show (1984), [TV programme], ZDF, 8 December.
Top of the Pops (1984), [TV programme], BBC 1, 8 November.
Top of the Pops (1985), [TV programme], BBC 1, 23 May.
Tracking Down Maggie (1994), [TV programme], Channel 4, 19 May.
The Vicar of Dibley (1994–2007), [TV programme], BBC 1.
Wacko about Jacko (2005), [TV programme], Channel 1, 4 January.
Watch the Sound with Mark Ronson (2021), [TV programme], Apply TV+.
The Wednesday Play, 'Cathy Come Home' (1966), [TV programme], BBC 1, 16 November.
The Wednesday Play, 'Alice in Wonderland' (1966), [TV programme], BBC 1, 28 December.
Wham! (2023), [TV programme], Netflix.
What's Happening! The Beatles in the USA (1964), [TV programme], CBS, 13 November.
When Pop Ruled My Life: The Fan's Story (2015), [TV programme], BBC 4, 29 May.
The X Factor (2004–18), [TV programme], ITV.

Index

20,000 Days on Earth, 12, 24, 58, 103–8, 194

access
    archival footage and 69, 70–9, 93, 96
    to creative process 3, 105–6, 110–13, 116–17, 125–6, 136, 193
    discourses of 3–4, 23–5, 26–7, 64
    by documentary makers 3, 15, 67, 80, 86, 92, 98, 103, 108, 149. *See also* backstage
    by fans 3, 155, 156, 158–60, 196
    and interiority 67, 80–81, 99, 111
Altamont 11, 88, 156, 201 n.11, 203 n.16
Anvil 5, 28
Amy 7, 11, 69, 166–7, 203 n.15
Andrews, Hannah 10, 11, 166–7, 196
AppleTV+ 8, 9
archival footage
    access to 3
    emulation of 45, 54, 70
    ethics of reuse 166–7
    as evidence of pastness 69–72, 74–5
    'foundness' 69–70, 78, 84
    home movies 79, 83–4, 98, 188
    legalities 71–2
    as marker of significance 70–4
    textural qualities of 69–70, 72–3, 202 n.3
    See also under access
Ariana Grande: Excuse Me, I Love You 8, 34, 51, 200 n.7
Asquith, Daisy, 154, 157, 180, 184. *See also Crazy About One Direction*
Auslander, Philip 30, 44, 46–7, 58, 65, 156, 163, 200 n.4
authenticity 13, 67, 155
    as an evaluative framework 14–15
    in performance 24–5, 58–9, 199 n.9
    self-reflection 3
    See also under observational documentary; performance

authorship 25, 30, 31, 37, 55–6, 102, 199 n.3. *See also under* Sheeran, Ed; songwriting; Swift, Taylor
Awesome; I Fuckin' Shot That! 43–4, 201 n.10

backstage 3, 23, 24–5, 67–8, 72
    as conceptual space, 64–5
    as element of pop stardom, 64–6, 81, 103–5
    as real space, 63–5
    theorization of, 63–6
    See also documentary backstage
Backstreet Boys 171, 173–5
Baker, Michael Brendan 2, 9, 29, 36
Barber, Simon 109–10, 114–17, 120, 132, 136, 140–1, 204 n.2
Baron, Jaimie 69–70, 72–3, 167
Beastie Boys *See Awesome; I Fuckin' Shot That!*
Beattie, Keith 9, 10, 12, 28, 57, 63, 65, 68, 70, 72, 135
Beatles, The 11, 21, 25, 37, 88, 191, 194
    'A Day in the Life' 130, 136, 206 n.22
    'Being for the Benefit of Mr. Kite' 130, 131, 134, 136, 205 n.15
    decision to stop touring 164–5, 208 n.11
    drug use 130
    fans 151, 163–70, 171, 176
    'Fixing a Hole' 136
    innovations in production 137–41, 149, 206 n.23
    'Lucy in the Sky with Diamonds' 130, 134, 136
    'Penny Lane' 130–2, 136, 165, 206 n.22
    relationship with Disney+ 8–9, 94
    'She's Leaving Home' 134, 136
    songwriting practices 130, 131
    'Yesterday' *See under* McCartney, Paul
    See also Let it Be (film); *Beatles Anthology, The*; *Beatles: Eight Days*

a Week – The Touring Years, The;
Beatles: Get Back, The; Harrison,
George; McCartney, Paul; Lennon,
John; *Sgt. Pepper's Lonely Hearts Club
Band* (album); *Sgt. Pepper's Musical
Revolution with Howard Goodall*;
Starr, Ringo; 'Strawberry Fields
Forever'
Beatles Anthology, The 94, 109, 112, 162–3, 165, 204 n.1
Beatles: Eight Days a Week – The Touring Years, The 94, 165
The Beatles: Get Back 8, 69, 89, 94–6, 113, 115–16, 204 n.7
Bendjelloul, Malik 89–93, 98
Beyoncé 21, 55
  as artist 31, 53, 70, 195
  as performer 33–4, 49, 54
  relationship with streaming services 8
  See also *Homecoming: A Film by Beyoncé*, *Renaissance: A Film by Beyoncé*
Bieber, Justin 142, 144, 148
  relationship with Selena Gomez 143
  See also *Justin Bieber: Never Say Never*
Billie 12, 21, 24, 69, 71–9
Billie Eilish: The World's A Little Blurry 4, 8, 12, 24, 80, 82–7, 98, 155, 204 n.4
Blanco, Benny 142–6
Bowie, David 155, 181, 187, 194, 201 n.16. See also *Moonage Daydream*; *Ziggy Stardust and the Spiders from Mars*
Broomfield, Nick 70–1, 87, 97, 98, 104
Bruzzi, Stella 11, 12, 79, 87, 89, 104, 199 n.6, 203 n.14
Buena Vista Social Club 89–90, 92–3
Byrne, David 21, 34, 48, 53–4, 58–9

Cave, Nick 21, 58, 103–8, 180
celebrity 18
Chanan, Michael 9, 11, 16, 19
Channel 4 152, 184, 209 n.18
Charlie Is My Darling 113, 156, 204 n.4
'cinema of attractions' 33–5, 50–1
Classic Albums 7, 27, 113, 125–7, 130, 135, 137, 140
Coachella Festival 31, 33–4, 37, 49, 70, 201 n.11
Cobain: Montage of Heck 69, 202 n.2

colour 49–50
  black and white 37, 57, 74–8, 200 n.2, 201 n.9, 202 n.4
  See also colourization
colourization 74–7
  as historical method 75–6
comedy 5. *See also under* music documentary
concert film 23–4, 193
  as component of star image 28–30, 50–1
  commercial success of 28
  experience of 3, 28, 30, 44–5, 51–2, 57
  fantastical space of 56–8
  fragmentation 3, 27, 35–47, 59–61
  history of 11, 44, 45
  live audience and 27, 28, 32–5, 42–3, 46, 200 n.3
  point of view 30, 42–5, 59–60
  production of 31, 54–6, 60–1
  purpose of 28–30
  relationship with live event 28, 30–5, 42–3, 44–50, 202 n.20. *See also under* television
  shifting knowledge regimes 52–61
  staging the concert 38, 40–1, 52–4
Corner, John 6, 78, 126–9, 133, 135
Crazy About One Direction 152, 154, 157, 180, 183–4. See also Asquith, Daisy
creativity
  relationship with commerciality 110, 112, 145–9
  representation of 25, 111, 118–23, 133
  See also *under* songwriting
Criterion Collection 17, 179
Cutler, R. J., 82–7
Cyrus, Miley *See Hanah Montana and Miley Cyrus: Best of Both Worlds Concert*

Dance Craze 4, 199 n.5, 201–202 n.19
David Byrne's American Utopia 30, 37, 59–61, 200 n.3, 202 n.22
Deller, Jermy 156–7, 184, 189, 191, 209 n.17
Demme, Jonathan 32, 37, 40
Depeche Mode 21, 180, 185–7, 209 n.20, 209 n.21. See also *Depeche Mode: 101*; *Our Hobby is Depeche Mode*
Depeche Mode: 101 38, 40, 53, 55, 57, 88, 191, 201 n.13, 209 n.22

Dessner, Aaron 30, 96, 98. *See also* National, The
Devil and Daniel Johnnston, The 69, 80
direct cinema 4, 10–14, 16–17, 194
  aesthetics of 4, 11, 14–15, 102, 201 n.9
  crisis structure 88, 95, 116
  theorization of 10–12, 79–80, 82, 203 n.14
Disney+ 9. *See also under* Beatles, The
documentary
  as 'assertive' form 3, 24, 67–9, 74, 78–9, 83–4, 86–7, 91, 93, 103, 108, 193
  documentary boom 6–7
  technology 4, 34–5, 46, 49, 79, 82, 83, 142
  interactivity 96, 116–19, 121–4. *See also under* observational documentary
  journey narrative 88–103
  self-referentiality 13, 68, 72, 89, 100, 103–8. *See also under* music documentary
  See also music documentary; observational documentary; direct cinema; documentary backstage. *See under* performance
documentary backstage
  as a 'projected world' 66–7, 81, 83
  construction of 70–4, 76, 78–80, 84, 86–7, 89, 93, 96–7, 100, 103–5, 107, 116
  definition of 64, 66–8, 108, 193
Doherty, Thomas 5, 6, 42, 48
domesticity 3, 18, 31, 57, 81–7, 92, 99–100, 126, 177, 179–82, 196. *See also* family; intimacy
Donnelly, K. J. 17, 36–7
Dont Look Back 4, 9, 10–11, 15–17, 68, 79, 88, 157, 199 n7, 203 n.16
Duffett, Mark 151, 152, 155, 161, 162, 163, 168, 208 n.5
Dyer, Richard 22, 57–8, 67, 156
Dylan, Bob 8, 15–16, 88, 157, 194

Ed Sheeran: The Sum of It All 163, 199 n.5, 203 n.15
Ehrenreich, Barbara, Elizabeth Hess and Gloria Jacobs, *Remaking Love: The Feminisation of Sex* 151, 168–71
Eilish, Billie 21, 80, 82, 83–7, 98, 155, 203 n.10, 203 n.13 *See also Billie Eilish: The World's A Little Blurry*; *Happier than Ever: A Love Letter to Los Angeles*
Ellis, John 36, 47, 51, 78, 87–8, 96–7

family 81–3, 85–7, 96, 98–100, 173–6, 203 n.12. *See also* domesticity; intimacy
fan studies 151, 207 n.1
fans
  as component of star image 23, 25, 152, 154–7
  collecting 173–4, 177, 178–83
  ethics of representation 25–6, 166–8, 183–4, 193–4
  interaction with stars 152, 154–9
  life stage and 171–7, 209 n.14
  as 'mob' 152–3, 161–5, 167–8
  pathologization of 26, 153–4, 157, 184
  as pedagogical figure 152, 156–8, 161, 191
  performance of 154, 208 n.4
  pop vs rock 152, 154, 161, 163–6, 169–70
  position outside of music industry 151
  power structures between star and fan 25–6, 158–60, 166–7
  screaming 161–9
Feuer, Jane 22, 53, 148
film, textuality of 45, 54, 70, 74–5
Finlay, Jeanie 177–84
Folklore: The Long Pond Sessions 4, 29, 30, 38, 156
Frith, Simon 5, 7, 10, 112, 118, 141

Gaga: Five Foot Two 8, 80–1
Gahan, Dave 55, 185, 187, 191
  'Dave Day' 187–9
Geri 4, 80, 199 n.6
Gimme Shelter 4, 11, 16–17, 70, 79, 88, 156, 201 n.11, 202 n.21, 203 n.16
Gomez, Selena 58, 80, 203 n.10, 203 n.11 *See also Selena Gomez: My Mind and Me. See also under* Bieber, Justin
Goodall, Howard 7, 126, 130, 132–5, 139, 164–5, 205 n.12. *See also Sgt. Pepper's Musical Revolution with Howard Goodall*
Gore, Martin 185, 187, 189, 209 n.20
Grainge, Paul 74–5, 77–8, 203 n.6

Grande, Ariana 57. *See also Ariana Grande: Excuse Me, I Love You*

Hanah Montana and Miley Cyrus: Best of Both Worlds Concert 35, 200 n.1
Happier than Ever: A Love Letter to Los Angeles 32
Harrison, George 115, 129–31, 165, 206 n.19
Hepworth, David 18, 19, 65
Hills, Matt 152–3, 156–7, 171, 183–4, 201 n.18, 208 n.4
Holiday, Billie 71–4, 76–7. *See also Billie*
home *See* domesticity
Homecoming: A Film by Beyoncé 8, 31–4, 37–8, 45–6, 49, 53–4, 57, 60, 70, 156, 195, 201 n.9, 201 n.11, 201 n.14, 202 n.4

I Used to Be Normal: A Boyband Fangirl Story 25, 153, 170–7, 180, 184, 209 n.19
idol culture 159–60
In Bed With Madonna See Madonna: Truth or Dare
intimacy 23–4, 27, 32, 34, 67, 80, 81, 83, 86, 87, 92, 98, 100, 108, 160, 208 n.6
 and risk 67, 160
 See also under observational documentary
It All Begins with a Song 113, 116–25, 141, 144–5

Jackson Michael 170. *See also Michael Jackson's This Is It*; *Wacko About Jacko*
Jackson, Peter 8, 94–6, 113
Jacobs, Jason 32, 36
Jagger, Mick 55–6, 113, 156, 203 n.16
James, David E. 10–11, 14, 16–17, 156
jazz 11–12, 17, 21, 70–2, 175
Jazz on a Summer's Day 9, 11, 16
Jenkins, Henry 154, 159, 207 n.1, 208 n.7
Jensen, Joli 152–3, 156, 161–2, 176, 207 n.2
Jones, Bethan 152, 154, 184, 208 n.4
Jones, Mike 18, 22, 109–12, 116–17, 119, 136, 146, 147
Journey to Fearless 64–5, 155
Justin Bieber: Never Say Never 17, 35, 38, 51, 53, 200 n.1, 201 n.10, 203 n.15

Kael, Pauline 6, 11
Katy Perry: Part of Me 12, 17, 200 n.6, 38–42, 45, 51, 53, 80, 203 n.15, 208 n.6
Kuehl, Linda Lipnack 71–4

Lady Gaga 8. *See also Gaga: Five Foot Two*
Last Waltz, The 11, 29, 37–8, 40, 201 n.11
Lee, Spike 30, 37, 59
Lennon, John 125, 126, 130, 132, 136–8, 140, 205 n.17
Let it Be (film) 8, 94–6, 116, 203 n.17, 204 n.7
Lewis Capaldi: How I'm Feeling Now 80, 199 n.5, 201 n.10, 203 n.15
Lindsay-Hogg, Michael 94–6
Long, Paul 10, 109–10, 114–17, 120, 132, 136, 140–1, 196, 200 n.14, 204 n.2
Lou Reed: Berlin 37, 200 n.3
Lury, Karen 127–9

MacCannell, Dean 63, 67–8
Madonna: Truth or Dare 19, 37–9, 48, 57, 66, 201 n.9, 202 n.4
'Making of Sgt. Pepper, The' (*South Bank Show* episode) 126–7, 129–31, 136–40, 165
Mamber, Stephen 88, 116, 200 n.11
Mapping the Rockumentary (Iversen and MacKenzie) 5, 6, 10, 11, 14, 16
Marquis, Elizabeth 47–8, 179
Martin, George 126–7, 129–30, 132, 136–40, 205 n.17
McCartney, Paul 125–7, 129, 136, 139, 165, 168–9
 articulating process of songwriting 130, 131–2
 realizing songs prior to recording 136, 206 n.19
 writing 'Get Back' 113, 115–16, 204 n.6
 writing 'Yesterday' 109, 112–14, 123, 131, 141, 204 n.2
McCartney 3,2,1 8, 9, 127–8
Michael Jackson's This Is It 17, 53, 200 n.1
Miss Americana 8, 80–2, 113, 158, 203 n.15, 204 n.4
Mission to Lars 152, 208 n.5
Mistaken for Strangers 12, 24, 89, 94, 96–103, 116

mockumentary 5, 6, 82. *See also This is Spinal Tap*. *See also under* music documentary
Monterey Pop 11, 17, 28, 37, 44, 45, 47, 70, 201 n.13, 202 n.22
Moonage Daydream 69, 201 n.16, 202 n.2
Morgen, Brett 201 n.16, 202 n.2
MTV 5, 44, 199 n.8
music documentary
 availability of 13
 as commercial product 9, 14–23, 28, 65–6, 93, 193
 as component of star image 16, 18–20, 22–4, 26, 80–1, 104–6, 110–11, 144, 149, 193. *See also under* concert films; pop stardom
 contemporary relevance 1–2, 7–9
 Covid-19 pandemic affect on 12–13, 29, 32
 critical reception 2, 5–6, 7–8, 18–19, 93, 194
 depictions of mental health 30, 203 n.10. *See also* intimacy; privacy
 distribution of 7–8, 12–13, 16–17
 emotional aspects of 18, 80–1, 101–2, 181–3
 as 'event cinema' 2
 history of 4, 6, 9–12
 narrative form 87–91, 98–9, 102–3
 parody 5–6, 82, 127–8. *See also* mockumentary; *This is Spinal Tap*
 politics 70, 90–1, 93, 159, 173–4, 185–91, 195, 205 n.16
 production technologies 4–5, 34–5, 49
 self-reflexivity 5–6, 12, 13, 15
 social media 5, 85, 196
 streaming services 2, 5, 7–8
 television and 7. *See also* television
 See also access
Music Documentary: Acid Rock to Electropop (Edgar, Fairclough-Isaacs and Halligan) 10, 14–19
musical 22, 52–3, 57–8, 148

National, The 94, 96–101
Negus, Keith 110, 146–7
Netflix 8, 9, 200 n.5
Nichols, Bill 2, 79, 84, 167, 200 n.11
Niebling, Laura 10, 16

No Distance Left to Run, 5, 202 n.21

observational documentary
 authenticity 14–15, 74, 79–80
 immediacy 15
 interactivity 80, 82
 intimacy 80, 84
 invisibility 95
 limitations of 120–2
 See also direct cinema
One Direction 169, 171, 175–6. *See also Crazy About One Direction*
Our Hobby is Depeche Mode 25, 153, 156–7, 170, 184–91, 209 n.17, 207 n.3, 209 n.17

Pennebaker, D. A. 15, 17, 28, 47, 55, 57, 201 n.13, 203 n.16
performance
 concert 27–30, 32, 47–51, 58, 65, 101–2, 164–5, 193
 documentary 14–15, 24–5, 63, 80, 82, 104–5, 121, 208 n.13
Perry, Katy 12, 21. *See also Katy Perry: Part of Me*
Pillai, Nicolas 10, 196, 200 n.14
Plantinga, Carl 57, 63, 66–7
pop music
 authorship and 141. *See also under* Sheeran, Ed; songwriting; Swift, Taylor
 definition 18, 20–1
 gender 18, 21–2, 158, 165–9, 206–7 n.24
 opposition with rock 17–18, 163–6
 value 14, 17–19, 165–6
 See also 'pop-rock'. *See also under* fans; rock music
'pop-rock' 20–1
pop stardom 2–4, 18–23, 104
 industrial position 21–3, 170
 as labour 22–3, 54, 96, 126, 142, 193
 as myth 21–3, 105–6
 public image 106–8, 151. *See also under* fans; music documentary; stardom; songwriting
 reception 26
Posters Came From the Walls, The. *See Our Hobby is Depeche Mode*
privacy 3, 38–9, 47, 64, 67, 80, 180

public sphere 17–18, 163–4, 180, 192
Pulp: A Film about Life, Death & Supermarkets 152, 208 n.13

Railton, Diane 17–18, 162–4
reality television 18–19, 65, 81
Richards, Keith 56, 65, 113
rock music
  associations with seriousness 13, 17–19, 164–6
  definition 17–18, 20–1
  gender 18, 164–6, 208 n.10
  opposition with pop 17–18, 132, 164
  See also 'pop-rock'. *See also under* fans; pop music
Rodriguez, Sixto 28, 90–3
Rolling Stone (magazine) 17, 166
Rolling Stones, The 16, 55–6, 88, 156, 170, 194, 204–5 n.10. *See also Charlie Is My Darling*; *Gimme Shelter*, Jagger, Mick; Richards, Keith, *Shine A Light*; *Sympathy for the Devil*; Watts, Charlie
Romney, Jonathan 10, 15–16, 63–6, 194
Rosher, Jenna 82–4, 87
Rothman, William 10, 15, 16

Saunders, Dave 10, 11, 79, 200 n.11
Scannell, Paddy, 31–2, 48
Scorsese, Martin 19, 40, 55–6
Searching for Sugar Man 7, 11, 24, 88–93, 98, 102
Selena Gomez: My Mind and Me 8, 58, 80, 143, 203 n.11, 203 n.15
Sgt. Pepper's Lonely Hearts Club Band (album), 25, 125–7, 129–41, 164–5
Sgt. Pepper's Musical Revolution with Howard Goodall 126, 131–40, 164
Sheeran, Ed 8, 12, 25, 116
  authorship of songs 142–9, 207 n.25
  public image 144
  'Love Yourself' 142–4, 148
  'Shape of You' 145–9, 207 n.25, 207 n.27, 207 n.28
  See also Ed Sheeran: The Sum of It All; *Songwriter*
Shine A Light 55–7, 202 n.4
Shut Up and Play the Hits 38, 40, 201 n.11
Smith, Caitlyn 120–3, 124
songwriting

authorship 25, 112, 141–9, 206–7 n.24, 207 n.25
  collaboration 120–1, 123, 143, 145, 204 n.4, 206–7 n.24
  as component of star image 25, 105–6, 110–13, 140–1, 144–5, 149
  inspiration 112, 114–15, 117, 130–1, 133–5, 138, 141
  as labour 25, 110, 112, 114–15, 117, 120, 123–6, 141
  as 'magic' 109–10, 114, 117–18, 123, 141, 204 n.2
  production 85, 113, 125–41, 147–8
  relationship with music industry 110, 125, 141, 144–6
  representation of, 111–12, 118–24, 145, 147–8
  routines of 111–15, 130, 142, 145
  stories about 109, 112–13, 117–18, 130–1, 135–7, 141, 143, 146–9, 204 n.2, 206 n.22
  understanding of 105–7, 109, 116
Song Exploder 8, 9, 113, 125
Song Remains the Same, The 37, 200 n.8
Songwriter 8, 12, 25, 116, 142–9
Sontag, Susan 32, 48, 51
Sound it Out 25, 153, 170, 177–83, 190
Stahl, Matt 12, 19, 21–2, 158
stardom 51, 67, 156. *See also* pop stardom
Status Quo 178–9, 181, 184, 185, 208 n.12
Starr, Ringo 115, 125–6, 165
Stop Making Sense 6, 32, 34–5, 37, 40, 48–9, 53–4, 199 n.5, 200 n.3, 201 n.17, 202 n.22
Strachan, Robert and Marion Leonard, 'Rockumentary: Reel to Real: Cinema Verité, Rock Authenticity and the Rock Documentary' 12, 14–15, 21, 63, 65–6
'Strawberry Fields Forever' 129, 130–3, 135–40, 165, 205 n.14, 205 n.17
streaming 7–9
  precarity 13, 196
  See also Netflix; Disney+. *See also under* Beatles, The; Beyoncé; Swift, Taylor
Swift, Taylor
  authorship 199 n.3, 206–7 n.24
  family 64, 203 n.12
  fans, relationship with 155, 157–8

mental health 80, 203 n.10
relationship with streaming services 8
star image 29–30, 155, 200 n.2
See also Folklore: The Long Pond Sessions; Journey to Fearless; Miss Americana; Taylor Swift: The Eras Tour; Taylor Swift: Reputation Stadium Tour
Sympathy for the Devil (film) 204–5 n.10

Take That 21, 169, 171, 173, 185
Talking Heads *See* David Byrne; *Stop Making Sense*
Taylor Swift: The Eras Tour 1–2, 4, 9, 29, 48, 197, 199 n.1, 199 n.2, 199 n.4, 200 n.1
Taylor Swift: Reputation Stadium Tour 8, 13, 29, 51, 200 n.7
television
  aesthetics 205 n.18
  archiving 13, 203 n.8
  broadcasting 187–8
  documentary aesthetics 126–9, 132–5, 137–8, 195–6
  domesticity 126, 200 n.5
  eventfulness 30–2, 42
  fragmentation 36
  hybridity 19
  liveness 31–2, 44
  scheduling 184
  technologies 76–7, 201 n.18, 203 n.7, 203 n.9
  viewing practices 151
  See also reality television

This is Spinal Tap 5, 6
See also mockumentary. *See under* music documentary
Tokyo Idols 25, 159–61
Tweedy, Jeff 109, 114–15, 117–18, 205 n.11

U2: *Rattle and Hum* 5–6, 28, 37–40, 57, 201 n.9, 202 n.20, 202 n.21, 202 n.4

Velvet Underground, The 8, 69, 202 n.2

Wacko About Jacko 152, 157, 183–4
Wall, Tim 10, 196, 200 n.14
Watts, Charlie 55, 203 n.16
Wenders, Wim 89, 90, 93
Weston, Leanne 7, 74–55, 196
Westrup, Laurel 11, 28, 30, 42, 44–6, 201 n.13
What Happened, Miss Simone? 8, 69, 88–9, 199 n.10
What's Happening! The Beatles in the USA, 10–11, 88
When Pop Ruled My Life: The Fan's Story 162, 165–70
Whitehead, Forest Glen 122–3, 144
Whitney: Can I Be Me 70–1, 78
Williams, Alan, 125–7, 130, 137, 140, 196
Williams, Raymond 2, 36, 153
Winston, Brian 14, 80, 200 n.11
Woodstock 11, 16, 36
Wootton, Adrian 28

YouTube 5, 44

Ziggy Stardust and the Spiders from Mars 37, 38, 199 n.5